W9-BOO-118

About Island Press

Island Press is the only nonprofit organization in the United States whose principal purpose is the publication of books on environmental issues and natural resource management. We provide solutions-oriented information to professionals, public officials, business and community leaders, and concerned citizens who are shaping responses to environmental problems.

In 1999, Island Press celebrates its fifteenth anniversary as the leading provider of timely and practical books that take a multidisciplinary approach to critical environmental concerns. Our growing list of titles reflects our commitment to bringing the best of an expanding body of literature to the environmental community throughout North America and the world.

Support for Island Press is provided by The Jenifer Altman Foundation, The Bullitt Foundation, The Mary Flagler Cary Charitable Trust, The Nathan Cummings Foundation, The Geraldine R. Dodge Foundation, The Charles Engelhard Foundation, The Ford Foundation, The Vira I. Heinz Endowment, The W. Alton Jones Foundation, The John D. and Catherine T. MacArthur Foundation, The Andrew W. Mellon Foundation, The Charles Stewart Mott Foundation, The Curtis and Edith Munson Foundation, The National Fish and Wildlife Foundation, The National Science Foundation, The New-Land Foundation, The David and Lucile Packard Foundation, The Pew Charitable Trusts, The Surdna Foundation, The Winslow Foundation, and individual donors.

About The H. John Heinz III Center

The H. John Heinz III Center for Science, Economics and the Environment, a nonprofit institution, continues the work of Senator John Heinz by improving the scientific and economic foundation for environmental policy. The Heinz Center's distinctive contribution is to create new mechanisms for collaboration among the four major sectors essential to solving environmental problems. Environmental organizations, industry, government, and academia all play important roles in defining the agenda that shapes our common future. The Heinz Center provides a venue for these sectors to work together to address challenging issues.

About the NOAA Coastal Services Center

The NOAA Coastal Services Center's mission is to provide information, education, and technology transfer to the coastal community for improved decisionmaking. With a strong emphasis on partnerships, the Center works with local, state, and federal officials to determine specific coastal management issues or challenges. NOAA CSC helps these organizations by providing training, data, or information that was previously unavailable or underutilized.

About The Heinz Center's Risk, Vulnerability and True Costs of Coastal Hazards Study

The Heinz Center's Risk, Vulnerability and True Costs of Coastal Hazards study was conducted under the terms of a joint project agreement between The Heinz Center and the National Oceanic and Atmospheric Administration's Coastal Services Center. Funds were provided by the United States Geological Survey, the Federal Emergency Management Agency, the National Oceanic and Atmospheric Administration, the Andrew W. Mellon Foundation, and The Heinz Center. This report does not necessarily reflect the policies or views of individual members of the Panel on Risk, Vulnerability, and the True Costs of Coastal Hazards, or the organizations or agencies that employ these individuals.

The
Hidden Costs
of Coastal
Hazards

The Hidden Costs *of* Coastal Hazards

IMPLICATIONS for RISK ASSESSMENT and MITIGATION

The H. John Heinz III Center for Science,
Economics and the Environment

ISLAND PRESS
Washington, D.C. • Covelo, California

Copyright © 2000 by Island Press

All rights reserved under International and Pan-American Copyright Conventions. No part of this book may be reproduced in any form or by any means without permission in writing from the publisher: Island Press, 1718 Connecticut Avenue, N.W., Suite 300, Washington, DC 20009.

ISLAND PRESS is a trademark of The Center for Resource Economics.

Library of Congress Cataloging-in-Publication Data
The hidden costs of coastal hazards : implications for risk assessment
  and mitigation / a multi-sector, collaborative project of the H.
John Heinz III Center for Science, Economics and the Environment.
     p.   cm.
  Includes bibliographical references and index.
  ISBN 1–55963–756–0 (paper)
  1. Coastal zone management.   2. Regional planning.   I. H. John
Heinz III Center for Science, Economics and the Environment.
HT391.H525   2000   99-37171
333.91'7—dc21   CIP

Printed on recycled, acid-free paper

Manufactured in the United States of America
10 9 8 7 6 5 4 3 2 1

The following poem was written in the aftermath of 1989's Hurricane Hugo.

Carolina Umbra
by Marjory Wentworth

Boats fly out of the Atlantic
and moor themselves in my backyard
where tiny flowers, forgotten
by the wind, toss their astral heads
from side to side. Mouths ablaze, open,
and filling with rain.

After the Hurricane, you could see
the snapped-open drawbridge slide
beneath the waves on the evening news.
You go cold imagining
such enormous fingers of wind
that split a steel hinge until
its jaw opens toward heaven.

Above the twisted house,
above this island, where the torn
churches have no roofs, and houses
move themselves around the streets
as if they were made of paper;
tangled high in the oak branches,
my son's crib quilt waves its pastel flag.

But the cribrail is rusted shut.
And you can't see my children
huddled together on the one dry bed
of this home filling with birds

that nest in corners of windowless rooms,
or insects breeding in the damp sand
smeared like paint over the swollen floors.

The storm will not roar in your sleep
tonight, as if the unconscious
articulations of an animal aware
of the end of its life were trapped
in the many cages of your brain.

The tedium of nights
grows beyond the absolute
black of this world without light,
where human beings, born on the mud
floors of unnamed cages, are exposed
to eternal, unforgiving winds.

You can't see grief darken the wind
rising over Sullivan's Island. Tonight,
as the burning mountains of debris
illuminate the sky for hundreds of miles,
I see only the objects of my life
dissolving in a path of smoke.

All the lost and scattered hours
are falling completely out of time,
where endless rows of shredded trees wait
with the patience of unburied
skeletons, accumulating in the shadows.

Contents

Foreword

The Hidden Costs of Coastal Hazards is a ground-breaking analysis of methods for understanding the full impacts of coastal hazards, and of what this could mean for measures to deal with them constructively.

While it focuses on problems in the coastal zone, the same approach is appropriate for hazards in other parts of the nation. If the steps recommended by The Heinz Center were to be pursued, the public policy on dealing with natural hazards would be improved in at least three basic ways: methods of estimating costs and benefits of extreme events would be improved, the analysis of risk and vulnerability would be defined, and the measures necessary for achieving genuine community mitigation would be advanced.

Some observers would note that the first U.S. effort to lay the groundwork for national land-use planning was in the Coastal Zone Management Act of 1972. Much was accomplished under that legislation in establishing appropriate state agencies and supporting activities by the National Oceanic and Atmospheric Administration, but a truly comprehensive program did not emerge. Now, after 27 years, the specifications for such an effort are outlined.

In addition to its detailed appraisal of concrete experience with Hurricane Hugo in the Charleston area, the report draws from a wide variety of hazard and land-use studies for the entire country. Many of the findings and recommendations are applicable to noncoastal areas. The suggestions made, for example, to prepare more nearly precise estimates of social and health effects and losses sustained by the business community would be useful in computing the losses from inland floods or tornadoes.

If this report were to lead only to the design and operation of a more comprehensive and accurate estimation of the social and environmental losses from coastal natural hazards it would be highly useful. However, its potential significance is far greater. It could inspire genuine improvements in methods of estimating losses, in examining risk and vulnerability, and in down-to-earth planning of mitigation measures. The recommended steps could lead to truly disaster-resistant and sustainable communities.

GILBERT WHITE
University of Colorado at Boulder

Preface

In 1996, representatives of The H. John Heinz III Center for Science, Economics and the Environment and the National Oceanic and Atmospheric Administration's Coastal Services Center (CSC) began discussions of the need for an improved understanding and accounting of all costs associated with weather-related coastal hazards. Both The Heinz Center and the CSC place a strong emphasis on partnerships with local, state, and federal officials and on fostering collaboration among industry, environmental organizations, government, and academia.

Because of the traditionally limited mission objectives of government agencies and the confidential nature of much insurance industry information, The Heinz Center and the CSC decided to convene a panel of experts who could help identify and develop new strategies to reduce costs associated with rapidly increasing coastal development activities. In the course of determining the scope of the work involved in such a study, the U.S. Geological Survey (USGS), the Andrew W. Mellon Foundation, and the Federal Emergency Management Agency (FEMA) became sponsors and supporters of the project's goals as well.

Project Management

The H. John Heinz III Center for Science, Economics and the Environment is a nonprofit institution dedicated to improving the scientific and economic foundation for environmental policy. The center is committed to fostering collaboration among four sectors—industry, environmental organizations, government, and academia—each of which plays an important role in solving environmental problems. The center concentrates its efforts on emerging issues; that is, environmental problems likely to confront policy makers within two to five years. This commitment made the center ideally suited, to bring all parties to the table to conduct this study.

The CSC works to provide information, education, and technology transfer services to the coastal community for improved decision making. With a strong emphasis on partnerships, the CSC works with local, state, and federal officials to determine specific coastal management issues or challenges. The CSC helps these organizations by providing training, data, or information that was previously unavailable or underutilized.

Working as partners with the CSC, in October 1997 The Heinz Center appointed the Panel on Risk, Vulnerability, and the True Costs of Coastal Hazards to carry out the study and research necessary to address the tasks outlined in the following section on the scope of work. The 23 members of the panel volunteered their time to work on this project and met four times during the study period.

After two meetings, the panel decided to focus on one large coastal hazard event in gathering data and information on direct and indirect costs and impacts. The panel chose Hurricane Hugo, a major disaster that struck the South Carolina region in 1989. A draft risk, vulnerability, and cost assessment framework was developed after the first meeting and continued to evolve as more information was gathered. The panel was divided into four working groups to focus on four categories of costs: costs to the natural environment, costs to the built environment, social and family costs, and business costs. A workshop was held in March 1998 in Charleston, where approximately 30 persons were interviewed (see appendix B) about the direct and indirect impacts and costs associated with Hurricane Hugo. Each working group developed a list of questions, which were sent to the invited participants prior to the workshop (see appendix A) and used during the interview sessions in Charleston. After the panel's third meeting, the members developed their report outline and began drafting this report.

The Heinz Center provided the primary project management for the study, with the generous assistance and cooperation of the staff of the CSC. The CSC also furnished cost data, photos, and maps related to Hurricane Hugo. The USGS and FEMA also assisted the panel by providing maps, figures, and data.

Scope of Work

The Heinz panel's task was to develop an improved framework for community-level risk and vulnerability assessment that factors in relevant economic, social, environmental, and regulatory issues not now considered. Particular emphasis was given to developing an understanding of the full range of un-reported or hidden economic cost categories associated with weather-related hazard events. Traditional risk and vulnerability assessment methods used by coastal communities generally have not incorporated such unreported or hid-den costs to families, natural resources, or community support systems, even though these are important components of the total cost of extreme events, nor have evaluations of potential measures for mitigating future losses taken these impacts into account.

It was envisioned that an improved understanding of the full range of economic costs, including normally unreported costs, would allow for more cost-effective and appropriate public and private investment in hazard miti-gation. Tasks for the panel included:

- identifying the full range of cost categories associated with weather-related coastal hazards;
- analyzing existing community-based risk and vulnerability assessment methodologies and identifying their strengths and weaknesses;
- developing an improved, comprehensive framework for standardizing community-level risk and vulnerability assessment methods incorporating the full range of associated costs; and
- suggesting the types of mitigation strategies that might be considered to reduce future costs resulting from coastal hazards.

Because of the breadth and diversity of knowledge needed to approach these tasks, the panel included 23 whose combined expertise spanned the four sectors of government, industry, academia, and environmental organizations. The individual expertise represented on the panel included economics, environmental science and engineering, ecology, coastal geology, emergency preparedness, architecture, geography, oceanography, statistics, sociology, state emergency management, meteorology, coastal engineering, law, and ecosystem restoration.

While The Heinz Center study was under way, the National Research Council (NRC) Board on Natural Disasters appointed a committee to conduct a study on the losses resulting from natural disasters. The NRC report includes recommendations on which losses should be included when estimating the total costs of a natural disaster. The NRC report, *Impact of Natural Disasters: A Framework for Loss Estimation* is available through the National Academy Press, Washington, D.C.

We would like to take this opportunity to thank the staffs of The Heinz Center, NOAA's Coastal Services Center, FEMA, and the USGS, who helped locate the data, maps, and other information needed by the panel during the study. We especially thank Margaret Davidson, Paul Scholz, Sandy Ward, and Caroline Kurrus of the CSC, who initiated the study and contributed data and other information to the panel. Special thanks go to Rud Platt, who served as vice chair of the panel and made sure that we recognized the current status of public policy with respect to coastal hazards; Allison Sondak, research assistant at The Heinz Center, who took the lead in writing chapter 2 and assisted in organizing the panel's meetings, workshop, and other activities; Jim Good, who took the lead in writing chapter 3 and helped organize the Charleston workshop; and Roger Pielke Jr., who took the lead in writing chapter 4. Four other panel members played a key role in coordinating, analyzing, and writing material for the four-sector analysis: Don Geis (built environment), Molly Macauley (business community), Betty Morrow (social, health, and safety), and Virginia Burkett (natural resources and ecosystems). Sheila David, The Heinz Center project manager, deserves special thanks for the way she organized the panel and its activities, meetings, and report with both good humor and firmness. She made working on the project an enjoyable, productive, and rewarding experience for all panel members.

This report is directed to decisionmakers—both policymakers and planners—who are interested in learning about the categories of costs and risk associated with weather-related coastal hazards. This audience includes legislators who establish broad policy and programs and local government officials who develop and implement specific mitigation strategies and policies, such as land-use planning, building codes, and evacuation plans. Another key audience is private-sector decision makers, including lenders, investors, developers, and insurers of coastal property. In addition, social and natural scientists may be interested in the research needs outlined in this report.

HOWARD KUNREUTHER
Chair

Acknowledgments

Many individuals assisted the panel in its task by participating in panel meetings, providing cost data, recommending individuals to be interviewed about the impacts and costs of Hurricane Hugo, and providing background information to the panel. We express our appreciation to the following people for their unique contributions to this project:

Bob Bacon, South Carolina Sea Grant Extension Program, Charleston, SC; David Baumann, South Carolina Department of Natural Resources, Bonneau, SC; Karen Clark, Applied Insurance Research, Boston, MA; Susan Cutter, University of South Carolina, Columbia, SC; Jeanine DiStefano Petterson, Natural Hazards Center, Boulder, CO; Claire Drury, Federal Emergency Management Agency, Washington, DC; Mary Edna Fraser, Artist, Charleston, SC; Mary Graham, Charleston Chamber of Commerce, Charleston, SC; Steve Grantham, Florida Division of Emergency Management, Tallahassee, FL; John Hewell, Trident United Way, Charleston, SC; Interviewees at Charleston Meeting (see appendix A); Gil Jamieson, Federal Emergency Management Agency, Washington, DC; John Knott Jr., Dewees Island, SC; Frank Koutnik, Florida Division of Emergency Management, Tallahassee, FL; Meredith Krejny, Heinz Center Intern, Washington, DC; Scott Lawson, Risk Management Solutions, Menlo Park, CA; Diana McClure, Institute for Business and Home Safety, Boston, MA; John Miglarese, South Carolina Department of Natural Resources, Charleston, SC; Mary Fran Myers, Natural Hazards Center, Boulder, CO; Bill Robertson, The Andrew W. Mellon Foundation, New York, NY; Heather Rogers, Coastal Services Center Intern, Charleston, SC; Peter Sparks, Clemson University, Clemson, SC; John Tedeschi, EQECAT, San Francisco, CA; Marjory Wentworth, Poet, Charleston, SC; and Jeff Williams, U.S. Geological Survey, Reston, VA.

The Heinz Center appreciates the thoughtful critiques provided by the reviewers. The reviewers do not, however, necessarily approve, disapprove, or endorse this report. The Heinz Center assumes full responsibility for the report and the accuracy of its contents and acknowledges the contributions of the following reviewers:

Laurel Addy, South Carolina Department of Social Services, Columbia, SC; Philip Berke, University of North Carolina, Chapel Hill, NC; David Brower, University of North Carolina, Chapel Hill, NC; Hal Cochrane, Colorado State University, Fort Collins, CO; Paul Fischbeck, Carnegie Mellon University, Pittsburgh, PA; Frank Koutnik, Florida Division of Emergency Management, Tallahassee, FL; Robert Litan, The Brookings Institution, Washington, DC; and Glen Stapleton, Francis Marion National Forest, Cordesville, SC.

Panel on Risk, Vulnerability, and the True Costs of Coastal Hazards

Howard Kunreuther, Chair, The Wharton School, University of Pennsylvania, Philadelphia, PA

Rutherford Platt, Vice Chair, University of Massachusetts, Amherst, MA

Stephen B. Baruch, Stephen B. Baruch & Associates, LLC, Los Altos, CA

Richard Bernknopf, U.S. Geological Survey, Menlo Park, CA

Michael Buckley, Federal Emergency Management Agency, Washington, DC

Virginia Burkett, U.S. Geological Survey, Lafayette, LA

David Conrad, National Wildlife Federation, Washington, DC

Todd Davison, Federal Emergency Management Agency, Atlanta, GA

Ken Deutsch, American Red Cross, Falls Church, VA

Donald E. Geis, Geis Design-Research Associates, Potomac, MD

James Good, Oregon State University, Corvallis, OR

Martin Jannereth, Michigan Department of Environmental Quality, Lansing, MI

Anthony Knap, Bermuda Biological Station for Research, Inc., Ferry Reach, Bermuda

Hugh Lane Jr., The Bank of South Carolina, Charleston, SC

Greta Ljung, Institute for Business and Home Safety, Boston, MA

Molly Macauley, Resources for the Future, Washington, DC

Dennis Mileti, Natural Hazards Center, Boulder, CO

Todd Miller, North Carolina Coastal Federation, Newport, NC

Betty Hearn Morrow, Florida International University, Miami, FL

Joseph Myers, Florida Division of Emergency Management, Tallahassee, FL

Roger A. Pielke Jr., National Center for Atmospheric Research, Boulder, CO

Anthony Pratt, Delaware Department of Natural Resources, Dover, DE

James T. B. Tripp, Environmental Defense Fund, New York, NY

Heinz Center Project Management Staff

Sheila D. David, Project Manager

Allison Sondak, Research Assistant

National Oceanic and Atmospheric Administration Coastal Services Center Project Staff

Margaret Davidson, Director

Paul Scholz, Coastal Management Services Branch Chief

Sandra Ward, Coastal Hazards Program Manager

Caroline Kurrus, Coastal Planner

Russell Jackson, Coastal Hazards Program Analyst

Executive Summary

The coastal regions of the United States include some of the most diverse and dynamic environments on earth. From the rugged, rocky shores of Washington's Olympic coast to the coral reefs of southern Florida, the nearly 88,000 miles of U.S. ocean, estuarine, and Great Lakes shorelines exhibit a stunning array of physical, natural, and human diversity. Much of this physical and natural diversity is associated with global, regional, and local geologic processes. The physical and natural environment are, in turn, further shaped by weather events and patterns operating at a variety of spatial and temporal scales. Familiar examples include hurricanes, nor'easters, winter storms along the west coast, and El Niño–related storms, floods, and droughts. Along undeveloped coasts, these natural events constantly reshape shorelines as they have for centuries, cutting new inlets, eroding some areas, and accreting new beaches in others. However, once a coastal area has been developed and become a home to humans, these weather events can become deadly and costly, and in this context the terminology is transformed: what were once mere weather events become coastal hazards or, even worse, coastal disasters.

Historically, settlements were drawn to the coasts for convenient pursuit of fishing and whaling, as ports serving ocean trade routes, and as centers of social interaction and civilization along waterways. Many of the world's leading cities, such as New York, San Francisco, London, Tokyo-Yokohama, Hong Kong, Singapore, and Shanghai, are located near the water's edge. As of 1998, eight of the ten largest American cities were situated on the oceans or Great Lakes. Beyond the cities that have evolved around deepwater harbors and protected waterways, the tide of humanity has flowed to all parts of the U.S. coastline. People are drawn by the millions to the elemental, visually pleasing, and emotionally restorative shores of the oceans and the Great Lakes.

Those stretches of the coast not held in public or conservation status attract residential, commercial, and recreational investment. Ribbons of intense development follow the narrow strands of beaches and encroach on estuarine wetlands and maritime forest. In addition to the many benefits of living on the coast, population growth and development have brought many problems in their wake: pollution of nearshore waters, loss of valuable coastal wetlands, degradation of major fisheries, traffic congestion, visual blight, and overcrowding of recreational areas. Such development has also invited ever-rising costs, both economic and nonmonetary, imposed by weather-related coastal hazards. This book explores the implications of this increased vulnerability of the United States to coastal disasters.

As coastal communities have grown, the nation has experienced higher property losses, relief costs, more business interruptions and failures, social disruption and dislocation, and natural resource damages associated with coastal hazards. Given the clear trends—continued human migration to the coast, burgeoning growth in coastal tourism, and dramatically escalating investment in hazardous coastal locations—the prospects for controlling these costs are not good. A greater loss of life associated with weather-related coastal hazards has been seen in the mid- to late 1990s, both in the United States and globally. Although better forecasts and warning processes have helped save lives by providing more lead time to evacuate, the tremendous growth of development and human population in coastal regions is proceeding so rapidly that an increase in the loss of life related to coastal disasters can be expected in the future. Implementation of mitigation measures to prepare for and reduce the impacts of coastal disasters in threatened communities has not followed the growth of development on U.S. coasts. Although a hurricane landfall at any particular coastal location is relatively rare for the U.S. and Gulf coasts, hurricane landfalls somewhere in this region are almost certain every year. Fundamental changes are needed to address the risks of weather-related coastal hazards and the increasing vulnerability of coastal communities' economies, social systems, and governmental and private institutions.

The costs currently reported are typically limited to insured and uninsured property losses and official disaster relief expenditures. Even these limited cost data are uneven in availability and consistency. A much broader understanding of the categories and range of coastal hazard costs is needed. These include not only the losses to the built environment but also additional impacts, such as

- uninsured business interruption costs,
- social and family disruptions and health costs, and
- costs of the damages to natural resources and ecosystem services.

Communities need a better understanding of what types of mitigation approaches can reduce the range of coastal hazard costs. This book suggests a wide range of techniques for reducing losses to property as well as for protecting natural resources. A new framework for risk and cost assessment should enable communities to rank a set of cost-effective hazard mitigation measures that can be undertaken given limited resources for implementation and enforcement. Each community potentially affected by hazards must evaluate its own vulnerability to specific hazards and determine the need for alternative mitigation measures. These analyses may be placed higher on the local and state political agenda if policymakers have a fuller appreciation of the wide range of potential losses that may occur if a disaster affects their region. In this sense, this book should be viewed as a starting point for a more detailed analysis of the hidden costs of disasters.

Costs of Coastal Hazards

Accounting for the full range of costs of coastal hazards and disasters—both reported and unreported or hidden costs—is an enormous challenge. Yet an improved understanding of the costs of hazards and disasters is essential for accurate risk assessment and wise investment of mitigation dollars. This study found that the typically reported costs of coastal hazards and disasters are greatly underestimated. Often unaccounted for are the costs to the business community; costs to individuals, families, and neighborhoods; costs to public and private social institutions; and costs to natural resources and the environment. In addition, the costs to people far from the immediate disaster, who give directly to private relief efforts and indirectly through their tax contributions, are not recognized explicitly. Finally, one must consider that disasters do create benefits to some stakeholders (e.g., contractors) and to regions unaffected by the disaster; this report focuses only on the costs associated with coastal hazards.

Significant improvements can and should be made in coastal hazard and disaster cost accounting. Some of these can be made with a modest effort and investment. Other changes will require significant resources, improved intergovernmental and public–private cooperation, and political support and will. In considering these changes, the panel makes the following recommendations:

• The Federal Emergency Management Agency (FEMA), the National Emergency Management Association, the Institute for Business and Home Safety, and the American Red Cross and other voluntary disaster relief organizations should collectively convene a task force of their governmental and nongovernmental counterparts to identify ways to improve and coordinate disaster cost data collection, reporting, and accessibility.

—An important objective for such a task force would be to find ways to better incorporate the hidden costs of coastal hazards and disasters as identified in this report.

—Cost data of all types should be made more accessible by being located at, or linked to, a single World Wide Web site.

- Current methodologies and databases used by federal and federally mandated disaster response agencies to report expenditures associated with a given event should be expanded to include a more complete range of costs, consistent with the business, social, and natural resources categories recommended in this report.

—Protocols should be developed to promote consistency among diverse databases with respect to geographical scale, reporting period (e.g., fiscal year), and purpose.

—Where it is inappropriate for existing databases to incorporate these data, new record keeping and reporting mechanisms should be established.

—New information collected should, at a minimum, include location, type of loss, cause of loss, and actual or estimated dollar amounts in all four categories: business, social, natural resources, and built environment.

- Existing and new databases should record the geographic location of losses down to at least the zip code level. This would be especially valuable to municipal, county, and state officials who need these data to analyze risk and decide on appropriate mitigation strategies and investments. These data, when displayed using a geographic information system (GIS), would also be useful for public education and guidance of mitigation at all levels.

—The Institute for Business and Home Safety (IBHS) database of paid insured catastrophe losses provides information about insured losses by zip code for post-1994 events. If such information were available from FEMA and other sources, results might be combined into a single estimate of losses by zip code, thereby providing an improved picture of the geographic distribution of losses.

- Post-disaster reports for hurricanes and other disasters, currently written by state agencies and others, should be expanded to address the business, social, health, and natural resource and ecosystem impacts and costs.

—To implement this new structure, state emergency managers, in cooperation with federal agencies and private-sector representatives, should enhance their existing stakeholder network from each of these categories in advance. Then, when a disaster strikes, post-disaster teams can be mobilized quickly.

—A periodic update procedure should provide for a more complete accounting of the long-term and often unreported costs that accrue in the years following a disaster.

—Sector-specific post-disaster teams for business and employment, housing, human resources, and health and environment should be assembled following a disaster. The North Carolina Disaster Recovery Task Force on Hurricane Fran serves as a possible state-level model.

• Individual communities should consider implementing community-based post-disaster damage and loss reporting. A comprehensive pre-disaster assessment of the full range of potential costs at the community level would provide a basis for establishing such a reporting process.

• An intensive, intergovernmental research effort is needed to identify federal, state, and local public policies that directly or indirectly promote growth and development that increase the vulnerability of communities to coastal disasters.

• The policies so identified and the programs that flow from them should be changed to include "natural hazard vulnerability and mitigation needs" as key criteria in decision-making processes.

• At the federal level, NOAA and FEMA should take the lead in this research; at the state level, coastal zone management programs, in alliance with economic development and emergency management agencies, should lead the way.

Improving Risk and Vulnerability Assessment

Assessment of risk and vulnerability is important because it is directly related to the quality of the decisions made regarding how to reduce societal and environmental exposure to coastal hazard impacts. The risk and vulnerability of an area can be overestimated, hidden, or unreported, leading to incorrect estimates of the expected costs and benefits of development and mitigation options. Conventional risk assessment has tended to emphasize that which has been (or can be) measured quantitatively. This approach has worked well for those concerned parties whose costs fall exclusively into these categories. However, for many other stakeholders (higher risk groups are discussed in detail in chapter 4), environmental and social impact costs are not expressed well in conventional categories of risk assessment. Consequently, new methods of vulnerability assessment should be designed to go beyond the limitations of conventional risk assessment using mechanisms such as community vulnerability maps. Much work remains to be done to promote integrated assessments of risk and vulnerability to improve the decision-making process.

Based on its review of risk and vulnerability assessment in relation to coastal hazards, the panel makes the following recommendations:

- Vulnerability studies conducted by federal, state, or local agencies should incorporate a broader set of potential losses and costs than is typical in traditional assessments. In addition to potential damage to the built environment, such a study should consider the characteristics of individuals and families at risk and environmental vulnerabilities of the community or region.
- Community vulnerability assessments should include evaluations of the circumstances and locations of concentrations of high-risk groups, such as the poor, elderly, handicapped, women living alone, female-headed households, families with low ratios of adults to dependents, ethnic minorities, renters, recent residents including immigrants, transients, tourists, and the homeless.
- Research is needed on the physical, emotional, and social effects of disasters on both men and women of varying age, ethnicity, and social class. Such research will explain the effects of social, economic, and political status on disaster response at household, neighborhood, and community levels.
- Risk assessments of coastal hazards should delineate the uncertainty (e.g., confidence intervals) associated with the likelihood of disasters and the potential losses should a disaster occur.
- Existing research on business costs related to coastal hazards is quite limited, and that which is available focuses on businesses with fewer than 50 employees. Therefore, more studies should be undertaken focusing on the vulnerability of and costs to both large and small businesses, and the impacts of business interruption on the affected community.
- Communities should develop and maintain up-to-date databases of existing building stock, critical facilities such as hospitals and evacuation centers, public utilities, and public buildings. The recorded information should include location of these facilities and their property or replacement values. This information would be valuable as input to HAZUS (Hazards U.S.) and other GIS mapping tools. Community vulnerability maps should be developed that include the locations of high-risk households and congregate living facilities.

Developing and Evaluating Mitigation Strategies

The previous findings and recommendations highlight the need for reliable cost data related to coastal hazards and for new databases listing unreported costs. Such data would assist federal, state, and local governments in delineating the full range of costs of a coastal disaster, a first step in the development of mitigation strategies. Hazard mitigation is defined by FEMA as "sustained action to reduce or eliminate the long-term risk to people and property from hazards and their effects."

A paradigm shift in hazard mitigation is beginning to occur. Model state programs in Florida and elsewhere are designed to foster more disaster resistant communities, and some private business and insurance industry initiatives have had similar goals. There has also been a new focus on intergovernmental and public–private collaboration aimed at reducing hazard vulnerability. However, some of these efforts must still be characterized as pilot programs, while others, especially in Florida, are expanding. The more successful of these programs may eventually be institutionalized and expanded to other states and regions.

Foresight in the design and management of the built environment is key to effective coastal hazard mitigation. It is through the process of developing and redeveloping safer communities—disaster resistant communities—that it is possible to achieve significant reductions in the costs of coastal hazards. This book defines a disaster resistant community (DRC) as a community or region developed or redeveloped to minimize the human, environmental, and property losses and the social and economic disruption caused by natural disasters.

Traditional approaches to mitigation, land-use planning, flood proofing, elevated structures, and building codes, although important, are no longer enough. A community-based approach is required that integrates the principles and techniques of mitigation into the very manner in which communities are developed and redeveloped. This can be done through the existing planning-development process available in almost every community. An improved understanding of natural systems and appropriate siting, design, and construction of the built environment are essential to advances in hurricane and weather-related hazard mitigation.

Damage to natural ecosystems and resources during and after a hurricane or major storm is inevitable. However, communities, public agencies, and individuals can help reduce the vulnerability of natural ecosystems and resources to coastal hazards by preventing releases of hazardous waste with proper handling, storage, and contingency planning. Sound planning and siting of development and infrastructure consistent with realistic coastal disaster scenarios is an important environmental protection tool. Preserving and restoring floodplains and wetlands would allow these areas to serve as storm and erosion buffers and as temporary storage of floodwaters. Strict enforcement of building codes may result in less debris released into the environment with the result that less space would be taken from valuable landfill capacity. Protection of beaches, dunes, and native vegetation, and appropriate building construction setbacks that take into consideration natural coastal processes may help to minimize damage to critical habitats. This would also lessen the need for expensive beach restoration that can further degrade turtle nests and shorebird habitats.

The domain of benefit–cost analysis must be expanded to include the evaluation of the relative effectiveness of different mitigation strategies. As the panel has recommended, the concept of costs must be broadened to incorporate many of the hidden costs and impacts of coastal disasters. A successful mitigation strategy requires that interested parties interact so that each feels net gains will be achieved if specific measures are implemented. The Project Impact program run by FEMA, the IBHS Showcase Community program, and the Disaster Recovery Business Alliance (described in chapter 5) are new initiatives that bring key stakeholders together to develop strategies for reducing future losses from natural hazards.

Based on its analysis of mitigation strategies, the panel makes the following recommendations:

- Communities can follow a number of general steps to help plan and create a disaster resistant community. To be successful, the plan must be developed and supported by a full range of local players—government officials, developers, the citizenry, financial and insurance institutions, business leaders, and state and federal governments. The five steps in such a process are:
  1. promote public awareness;
  2. maintain a comprehensive perspective;
  3. integrate mitigation planning into the local decision-making process;
  4. conduct a community risk analysis; and
  5. create and use a disaster resource network.

  Further information about these steps is provided in chapter 5.

- Existing community-based hazard mitigation planning models should be expanded to include not only the risk to the built environment but also business, social, and natural resource or ecosystem risks and vulnerabilities.

- Communities should consider establishing a local hazard mitigation committee composed of individuals who represent key stakeholders from the community as well as state and federal officials who have expertise in hazard mitigation. Such a committee can play an important role in developing and evaluating mitigation strategies.
- Existing building codes must be enforced.
- Empirically based model programs for reducing the risk of coastal hazards are needed. These programs should factor in the impacts and costs associated with the built environment, business, social concerns, and natural resources.
- All levels of government (federal, state, and local) should examine their current programs and policies to determine whether they are acting as disincentives to mitigation efforts.
- To reduce the indirect effects of a coastal hazard event, community disaster plans should provide for prompt response to the social needs of the affected community by placing a higher priority on the restoration of schools, recreational facilities, family counseling programs, daycare centers, and shelters for abused women and children, in addition to hospitals. The plans also should promote neighborhood-level response networks and initiatives.
- To deal with the broader set of costs of coastal hazards, there is a need for a mitigation strategy that combines a number of policy tools, including building codes, land-use planning (e.g., zoning), incentives (e.g., subsidies, fines), taxation (e.g., property taxes), and insurance. Developing and implementing these policy tools will require an integrated effort by a number of the concerned parties, including contractors and developers, real estate agents, banks and financial institutions, insurers, and public-sector agencies.
- A partnership with the insurance industry should be developed and an analysis of the industry undertaken to determine how it can play a more creative role in encouraging mitigation through linkages with other policy tools as well as with other interested parties such as financial institutions, developers, and the real estate community. Insurance rates should reflect the risk associated with the hazard so that appropriate premium reductions can be given to property owners who adopt loss-reduction measures. If rates are suppressed in high-hazard areas, as they appear to be in some states, then one cannot expect insurance to be used effectively as a policy tool for encouraging adoption of mitigation measures.

A Framework for Community Planning

Although this study focuses on weather-related coastal hazards, the panel developed a framework that can be used to address a broad range of natural hazards and incorporates the concerns of the key interested parties. To the panel's knowledge, this is the first attempt to incorporate a broad set of impacts that a community should consider in determining if a particular strategy is attractive enough to adopt.

The Risk and Cost Assessment framework (figure ES.1) is organized around three principles:

1. The importance of developing a broad set of alternative mitigation and preparedness strategies, recognizing the relevance of the status quo but not being restricted by current policy.
2. The importance of characterizing the potential losses from disasters of different magnitudes by linking risk assessment with the vulnerability of the region.
3. The need to incorporate a very broad range of economic, business, social, and environmental costs (both immediate and incurred over time) associated with weather-related hazard events when evaluating alternative mitigation and preparedness strategies.

The Risk and Cost Assessment framework serves as a conceptual planning tool, which a coastal community can use to develop mitigation strategies that respond to its physical location, development patterns, social institutions, and resulting vulnerabilities. The Heinz panel framework proposes that risk and vulnerability result from a combination of natural conditions and societal conditions. The framework also emphasizes the importance of developing strategies for preparedness and mitigation that take into account a broad set of direct and indirect costs. Finally, an evaluation of these strategies needs to consider the impact on individual stakeholder groups as well as on society. In developing alternative mitigation and preparedness strategies, it is essential to first examine the current set of programs and evaluate their performance. Then, one or more elements may be varied to determine how the status quo would be affected.

The recommendations offered in this book suggest a wide range of activities that should be pursued locally and regionally. In particular, the panel strongly urges community and regional leaders to rethink the potential costs resulting from future disasters and to take the necessary steps now to mitigate these impacts.

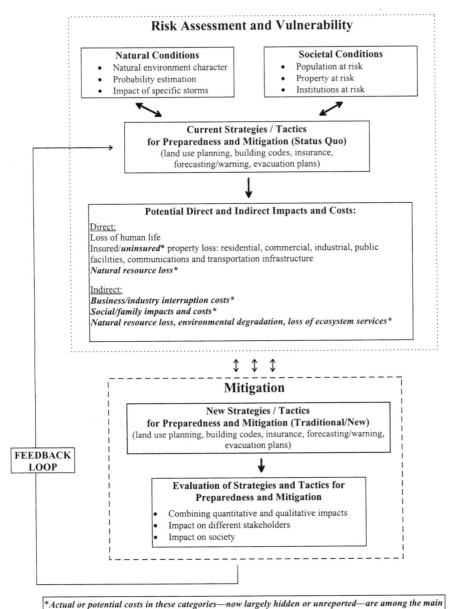

Figure ES.1. Risk and Cost Assessment Framework.

Chapter 1

Setting the Stage

Nature to be commanded must be obeyed.
                           —Sir Francis Bacon

Humans have been attracted to the coast for millennia. Food is abundant; coastal waters provide easy transport; and the elemental, aesthetic appeal of the ocean and beaches draws people who want to live, work, and play in their proximity. The twentieth century has brought unprecedented growth in coastal populations, and this trend has stimulated industrial, commercial, recreational, and residential development in coastal areas. Growth and development have brought people pleasure as well as problems, including pollution of nearshore waters, loss of valuable coastal wetlands, degradation of major fishery resources, and crowding of recreational areas. Rapid growth in development has also increased the nation's vulnerability to weather-related coastal hazards, as more people choose to live in areas plagued by coastal storms. This book explores the implications of this increased vulnerability.

A paradigm shift is already occurring. For example, a new federal emergency management philosophy is putting a new, strong emphasis on advanced planning and damage prevention. Model state programs are designed to foster more disaster resistant communities, and some private business and insurance industry initiatives have had similar goals. There has also been a new focus on intergovernmental and public–private collaboration aimed at reducing hazard vulnerability. However, many of these efforts must still be characterized as pilot programs.

The term "hidden costs," as used in this book, refers to the unreported hidden or undocumented costs related to coastal hazards. These hidden costs, coupled with the reported costs, constitute the true costs of a coastal hazard. Many of the hidden costs cannot be quantified or reported in dollar terms.

1

Furthermore, the true costs of a particular coastal hazard cannot be summed to a bottom-line figure because they are based on different measures (e.g., insured losses and injuries) and different time and spatial scales. Rather than providing a bottom line, the concept of "true costs" provides a way to look at the complex tapestry of coastal hazards and the corresponding richness and subtlety needed for accurate and useful risk and vulnerability assessment.

Both the economic and the noneconomic costs of disasters fall unevenly on different classes of victims and stakeholders. Table 1.1 illustrates the approximate incidence of various major and minor costs borne by a range of cost-bearing entities, including victims ("unreimbursed"), private insurance companies, the American Red Cross, states, and various federal programs. This table indicates roughly how the different kinds of costs are likely to be distributed under current U.S. disaster policies, without attempting to quantify the impacts. As indicated, many costs are shared among several different loss-bearers; seldom, if ever, do individuals and commercial victims emerge from disasters with no residual losses. But, depending on their insurance coverage and eligibility for federal assistance of various types, victims can transfer much of the economic consequences of disaster damage to other levels of society.

An important feature of table 1.1 is the category "Government Response." Often, the governmental costs of disasters are thought to include only the direct transfer payments made to individuals, businesses, or state and local governments as grants, loans, or federal insurance payments (for floods or crops). But the costs to the federal government of administering these programs are likely to be substantial. In addition to the Federal Emergency Management Agency (FEMA), a variety of other federal agencies respond to coastal hazard events. They include the U.S. Army Corps of Engineers, the Environmental Protection Agency, the Small Business Administration, and the Departments of Agriculture, Transportation, and Housing and Urban Development.

Sending governmental staff and consultants into the field, setting up disaster field offices, assessing damage, and facilitating the recovery process require an enormous commitment of federal resources. Some of these expenses are covered by the regular operating budgets of federal agencies such as FEMA. Other administrative or "overhead" costs are paid from supplementary appropriations following major disasters. The costs of rendering assistance are usually not distinguished from the assistance itself in governmental accounting practices.

A much broader understanding is needed of the costs of coastal hazards, including the costs of

Table 1.1. Typical Distribution of Financial and Other Impacts of a Coastal Disaster

Type of Impact	Nonfederal	Federal[a]							
	Unreimbursed	Private Insurance	American Red Cross	State	National Flood Insurance Program	Small Business Administration	FEMA Individual Assistance	FEMA Public Assistance	Other Federal
Built Environment									
Private	XXX	XXX			XXX	XXX		XXX	
Public	X	X		X					
Business	XXX	XXX	X			XXX			
Social	XXX		XXX	XXX			XXX		XXX
Natural Resources	XXX								
Agricultural	XXX	X							XXX
Government									
Response									
Local	X	X		X				XXX	
State	X							XXX	
Federal[a]									

[a] Federal administrative costs are absorbed by relevant program or supplementary appropriation.

XXX = Major Cost

X = Minor Cost

- uninsured business interruptions;
- social and family disruptions and health problems; and
- damages to natural resources and ecosystem services.

Finally, communities need a better understanding of how mitigation can help lower these costs. Society has very limited hazard mitigation dollars to invest. Which actions will be the most cost effective, considering the true range of costs incurred? This book explores these issues by taking a structured approach to the problem, suggesting a new framework for community-based hazard mitigation, and making recommendations to help address these questions.

The balance of this chapter describes the coasts of the continental United States and associated development activities. It outlines the geographic reach of coastal hazards, and current public polices that help or hinder communities attempting to deal with coastal hazards. The policy overview is provided to give the reader a general understanding of the complexities and players involved.

Types of Coasts, Human Activities, and Coastal Development

The coasts of the United States are extremely diverse, and human activities add another layer of complexity to the natural processes of ever-changing coastlines. Human actions have direct and indirect effects on coastal areas. An example of an indirect effect is sediment starvation caused by the damming of rivers, which affects the amount of sediment carried to wetlands. Another human action that affects coasts is the removal of dune grasses and disturbance of coastal landforms, promoting increased erosion (Williams 1995). The major physical coastal landforms include:

- crystalline bedrock (e.g., central and eastern Maine coast);
- eroding bluffs and cliffs (e.g., outer Cape Cod; parts of Long Island, New York; Great Lakes);
- pocket beaches between headlands (e.g., southern New England; California; Oregon);
- strandplain beaches (e.g., Myrtle Beach, South Carolina; Holly Beach, Louisiana);
- barrier islands (e.g., generally along Atlantic and Gulf of Mexico ocean coasts);
- coral reef and mangrove (e.g., southern Florida, Hawaii, Puerto Rico);

- coastal wetlands (e.g., southern Louisiana; elsewhere generally landward of barrier beaches); and
- deltaic coasts (e.g., coastal Louisiana, Mississippi, Texas) (National Research Council, 1990).

These varying types of physical coasts lend themselves to human activities in different ways. Beaches, both on coastal barriers and on mainland strandplain, obviously attract public and private recreational use, along with related residential, commercial, and public development of all kinds. Pocket beaches and coves typical of southern New England tend to be bordered by villages, wharves, older homes, and newer condominiums and marinas. Bluffs and cliffs along the Pacific coast and Great Lakes become lined with single rows of higher-priced homes, providing spectacular views but often no direct access to the water. These physical patterns operate in conjunction with other factors—location, accessibility, suitability for boating and fishing, market image, and historical patterns of usage—to shape the human use of coasts.

What Is a Coastal Community?

Much is said in this book and elsewhere about the role of coastal communities in planning for and mitigating the effects of coastal disasters. But the meaning of "coastal community" varies widely among states, and locally, from one segment of coast to another. In addition, units of local jurisdiction seldom correspond to physical clusters of coastal development. It is therefore important to recognize that the concept of "coastal community" has different meanings in different places and political contexts in the United States.

Coastal New England, as an example, differs from the rest of the United States in that all land (regardless of state), lies within incorporated towns and cities. In other words, there is no unincorporated land on the New England coast. Each town or city is vested under state law with the power to plan and zone land use, enforce the state wetlands laws, and regulate new subdivisions, among other powers. This practice provides a readily identifiable unit of local government for each segment of coast. However, because these local units usually extend well inland, the coast is often of secondary importance when it comes to setting priorities among municipal issues.

The rest of the Atlantic and Gulf of Mexico coastline is governed by either local incorporated municipalities (e.g., cities, towns, villages, boroughs) or counties covering unincorporated areas. Some coastal municipalities are limited entirely to all or a portion of a coastal barrier (e.g., Beach Haven, New Jersey; Folly Beach, South Carolina; Sand Key, Florida). The barrier shore of New Jersey is segmented into small coastal jurisdictions that can be compared to "beads on a string." Other coastal segments may be located within a mainland city (e.g., New York City), to which coastal hazard mitigation may be of limited interest.

On the Pacific coast, cities and counties divide planning and hazards management responsibilities for areas under their jurisdiction, with policy guidance from state coastal management programs. Local coastal plans in Washington, Oregon, and California play an important role in hazard mitigation through land use controls, but the strength and effectiveness of these strategies and the tools employed vary widely from jurisdiction to jurisdiction. Further, none of these states has standardized building setback construction rules (e.g., each jurisdiction uses its own methods, and few are based on good scientific information). All three states also permit seawalls and revetments in some areas.

Complicating mitigation efforts in these three states is the nature of coastal hazards and risks. Erosion caused by winter storms is highly episodic with respect to which properties are affected. Thus it is difficult to predict vulnerability at any specific site. The potential for very large and destructive local earthquakes and tsunamis in the Pacific Northwest is a relatively recent discovery that presents huge challenges for those concerned about life, safety, lifelines, and infrastructure. Such events would require funds beyond local resources yet still need local planning and response efforts.

Coastal Land Use

Much public attention is directed to a particular subclass of coastal land use, namely expensive summer or retirement residential development. This type of development has sprouted along many accessible barrier shorelines since the 1960s, and it accounts for an important category of investment at risk from coastal hazards. However, this type of oceanfront development is not the sole form of coastal land use. Indeed, the coasts are characterized by a wide diversity of development from one location to another. Even in close proximity to intense development, substantial areas of preserved natural coastline can be found.

By way of illustration, consider the short stretch of Atlantic coast extending from Ipswich, Massachusetts, to Portsmouth, New Hampshire, a distance of approximately 25 miles. The natural landforms of this coast consist of a series of narrow coastal barriers, punctuated by a few areas of bedrock outcrop and glacial deposits and interrupted by inlets and river mouths (most notably the Merrimack River). Behind the barriers lie sizable areas of saltmarsh interwoven with tidal creeks but little open water.

Settlement of this segment of coast dates back to the seventeenth century and has proceeded in spurts in response to different economic and social forces ever since. Starting at the southern end, in the towns of Ipswich and Newbury, Massachusetts, the natural barrier beaches, dunes, and woodlands are largely preserved through the efforts of federal, state, town, and nonprofit organizations. Cranes Beach in Ipswich is managed by the Trustees for Public Reservations, Inc. Much of Plum Island, across an inlet from Cranes Beach, is included in the Parker River Wildlife Refuge, operated by the U.S. Fish and Wildlife Service. Continuing north, there is an abrupt transition from the wildlife refuge to a highly developed area of shore cottages built on small lots. This is the developed part of Plum Island; it dates back to the 1920s and is divided between two towns. In 1998, island residents were trying to decide whether to tax themselves to import sewer and water service from the "mainland." Roughly a mile west of Plum Island, on the south side of the Merrimack River, lies the center of Newburyport, a historic community of ship captains' homes, old port buildings, and a wooden boat–building establishment on the National Historic Register.

Crossing the Merrimack River, a very different coastal community is encountered at Salisbury Beach, Massachusetts. A state beach at the north side of the Merrimack River mouth lies next to a 1950s-era amusement park. The beach in front of the commercial district is covered with collapsing pavilions extending out on pilings into the water. There is a very small dry-sand portion of the beach in this area, and Salisbury stakes its future on the development of an oceanfront casino.

Continuing north, the shore road (Route 1A) is lined on both sides by vacation cottages ranging from shacks and mobile homes to more auspicious dwellings and condos. Crossing the state line, beachfront development appears to be more recent and of a more year-round character than in Salisbury. The Seabrook Nuclear Plant lies across a narrow estuary, probably discouraging further investment in the immediate area, which is clearly subject to evacuation limitations in the event of an accident. But within one mile lies the thriving summer resort of Hampton Beach. A couple of miles of bars, T-shirt outlets, and rental units face the ocean across from a four-lane highway, parking, an imposing seawall, and a fairly wide beach. Directly north of Hampton Beach is the town of Rye, New Hampshire, where the shore turns rocky and the houses are million-dollar homes set amid lawns, gardens, and rock walls. At the Portsmouth city limits, the scene abruptly changes again as Route 1A enters the twisting, crowded neighborhoods of an old port town now vigorously marketing itself as a tourist destination.

New England is atypical among U.S. coastal areas in terms of the diversity to be found within a relatively short distance. But the point of this detailed description is that it is difficult to generalize about coastal development anywhere. Some places are heavily developed, some less so, and some not at all. Some areas are devoted to mansions; others to mobile homes. Some areas are relatively safe from coastal hazards; others wait to be destroyed. The potential costs of weather-related coastal hazards, and the choice of coping strategies to reduce those costs, need to be calculated in light of the actual geographical circumstances of particular segments of coast and coastal communities.

The Geographic Reach of Coastal Hazards

This chapter addresses the effects of coastal hazards on three broad geographical areas of impact: open ocean coasts, estuarine areas, and inland areas affected by coastal hazards.

Open Ocean Coasts

The most obvious effects of coastal storms and hurricanes are visible immediately along the open ocean coast (approximately equivalent to "the coastal high-hazard zone" or "V zone" mapped by the National Flood Insurance Program). Whether situated on a coastal barrier or a mainland beach or bluff shore, the ocean–land interface is a place of great danger and sudden transformation during storms. The physical effects exerted on the open ocean coast include:

- storm surge flooding, which is especially damaging when it occurs in tandem with high tides or over several tidal cycles;
- storm-driven waves that crest high above the already elevated state of sea level at times of storm surge, which may overwash dune fields and built structures;
- erosion (both long term and episodic), which can undermine dunes, buildings, and artificial protective structures and cause bluffs to collapse;
- wind, which can damage roofs and windows, and even destroy entire buildings;
- rain, which causes water damage to the interior and contents of wind-damaged structures and contributes to inland stream flooding, disruption of transportation systems, and overflow of storm sewer systems;
- secondary effects, such as damage to second-tier structures when ocean-front houses are washed off their pilings or foundations, and the destruction of roads, septic systems, water lines, and other infrastructure;
- tsunamis, which are huge seismic sea waves triggered by undersea earth-

quakes and can travel thousands of miles at speeds of 300 to 400 miles per hour; and

- sea-level rise, which in the past century, has averaged about 1.5 millimeters per year worldwide.

Estuarine Areas

Coastal barriers stand between the open ocean and more-sheltered estuaries. Typically, the estuarine environment consists of highly diverse combinations of open water, tidal mudflats, saltmarshes, and other wetlands. Estuaries are characterized by the mixing of salt and fresh water as influenced by tidal cycles, storms, and variations in inland runoff. Estuaries in their natural state are areas of high biotic productivity and diversity of organisms, such as shellfish, finfish, birds, and plants, which they nurture, directly or indirectly.

Estuarine areas along the landward-facing shores of coastal barriers and along mainland shores and tidal river mouths are vulnerable to the effects of coastal hazards that affect the open coast. The natural estuarine habitat itself may be altered by extreme coastal events such as catastrophic hurricanes. A storm surge enters bays behind barriers through inlets or by overwash and breaches created by the storm itself. The high-water levels thereby introduced cause flooding to structures along bay shorelines. Sometimes water trapped in bays overwashes the barrier in reverse, forming an ebb tidal inlet that is destructive to structures in its path. Breaking waves are not usually a problem along estuarine shorelines, except when winds blow across a bay or sound with sufficient "fetch" (or breadth) to allow appreciable waves to develop. Bayshore erosion can also be a problem along broad bays or where the scour of tidal currents affects areas where wetlands have been disturbed. Wind and rain of course cause much damage in estuarine areas. On narrow barriers, bayside homes may be located behind oceanfront homes and thus be battered by debris from these other residences propelled by water or wind.

Inland Areas Affected by Coastal Hazards

Apart from the open ocean and estuarine zones of coastal damage, areas slightly farther inland, either on a wide coastal barrier or on the mainland, are vulnerable to both wind and flood damage as well as secondary effects from the disruption of infrastructure. In areas of steeper, unstable slopes, as along the Pacific Coast, inland storm effects may include rockslides or mudslides in the vicinity of the coast, and sometimes far inland. Inland flood damage results from either tidal storm surges, freshwater stream runoff, storm-sewer backup, or combinations of these. Beyond the reach of tidal flow, flooding is largely a function of heavy precipitation and inadequate (or nonexistent) storm sewer capacity. An indirect effect of coastal storms on inland areas may be saltwater intrusion into groundwater aquifers, and the resulting contamination of public and private water sources. Also, surface waters may be affected by turbidity from heavy storm runoff or various chemical and biological contaminants, such as those leaking from storage tanks or sewage treatment facilities. Wind hazards can penetrate 100–200 miles inland as seen in hurricanes Hugo and Fran. The inland wind damage in Fran was equal to the direct coastal damages.

All of this is to say that coastal hazards affect different geographical areas differently. On the one hand, to confine attention to "open ocean" coastal damage overlooks the broader areas along estuaries and inland areas that incur damage from coastal weather-related hazards. But the types of damage and resulting costs that arise in estuarine and inland settings are very different from those associated with the exposed open coast. Although the latter may be more dramatic and photogenic, in terms of damaged real estate, the effects elsewhere may be more insidious, more widely experienced, and ultimately more costly to individuals and to society. What society does in response, however, may be shaped more by the greater visibility and media attention accorded to the "front row" of oceanfront homes.

Current Public Policy

The costs of coastal hazards are influenced by state and federal laws as well as by local ordinances. More specifically, coastal communities (including cities, towns, and counties) are subject to both state and federal laws and policies concerning coastal development, wetlands, endangered species, waste management, and natural hazards. State governments empower local governments to engage in land use planning, zoning, and taxation. Most states also delegate authority to local governments to regulate subdivisions and provide local public infrastructure such as roads, schools, and parks, including coastal access facilities. Thirty-two of 35 states eligible to participate in the U.S. Coastal Zone Management Program (CZMP) have federally approved programs and receive funding to implement those programs; part of this funding goes toward management of development in areas vulnerable to coastal hazards. State coastal management programs meet federal guidelines in many ways, by networking pre-existing authorities, adopting new laws and programs, and developing and implementing new tools, such as building-construction setbacks. Details on specific state programs can be obtained from the National Oceanographic and Atmospheric Administration (NOAA) Office of Ocean and Coastal Resource Management (OCRM), the unit that oversees state programs; for further information, see their World Wide Web site at http://www.nos.noaa.gov/ocrm. Another good source of information on state coastal programs is the Coastal States Organization in Washington, D.C.

The federal government assumes many roles with respect to coastal hazards and has a wide range of agencies playing these roles, including the Department of Transportation, the Internal Revenue Service, the Federal Emergency Management Agency, the Department of Housing and Urban Development, and the Corps of Engineers. It is the primary source of disaster assistance, the rebuilder of damaged communities, and the principal champion of hazard mitigation. However, there is no comprehensive, consistent national policy on the problem of coastal hazards. As with other types of natural hazards, the enactment of new laws, policies, and programs has closely followed significant and well-publicized coastal disasters.

According to Platt et al. (1992), the formulation of a national policy on coastal hazards has been complicated by a number of factors:

1. the variability in coastal hazards depends on the physical type of shoreline, the effects of human intervention (i.e., coastal engineering), the available sand supply, and the geographic incidence of storms;
2. the multiplicity of units and levels of coastal management entities (e.g., private and public riparian landowners, municipalities, counties, special districts, states, and federal agencies that exercise authority over various aspects of coastal resource management);
3. the problem of cost sharing of hazard mitigation projects derived from the mixture of public and private interests in the coastal zone (e.g., public recreation vs. private homeowner or tenant use of beaches);
4. the lack of reliable long-term data with which to estimate potential risk from coastal hazards;
5. conflict between economic and environmental objectives in coastal management programs;
6. the variety of approaches to coastal hazard mitigation (e.g., shoreline armoring, sand trapping, beach nourishment, land-use controls, retreat);
7. the political representation in the U.S. Congress for coastal areas; and
8. the conflict between private property rights and public health, safety, and cost-saving goals.

Shoreline Protection and Beach Nourishment

The U.S. Corps of Engineers has a shoreline protection program that has evolved over the last 50 years in response to coastal storms and the resulting federal legislation. As of July 1993, the program consisted of 82 authorized projects along 226 miles of ocean and Great Lakes shoreline (U.S. Army Corps of Engineers, 1996). Such projects constitute less than 1 percent of the nation's total shoreline and about 8 percent of the critically eroding shore-line. Over time, the projects have evolved from hardened structures (e.g., groins, breakwaters, and seawalls) to soft structures (e.g., sand fills) and from an emphasis on erosion-control projects providing for recreational beaches to storm-damage-reduction projects providing incidental recreational benefits. Of the 82 projects, 26 were authorized in the late 1950s and early 1960s but were small in scope, with an average federal cost at the time of construction of $67,000 and an average physical length of about 0.6 miles.

The Corps of Engineers continues to conduct technical studies of coastal hazards through its Coastal Engineering Research Center (CERC) in Vicks-burg, Mississippi. When authorized by the Congress, the Corps also contin-ues to nourish beaches in many locations. The Corps currently has 57 pro-jects under way or proposed. These include the massive renourishment extending from Sea Bright to Asbury Park, New Jersey. The first 12 miles of this project are projected by the Corps to cost more than $1 billion, sug-gesting a cost approaching $3 billion for the entire 33-mile project (Pilkey and Dixon, 1996).

Federal Disaster Assistance

The Federal Disaster Assistance Program began modestly with the Disaster Relief Act of 1950 (P.L. 81-875), which marked the first of a series of laws that would progressively commit the nation to spending tens of billions of dollars on relief and recovery from natural disasters. Initially, its benefits were limited to covering local public costs; later, the benefits would be ex-tended to include private enterprise and individuals as well. After the Fed-eral Disaster Relief Act of 1970, the federal government assumed a perma-nent role as the primary source of funds and expertise to deal with major, and some not-so-major, disasters. As originally established by the Congress, the Federal Disaster Assistance Program was to be: limited as to the scope of fed-eral assistance to be supplied; contingent on a disaster declaration by the president that federal assistance is required to supplement state and local ca-pabilities; and limited as to amounts of federal funding to be allocated to dis-aster relief.

These limitations have been greatly eased over time, and disaster decla-rations by the president have been issued more readily and for wider areas than in the past. In fiscal year 1996, a record 72 declarations (weather-related coastal disasters and other natural disasters) were issued, followed by 49 in

Table 1.2. Presidential Major Disaster Declarations Requested and Granted, Fiscal Years 1984–1997

Fiscal Year	Number Requested	Number Declared	Percent Declared
1984	48	35	72
1985	32	19	59
1986	38	30	79
1987	32	24	75
1988	25	17	68
1989	43	29	67
1990	43	35	81
1991	52	39	75
1992	56	46	82
1993	51	39	76
1994	51	36	71
1995	45	29	64
1996	85	72	85
1997	66	49	74
1998	NA	62	NA
AVERAGES			
1984–1988	35	26	74
1988–1992	44	33	75
1993–1997	60	45	75

Source: General Accounting Office, 1995; Alan Rhinesmith, Office of Management and Budget.

1997, and 62 in 1998 (see table 1.2). In addition, the costs of disasters to the federal government have been rising dramatically. Between 1970 and 1981, 376 major disasters and 84 emergencies were declared, leading to direct federal disaster assistance costs of $3.8 billion (unadjusted for inflation) for that period (U.S. General Accounting Office, 1981). By contrast, between 1989 and 1994, 291 declarations cost the U.S. Treasury more than $34 billion (unadjusted for inflation) (Federal Emergency Management Agency, 1997).

The National Flood Insurance Program
The National Flood Insurance Program (NFIP), established by the Congress in 1968, combined protection against losses through insurance with land-use controls to limit future development in designated hazard areas. Under the NFIP, the federal government would map inland and coastal flood hazard areas throughout the nation; establish minimum land use and building standards to regulate future development in such areas; and within communities

that adopt and enforce such standards, offer affordable flood insurance to property owners. The NFIP thus introduced economic and legal measures to limit or redistribute the burdens of flood losses in an effort to reduce the need for either structural flood control projects or federal disaster assistance. The program did not initially cover coastal erosion losses. The 1973 Flood Disaster Act (P.L. 93-234) added "flood-related" coastal erosion as an insurable hazard under the NFIP.

In 1982, based on research findings on then recent hurricane damage, the Congress was persuaded that flood insurance and other federal benefits actually encourage development on coastal barriers. The Coastal Barrier Resources Act of 1982 (P.L. 97-348) designated a Coastal Barrier Resource System, within which federal incentives to new development would be prohibited. The system comprised nearly 200 segments of coastal barriers (expanded in 1990) that were neither developed nor in preserved status. Within these areas, the act prohibited the issuance of new flood insurance coverage and also suspended other federal assistance for highways, bridges, causeways, sewer and water systems, and shore protection projects. In other coastal areas not covered by the act, however, federal flood insurance and other benefits remain in effect.

The NFIP has had a significant impact on recent shoreline development in a vertical, if not a horizontal, direction. Structures built or substantially improved in communities where the NFIP is in effect must be elevated to or above the base (or 100-year) flood elevation. The first habitable floor of new (or "substantially improved") structures must be at or above the specified 100-year flood elevation (plus wave heights), or else insurance premiums will be prohibitive and a building permit may be denied by the local government. Elevation, however, does nothing to retard erosion: Retreating shorelines will simply continue to move toward and beneath the elevated structure until they eventually collapse.

Table 1.3 distinguishes coastal from noncoastal components of NFIP activity. "Coastal communities" include large municipalities and counties that extend far inland in some cases. Some of the data for "coastal communities," therefore, represent inland flood hazard areas. With that qualification, the NFIP is strongly oriented toward coastal communities, with 59 percent of its policies, 63 percent of coverage in force, and 63 percent of premium revenue pertaining to such places. Yet numbers of claims and total amounts paid in claims are lower for coastal communities than would be expected based on their share of program policies and coverage. Much of the insurance coverage in coastal areas has been spared a loss claim so far because many recent hurricanes have largely struck less populated areas. Another reason is that much

Table 1.3. National Flood Insurance Program Activity: Coastal and Noncoastal Communities as of March 31, 1997

Parameter	Coastal Communities (% of NFIP Total)		Noncoastal Communities (% of NFIP Total)	Total NFIP Activity
	Total Community[c]	V Zone Only		
Policies in force	2.1 mill. (58.7%)	77,298 (2.1%)	1.5 mill. (41.3%)	3.6 mill.
Insurance in force	$247 bill. (62.8%)	$4.1 bill. (2.2%)	$146 bill. (37.2%)	$393 bill.
Total premium[a]	$758 mill. (63.1%)	$27.5 mill.	$522 mill. (36.9%)	$1.3 bill.
Average premium	$352	$720	$343	$348
Average coverage	$114,520	$115,615 (post '81) $103,327 (other V)	$96,230	$106,960
Number of claims[b]	316,472 (48.8%)	24,084 (3.7%)	331,942 (51.2%)	648,414
Amount of paid losses[b]	$4.1 bill. (54.8%)	$406 mill. (5.4%)	$3.4 bill. (45.2%)	$7.5 bill.
Average loss[b]	$12,972	$25,359 (post '81) $14,645 (other V)	$10,215	$11,561

[a] For Fiscal Year 1997 through March 31, 1997.
[b] January 1, 1978 through March 31, 1997.
[c] Defined by FEMA as all communities containing a "coastal high hazard area" (V zone). Includes inland portions of such communities.
Source: Federal Emergency Management Agency unpublished data.

of the development in coastal areas is recent and is built using new building codes with higher wind resistance and other construction standards. Recent storms have proven that the losses to new (to code) construction are much less extensive. A direct hit by a category 3 or stronger hurricane on one of the principal metropolitan areas in the East or Southeast would generate several billion dollars in claims (Coch and Wolff, 1990).

Table 1.4 provides a different perspective on the coastal portion of the NFIP. This table summarizes data for coastal counties, by state. These data, of course, include some noncoastal activity. But in the Southeast, even inland flooding may be caused by coastal hurricanes, so this provides a good surrogate for NFIP exposure to coastal flooding. Florida stands out with coastal county coverage exceeding $190 billion, which constitutes 56 percent of all coastal county coverage in the nation, and 40 percent of the total NFIP coverage.

The last line of table 1.4 indicates that coastal counties collectively account for 71 percent of policies in force, 69 percent of premium revenue, and 73 percent of total coverage for the nation. Clearly, such counties also accounted for a heavy proportion of payments and repetitive losses, although exact percentages were not calculated because of different time periods for the databases used in compiling this table.

FEMA has declared mitigation to be the cornerstone of national disaster policy. In support of this goal, the Congress, in the 1994 Flood Insurance Reform Act, undertook the following measures to strengthen the NFIP:

- strengthened lender compliance with requirements that loans secured by flood-prone property are covered by flood insurance policies;
- provided NFIP coverage for "increased cost of compliance" in bringing flood-prone structures up to code;
- established a Flood Mitigation Assistance Program, financed with flood insurance premiums to cover 75 percent of the cost of state or local mitigation projects, including (A) demolition or relocation of structures on eroding shores; (B) elevation, relocation, demolition, or floodproofing of structures in floodplains; (C) acquisition of flood-prone properties; (D) minor physical mitigation projects; and (E) beach nourishment activities; and
- authorized a "Community Rating System" (CRS) allowing flood insurance rates to be reduced in communities that exceed minimum NFIP floodplain management requirements. (FEMA started to develop the CRS in 1989 as a way to encourage mitigation through the incentive of lower insurance rates, an approach widely used in the fire insurance industry.)

Coastal Zone Management

The Federal Coastal Zone Management Program was established by Congress in the Coastal Zone Management Act (CZMA) of 1972 (P.L. 92-583; 16 USC 1451 et seq.), based in part on recommendations in the report of the Stratton Commission (Commission on Marine Science, Engineering and Resources, 1969). The original act primarily reflected the concerns about coastal ecosystem degradation prevention and recreational needs, but was silent on coastal hazards. In 1976, the CZMA was amended to authorize grants to coastal states to develop "a planning process for assessing the effects

Table 1.4. National Flood Insurance Program Activity for Coastal Counties by State (Excluding Great Lakes)

	Policies in Force[a]	Premium Revenue[b] (thousands)	Total Coverage[b] (millions)	Number of Payments[a]	Total Claim Payments[a] (thousands)	Repetitive Loss Payments[c] (thousands)
Alabama	21,690	8,704	2,258	10,938	108,847	26,811
California	181,742	74,125	28,392	23,345	199,331	84,382
Connecticut	23,698	14,693	3,157	11,166	83,606	39,276
Delaware	15,247	6,708	1,848	2,589	15,305	6,021
Florida	1,624,220	532,534	190,850	92,456	1,069,313	178,681
Georgia	35,846	15,834	5,133	2,061	17,496	6,072
Hawaii	47,687	14,111	5,433	3,175	53,155	6,920
Louisiana	265,977	102,389	27,812	115,517	1,113,016	468.897
Maine	4,457	2,617	528	1,943	11,927	2,537
Maryland	31,470	7,972	2,706	1,890	10,899	505
Massachusetts	29,720	18,818	4,549	18,991	188,689	80,473
Mississippi	19,172	7,268	1,911	5,931	33,108	17,414
New Hampshire	1,915	991	181	1,002	5,193	964
New Jersey	121,128	61,447	15,165	41,095	296,846	130,630
New York	45,103	30,022	7,056	23,147	186,224	112,751
North Carolina	57,035	24,503	7,213	19,644	218,359	51,985
Oregon	9,038	4,194	1,120	1,059	9,050	2,349
Puerto Rico	42,495	13,242	2,198	14,106	65,088	32,028
Rhode Island	6,128	4,227	764	1,229	8,661	3,283
South Carolina	105,311	43,506	14,662	21,742	384,120	55,389
Texas	123,826	45,091	14,069	50,015	406,115	151,516
Virgin Islands	2,014	1,099	202	2,030	21,514	8.080
Virginia	9,913	4,408	1,139	1,096	3,695	1,110
Washington	7,632	3,302	819	1,355	16,489	3,579
TOTAL COASTAL COUNTIES	2,832,464	1,041,805	339,165	467,522	4,526,046	1,471,653
TOTAL NFIP	4,037,339	$1,549,107	$466,874	648,414[d]	$7,496,188[d]	$2,581,260[e]
COASTAL COUNTY % OF TOTAL NFIP	70.7	69.3	72.6	[f]	[f]	[f]

[a] Jan. 1, 1978–June 30, 1998.
[b] as of September 16, 1998.
[c] Jan. 1, 1978–Nov. 30, 1997.
[d] Jan. 1, 1978–March 31, 1997.
[e] Jan. 1, 1978–Aug. 19, 1995.
[f] Coastal percentages not calculated due to different time periods of coastal and total NFIP data.
Source: Federal Emergency Management Agency unpublished data.

of, and studying and evaluating ways to control, or lessen the impact of, shoreline erosion, and to restore areas adversely affected by such erosion." (P.L. 94-370, CZMA Sec. 305[b][9]). This still weak provision for hazards management was strengthened by 1980 amendments to the CZMA, wherein Congress encouraged states to use their full authority for "[t]he management of coastal development to minimize the loss of life and property caused by improper development in flood-prone, storm surge, geological hazard, and erosion-prone areas and in areas of subsidence and salt water intrusion, and by the destruction of natural protective features such as beaches, dunes, wet-lands, and barriers islands" (P.L. 94-464, CZMA Sec. 303[2][B]). In 1990, passage of the Coastal Zone Reauthorization Act (P.L. 101-508) provided ad-ditional impetus for states to address hazards. In a new CZMA Section 309, states were required to assess eight coastal issue areas, among them the man-agement of natural hazards and sea-level rise, and develop strategies for pro-gram improvement for the most important of these issues. In the assessment stage, 23 of 29 state coastal programs identified coastal hazards as a high pri-ority and 16 received special hazard management grants (Bernd-Cohen and Gordon, forthcoming, 1999).

Because states, and by delegation, local governments, are vested with the authority to regulate land use and development in the United States, state coastal management program responses to CZMA mandates are potentially very important to the overall coastal hazard mitigation picture. Bernd-Cohen and Gordon (forthcoming, 1999) asserts that states have responded well, using a variety of tools to manage coastal hazards, including building-con-struction setbacks (23 of 29 states studied), regulation of shore protection structures (28 states, including several with outright prohibitions on struc-tures), and mandatory land-use planning to restrict development in haz-ardous areas (9 states). Certain states have particularly strong CZM laws and programs for hazards management, with setbacks and other controls over new or rebuilt development along eroding coasts, for example, the North Carolina Coastal Area Management Act of 1974, the New York Coastal Ero-sion Act of 1981, and the South Carolina Beach Management Act of 1988 (as amended in 1990).

One frequent criticism of CZM programs is the relatively poor coordina-tion between state CZM efforts and implementation of the NFIP. This is par-ticularly true for states where local land-use planning plays only a minor role in state CZM efforts. Generally, the NFIP has been concerned with insurance and building practices at the level of municipalities and property owners, while CZM programs have been oriented to hazard assessment, large-scale planning projects, state-level regulation, and in some states, local land-use planning. Although CZM does contribute significantly to weather-related hazard mitigation, its promise has yet to be fully achieved.

Federal Incentives for Coastal Development

Contrary to the intent of the NFIP and CZMA to reduce vulnerability to coastal hazards, ample incentives have been provided to further growth and rebuilding along the coast. These incentives include various programs that support sewer and water service, highway and causeway access, and beach nourishment. Some of these are justified to support long-established communities, but too often they promote development in new areas, especially on barrier islands.

The 1982 Coastal Barrier Resources Act (CBRA) acknowledged that flood insurance and other federal benefits may serve to stimulate growth in hazardous coastal areas. However, in most coastal areas not covered by the CBRA, flood insurance coverage remains available for elevated structures located as far seaward as the mean high-water line, regardless of local erosion rates. The Congress has continued to fund beach nourishment projects. Disaster assistance continues to be provided despite the perseverance of some critics who demand a tightening of criteria for presidential declarations and a return to higher levels of nonfederal cost sharing. And the Small Business Administration disaster loan program extends credit at subsidized rates to finance reconstruction in hazardous locations.

The federal tax code exerts tremendous influence over land use and building practices in the United States, including the coasts. Clearly, much coastal real estate development benefits from tax deductions for investment property: deductions include virtually all of the costs of ownership (i.e., mortgage interest, taxes, maintenance, advertising, management). When personal use by the owner is limited to tax code guidelines or is nonexistent, annual depreciation can be deducted from the owner's taxable income. When a disaster occurs, a portion of the (noninsured) casualty loss may be deductible from taxable income as well. Detailed statistical evaluation of the effect of tax laws on development in hazardous areas is impossible because of privacy protections accorded to individual tax returns and the lack of any federal effort to aggregate the costs of specific classes of tax deductions.

What Is Missing from Public Policy?

A holistic view of coastal hazards is missing from current practices. This view would encompass a community's risk and vulnerability, including an accounting of the full range of costs of coastal hazards. In addition, research efforts should be undertaken to identify federal, state, and local public policies that directly or indirectly promote growth and development that increase coastal disaster vulnerability; these policies must be considered as well. These myriad policies and programs make implementation at the local level needlessly complicated. The result is numerous specialized "implementing experts," all of whom may be good at dealing with individual policies or programs. However, it is difficult for anyone to see beyond the trees to the forest of risk, vulnerability, and the wide range of economic costs of coastal hazards. Fundamental changes are needed to address the risks of weather-related coastal hazards and the increasing vulnerability of local and regional communities, economies, social systems, and governmental and private institutions.

Book Organization

The following chapters examine in greater detail many of the issues related to coastal hazards and the categories of costs incurred. Chapter 2 describes a "virtual field trip" to South Carolina to explore the devastating effects of 1989's Hurricane Hugo. Hurricane Hugo was chosen because of the rich data set available; the affected region's diverse range of industries (including manufacturing, shipping, and tourism); the boom in shoreline development evident in the area; and the presence of the National Oceanographic and Atmospheric Administration's Coastal Services Center, which facilitated the Heinz panel's interaction with the community. Furthermore, in the panel's judgment, enough time had passed since Hugo (approximately 10 years) to allow for the accumulation of significant information about the storm's effects and categories of costs, but not so much time that the hurricane's immense impact would be dulled in the minds of those who lived through the event.

Chapter 3 presents the panel's analysis of reported and unreported categories of costs resulting from coastal hazards and makes recommendations to improve cost accounting. Chapter 4 discusses the existing risk and vulnerability methods and how they could be used by communities. Chapter 5 evaluates the variety of mitigation and preparedness strategies for dealing with coastal hazards. Chapter 6 describes the linkages among costs, risk and vulnerability, and mitigation strategies and recommends a framework to be used by communities vulnerable to coastal hazards. Appendix A describes the Heinz panel's 1998 workshop in Charleston, South Carolina, and appendix B provides brief descriptions of models used by the insurance and reinsurance industries to estimate damage and risk. A glossary provides definitions for many of the technical terms used throughout the book.

References

Bernd-Cohen, T., and M. Gordon. (forthcoming 1999). State coastal program effectiveness in protecting beaches, dunes, bluffs, and rocky shores. *Coastal Management* 27(2).

Coch, N. K., and M. P. Wolff. 1990. Probable effects of a storm like Hurricane Hugo on Long Island, NY. *Northeastern Environmental Science* 9:33–47.

Commission on Marine Science, Engineering and Resources. 1969. *Our Nation and the Sea.* Washington, DC: U.S. Government Printing Office.

Federal Emergency Management Agency (FEMA). 1997. *Multi-hazard Identification and Risk Assessment.* Washington, DC: FEMA.

National Research Council. 1990. *Managing Coastal Erosion.* Washington, DC: National Academy Press.

Pilkey, O. H., and K. L. Dixon. 1996. *The Corps and the Shore.* Washington, DC: Island Press.

Platt, Rutherford H. et al. 1992. *Coastal Erosion: Has Retreat Sounded?* Program on Environment and Behavior Monograph, no. 53. Boulder: University of Colorado Institute of Behavioral Science, pp. 18–21.

U.S. Army Corps of Engineers. 1996. *Shoreline Protection and Beach Erosion Control Study.* Alexandria, VA: Institute for Water Resources.

U.S. General Accounting Office (GAO). 1995. *Disaster Assistance: Information on Expenditures and Proposals to Improve Effectiveness and Reduce Future Costs.* GAO/T-RCED-95-140. Washington, DC: GAO.

U.S. General Accounting Office (GAO). 1981. *Requests for Federal Disaster Assistance Need Better Evaluation.* GAO/CED 82-84. Washington, DC: GAO.

Williams, J. 1995. *Coasts in Crisis.* USGS Circular 1075. Washington, DC: U.S. Government Printing Office.

Chapter 2

Stormy Weather: Hurricane Hugo's Impact on the South Carolina Lowcountry

Such is the low situation of Charleston, that it is subject to be destroyed at any time by such an inundation, and the frequent warnings the people have had may justly fill them with a deep sense of their dependent condition, and with constant gratitude to Providence for their preservation.

—Alexander Hewatt, 1779

Hurricane Hugo blew away the Lowcountry I had known all my life. The spreading oak tree that once sheltered me from neighborhood bullies was toppled. Weathered beach houses on Sullivan's Island where I spent sun-tanned, barefoot weeks with my young daughters were rubble. The straightaway from Charleston to McClellanville was an endless expanse of broken trees. The Lowcountry had lost its innocence.

—Elsa McDowell, 1994

Coastal hazards take many forms, but major storms such as 1989's Hurricane Hugo are particularly useful in one respect: they expand society's understanding of the enormous cumulative effects of such hazards. A major event provides a tremendous learning opportunity, albeit an unwanted one. Accordingly, in an effort to learn more about the hidden, and often unreported, impacts and categories of costs resulting from a major coastal disaster, the Heinz panel invited 30 residents of the southern coastal region of South Car-

olina (known as the "Lowcountry" because of its low elevation) to a workshop
to discuss Hurricane Hugo.

This chapter uses the information collected at that workshop, along with
other primary and secondary sources, to create a "virtual field trip" that doc-
uments the event and some of its impacts. It is a very personal and emotion-
filled story—everyone who experienced Hugo has a story to tell about that
day and the days after the storm. It is almost impossible to describe the impact of the storm in words, but the experiences of some Lowcountry residents
illustrate the wrath of the hurricane. This chapter is not meant to be a comprehensive case study of Hugo, but instead will give the reader some idea of
how it felt to go through the event. The chapters that follow, particularly
chapter 3, will provide additional detailed examples of the impacts and categories of costs of Hugo and how the area, people, and institutions have
changed in its aftermath.

The Carolina Lowcountry

The Lowcountry (see figure 2.1) was first settled in 1670 by English
colonists, who were drawn to the area's potential for agriculture and access to
the Atlantic. Charleston, the region's largest city, was founded on the penin-
sula between the Ashley and Cooper Rivers. The city is surrounded by developed and undeveloped barrier islands, which are separated from the mainland by the rivers and the Intracoastal Waterway. The Lowcountry has a
subtropical climate, and because of its low elevation and many rivers, parts
of it are subject to frequent flooding. The many barrier islands in the area are
particularly at risk for flooding because of erosion that has been caused by
both sea-level rise and engineered structures meant to enhance navigation
and protect property (Lennon et al., 1996). The region has a long history of
weather-related disasters, having experienced countless major storms and
hurricanes. Terrestrial hazards have also taken a toll; the Lowcountry has
three major fault lines beneath it (the Woodstock Fault, the Charleston
Fault, and the Ashley River Fault) and, in 1886, the region experienced a
major earthquake estimated to have registered between 6.5 and 7.0 on the
Richter scale (Lennon et al., 1996).

The South Carolina Lowcountry is full of contrasts—from the sandy
beaches of Sullivan's Island one can see enormous container ships pulling
into Charleston harbor while dolphins play just feet away. This scene
serves as a symbol of the unusually varied economy of the Charleston area.
The region's largest employer is tourism—the barrier islands and down-

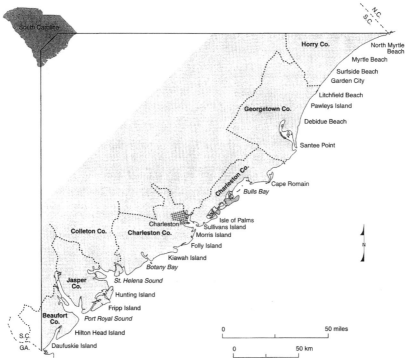

Figure 2.1. Map of the South Carolina Coast. (Lennon et al., 1996. Copyright 1996, Duke University Press. All rights reserved. Reprinted with permission.)

town Charleston draw about 3 million people each year (Charleston Metro Chamber of Commerce, 1998). Tourism has both a direct and an indirect impact on the region's economy. Visitors spend money directly and also contribute to other sectors, such as real estate and construction; in total, the tourism industry has an estimated $2.3 billion total economic impact on the area annually (Charleston Metro Chamber of Commerce, 1998). More traditional regional industries like forestry, fishing, and agriculture remain a very large part of the Carolina Lowcountry's economy as well, and these sectors continue to employ many area residents. Finally, the Lowcountry's relatively high wealth compared to the rest of South Carolina also depends on manufacturing and trade. The technological advances evident in these two sectors and other large businesses provide a stark contrast to the quaint architecture, beautiful beaches, and antebellum charm for which the region is known.

The Gathering Storm

Hurricane Hugo began as a tropical disturbance in the eastern Atlantic and became a tropical depression on September 11, 1989 (see figure 2.2). The depression was upgraded to a tropical storm named Hugo later that day. The storm continued on a westward path across the south Atlantic and was upgraded to a hurricane by September 14. At this point, the storm's winds were clocked at 75 miles per hour. The storm continued to strengthen, and by September 15, the winds reached 150 mph. Early in the morning on September 18, the storm hit Guadeloupe, the Virgin Islands, and Puerto Rico.

Guadeloupe was hit by 130 mph winds, 15 inches of rain, and a 10-foot storm surge. Five persons were killed by the storm, 80 were injured, and more than 10,000 people lost their homes (*The News and Courier* and *The Evening Post,* 1989). Six hours later, Hugo let loose on the Virgin Islands with winds of 140 mph, this time killing at least 9 and leaving thousands of people homeless (*The News and Courier* and *The Evening Post,* 1989; Rubin and Popkin, 1990). More than 90 percent of the buildings on St. Croix were destroyed or damaged (Lennon et al., 1996). Three hours later, the storm arrived at the eastern tip of Puerto Rico with sustained winds of 132 mph, a 7- to 8-foot storm surge, and approximately 15 inches of rain, causing heavy flooding and landslides. All told, 25 persons died, and more than 50,000 people were left homeless in the eastern Caribbean (*The News and Courier* and *The Evening Post,* 1989).

On the morning of September 21, 1989, hurricane warnings were issued for the East Coast of the United States from Florida to North Carolina. The hurricane eventually made landfall just north of Charleston Harbor after

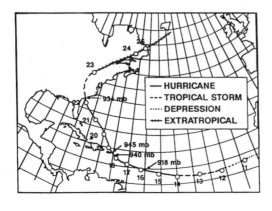

Figure 2.2. Hurricane Hugo Path. (Stauble et al., 1991. Reprinted with permission of the *Journal of Coastal Research.*)

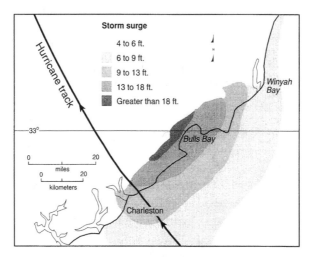

Figure 2.3. Hurricane Hugo Storm Surge Elevations along the South Carolina Coast. (Bush et al., 1996. Copyright 1996, Duke University Press. All rights reserved. Reprinted with permission.)

midnight on September 22. Storm-surge flooding in some areas was 15 to 20 feet above normal (see figure 2.3), and peak gusts were recorded in Charleston at 98 mph (Federal Emergency Management Agency, 1989). The eye of the storm was approximately 40 miles wide, with hurricane-force winds extending 140 miles in all directions, and tropical storm winds (50 to 60 mph) extending approximately 250 miles from the eye (Parker and Booth, 1989). Hugo continued in a northwest arc through the Carolinas, passing just west of Charlotte, North Carolina, through western Virginia, West Virginia, eastern Ohio, and toward Lake Erie. The nation's heavily developed Mid-Atlantic and Northeastern shores thus were spared its fury.

Hugo Hits the Lowcountry

On September 20, Charleston Mayor Joseph P. Riley warned Lowcountry residents that "there is no downside to being overly prepared. The citizenry must not be lulled into a false sense of security" (*The News and Courier* and *The Evening Post,* 1989). Police and emergency service workers were placed on alert and began to stockpile chainsaws and bulldozers, while hospitals and shelters prepared for the possible onslaught of hurricane victims. Sandbags were issued at Charleston City Hall. Most residents reluctantly boarded up their windows and doors as best they could, stocked up on emergency supplies at the supermarket and hardware store, and then made their way inland on Highway 26 to Columbia. The trip to Columbia, which usually takes only two hours, often took as long as eight hours because of the heavy traffic (*The News and Courier* and *The Evening Post,* 1989). Approximately 265,000 people were evacuated in just over 10 hours. This quick action undoubtedly prevented injuries and saved lives (Federal Emergency Management Agency, 1989).

Although evacuation orders from the governor for most of the Lowcountry were voluntary, a mandatory evacuation order was issued for residents of barrier islands, beaches, and peninsulas, except for residents of the city of Charleston (Baker, 1990). However, many barrier island residents did not want to leave their homes—police officers and emergency workers were forced to convince residents of the severity of the situation by ordering them out house by house in many places. On Sullivan's Island, Police Chief Jack Lillienthal told residents who were dead-set on staying that he would pick them up and carry them off the island if necessary (*The News and Courier* and *The Evening Post,* 1989). As it turns out, he was the last person to leave Sullivan's Island; just as he completed his trip across the Ben Sawyer Bridge, the only way off the island by car or truck, there was a terrible grinding sound—the bridge tore away from its foundation, and one end went down into the water as the other side tipped toward the sky.

Although residents of downtown Charleston who lived in one-story homes were told to evacuate, many other downtown residents chose to weather the storm. Some boat owners defied the evacuation orders as well, preferring to weather the storm on their boats; for some fishermen and shrimpers, these boats represented their entire livelihood. The nuclear submarine *Narwhal* was in the naval shipyard preparing for repairs when news of the hurricane was broadcast. The sub's crew decided to ride out the hurricane in port, but they eventually had to submerge because the sub was drifting uncontrollably—the submarine spent most of the storm at the bottom of the river.

Hurricane Hugo's Impacts

In writing this report, the Heinz panel chose to divide the reported and unreported costs and impacts of coastal hazards into four general categories that would help explain the myriad ways in which these disasters affect the world. The first of these categories is the built environment, which is probably what most people think of when imagining the impacts of a coastal hazard. This category encompasses damage to private property (e.g., homes and boats), public property (e.g., fire stations and hospitals), and many other parts of a community's infrastructure, such as roads, electric lines, water mains, and telephone wires. The second category, the business environment, is both a part of and separate from the built environment; whereas the physical plant of a business is part of the built environment, the total costs to business in the event of a coastal hazard are much higher than just those caused to buildings. For example, a business will experience losses if its suppliers are unable to deliver or if it cannot fill orders. Furthermore, losses to a business have ramifications for the entire community when workers are not able to earn money because their employer's business has failed. The loss of wages to employees is included in the third category examined by the panel—the social environment. This category includes damages on a human scale, such as injuries, deaths, long-term health problems, and emotional issues arising from the event itself and subsequent damages. In the fourth and final category, the panel examined losses and damages to the natural environment, such as beach erosion, harm to wildlife, and impaired ecosystem function. Each of these categories is discussed in more detail in chapter 3.

The four categories are loosely defined and interrelated. Damages to one category often flow into another. Imagine this scenario: a hazardous waste storage facility located in the floodplain is damaged by a hurricane and subsequently releases chemicals that flow into a surrounding estuary, which serves as a fish nursery. The number of fish caught that year is reduced greatly due to deaths of young fry, and local anglers who fish for a living lose their boats and are forced to go on welfare because they can no longer support themselves or their families. This scenario shows how one single event caused by a hurricane can have both short- and long-term effects in all four categories. These types of costs are almost impossible to categorize or quantify with any degree of accuracy because of ambiguities and overlaps among categories in who experiences losses and what exactly caused those losses. Anecdotal evidence provided by Lowcountry residents illustrates the broad range of losses caused by coastal hazards in all of the categories. Figures 2.4–2.7 are representative of the hurricane's myriad effects on the built, business, social, and natural environments.

It is important to acknowledge that many communities experience benefits from natural disasters, especially when the federal government invests money that otherwise would not have gone to the affected community. This investment can lead to immediate improvements in quality of life for certain individuals, such as those who are able to build nicer houses than before because of insurance payouts. In addition, certain business people, such as contractors and architects, are sure to enjoy an increased client base when an en-

Figure 2.4. Damage Caused by Hurricane Hugo. (*The News and Courier* and *The Evening Post,* 1989. Reprinted with permission of the *Post and Courier.*)

Figure 2.5. Damage Caused by Hurricane Hugo. (*The News and Courier* and *The Evening Post,* 1989. Reprinted with permission of the *Post and Courier.*)

Figure 2.6. Damage Caused by Hurricane Hugo. (*The News and Courier* and *The Evening Post,* 1989. Reprinted with permission of the *Post and Courier.*)

Figure 2.7. Damage Caused by Hurricane Hugo. (*The News and Courier* and *The Evening Post,* 1989. Reprinted with permission of the *Post and Courier.*)

tire community is forced to rebuild. A hurricane also may foster human connections, such as when neighbors get to know each other as they help each
other survive the aftermath of a storm. Finally, even the natural environment
can benefit from a coastal hazard, because certain ecosystems depend on periodic disturbances for self-renewal. In fact, the natural environment is by its
very nature *designed* to respond to and withstand events such as hurricanes.
For instance, if no artificial barriers have been constructed, barrier islands roll
over themselves and absorb the impact of storm-driven waves, thereby protecting the mainland behind them from storm damage.

Notwithstanding the possible benefits of a coastal hazard, the panel chose
to concentrate on the damages, on the grounds that the benefits that arise
from an event such as Hurricane Hugo tend to accrue narrowly to a few individuals and can never begin to offset the community-wide damages. As one
business owner put it: "Maybe some good did blow in from the ill wind
called Hugo. I say maybe because I assure you we never want to go through
it again" (Burbage, 1990).

Built Environment

Although the area to the north and east of Charleston County experienced
the most damage after Hurricane Hugo, few areas were left untouched. It has
been estimated that in the city of Charleston alone, 80 percent of all structures had roof damage after the event (*The News and Courier* and *The Evening
Post,* 1989). The photos shown in figures 2.4–2.8 help to illustrate the devastation inflicted on different areas of the built environment by Hugo. But
even though a picture may be worth a thousand words, it cannot tell the
whole story. Damages to the built environment have very real effects on people, who may have no electricity for weeks on end, or who may watch their
living rooms become swimming pools. The following stories sketch a more
complete picture of the range of impacts on the built environment associated
with Hurricane Hugo.

Boats Out of Water

One of the most famous images of Hurricane Hugo is of the *Guppy,* a sloop
thrown clear out of the Ashley River onto Lockwood Avenue in downtown
Charleston. Boats were tossed around like children's pool toys, slamming
into each other and running aground. Several boat owners were killed as they
tried to ride out the storm on their boats.

Franklyn Boardman was a lot luckier. He decided to stay on his 40-foot
sailboat, the *Chips III* (Frazier, 1994a). He was forced out of the municipal
marina in Charleston Harbor and decided to head up the Cooper River. As

the evening arrived, the water went from calm to turbid and the gentle wind was transformed into a ferocious squall. Boardman struggled for hours to keep the boat anchored, repeatedly crawling on his stomach out of the tenuous safety of the boat's cabin to check that his lines remained secure. Then, in his words: "All of a sudden I heard a sound like a freight train advancing. It grew louder and closer . . . the boat suddenly swung violently to port and then to starboard, raised a foot out of the water and then fell back down as the 52-foot mast exploded with the noise of a double barrel shotgun" (Frazier, 1994a). Boardman barely survived the storm, and five years later the *Chips III* remained unrepaired.

Terror in the Hospitals and Shelters

The Medical University of South Carolina could not evacuate its patients before Hugo hit. Hospital administrators were faced with the difficult task of telling staff members that they must leave their families and come to work to care for patients in the hospital. These patients were moved from place to place in the hospital as the hurricane threatened their well-being. Many of the windows in the hospital blew out because of the low atmospheric pressure caused by the hurricane, and hospital employees risked their lives protecting small children from the suction created by the broken windows. To keep patients on life-support systems alive, a few brave men endured the storm outside so that they could pump the fuel needed to keep the hospital's generator operating (*The News and Courier* and *The Evening Post,* 1989).

While the hospital served as a shelter for the sick, many residents weathered the storm in schools and other buildings designated as hurricane shelters. Most of these shelters provided safe refuge for Lowcountry residents, but some simply could not withstand the punishment Hugo inflicted. One shelter, Lincoln High School in McClellanville, had been surveyed improperly and was actually much closer to sea level than had originally been assessed. Evacuees who went to this shelter found themselves up to their necks in water. They were forced to punch out acoustical tiles in the ceiling so that children could be held up to breathe.

Safe at Home?

Sam Welsh and his wife, Nancy, thought that they could ride out the storm at their home in Awendaw. The house was built on a 5-foot concrete foundation and was located 13 feet above sea level, so the water would have to rise more than 18 feet just to reach the first floor. But Hugo had other plans for the Welshes: "The noise was unreal. It was like the house was ripping apart, rending. Things were bursting. I started to open the door. My wife yelled 'no,' but I opened it. The living room was a sea of marsh grass, and it started marching up the stairs. Flotsam forced us against the wall. We couldn't get out" (*The News and Courier* and *The Evening Post,* 1989).

After a few hours, the waters had risen so quickly that the couple was trapped in a small room on the second floor. The Welshes stood on chairs and tables as water rose toward the ceiling and then felt the house itself float free from its foundation. The couple was finally able to climb onto the back of a china cabinet that was floating around the room. The Welshes lost every-thing they owned—their home, two cars, and two boats, plus countless other possessions and memories. Shortly after their ordeal, Sam Welsh said: "It was a big mistake to stay through the storm" (*The News and Courier* and *The Evening Post,* 1989).

When Diane and Glenn Hughes finally were able to check their home in Folly Beach after the storm, they heard splashing in a nearby house. Inside their neighbor's home, they found a 6-foot-long, 250-pound dolphin swim-ming in the den. Using a door as a stretcher, they carried the disoriented dol-phin back to the ocean (Baxley, 1994). After washing back ashore once, the dolphin made it out to sea on its second attempt. Diane Hughes later said that she looked at the event as a message from God: "It was like the Lord said, 'He made it. Now you're going to make it'" (Baxley, 1994).

The "Invisible" Damage

Some of the damage to the built environment caused by Hugo could not be photographed, but it was very real, nonetheless. Damage to electrical lines created havoc in the Lowcountry. In Charleston, all three main transmission lines were above ground, and power outages were widespread—many resi-dents lost electricity for three weeks or more. Loss of electricity contributed to business losses and affected the community in countless ways, causing a lack of refrigeration, lighting, and hot water. Generators were in high de-mand after the event, and in hospitals and other places, their availability was a life-or-death issue. Luckily, most of the Lowcountry's telephone lines were underground, so, although phone communications were down during and immediately after the storm, phone service was restored quickly to most res-idents. Lowcountry residents were not so lucky, however, with regard to the area's infrastructure. Many roads and bridges could not withstand the storm's assault, and several barrier islands were inaccessible by car for weeks after Hugo.

Many types of damage to the built environment have long-term effects. Property damage was not always recognized in initial assessments made after Hurricane Hugo. James and Mary Jenkins of McClellanville appeared to be among the lucky ones immediately after the storm. When volunteer workers came into the community to assess damages and determine who needed aid or repairs, they were greeted by the Jenkinses' neat, green-and-white cinder block home with its tin roof in place (Frazier, 1994b). What the volunteers did not realize was that the Jenkinses' roof had peeled back in two places, and that they had attempted to repair it themselves by straightening out the tin. These makeshift repairs weakened the roof and by 1994 the damage was obvious—the inadequate roof let water seep into the house, damaging its wooden frame, and causing leaks and termite swarms during wet weather (Frazier, 1994b).

Business Environment

In Garden City, Sam's Corner restaurant was under 8 feet of water during Hugo; almost all of the kitchen equipment was ruined. Sam Baker, the restaurant's owner, recalled the day before the storm: "I guess you could say we were a little laid back about it. We moved a few things to keep them from getting wet, locked up and let it go at that. We thought there'd be a little water in here and we'd just sweep it away and reopen" (Steiger, 1990). Sam's Corner reopened 114 days later, after Baker had spent thousands of dollars on repairs and new equipment, which featured wheels so that it could be moved to safety the next time a hurricane threatened. Although Baker says he "only had about one-third of enough insurance to cover the damage" he never considered closing the store permanently (Steiger, 1990).

The Slotin family's business, George C. Birlant & Co., an English antique store located on King Street in Charleston, was similarly devastated by Hurricane Hugo. The roof was blown off the four-story, century-old building and the contents of the store were decimated. The Slotins lost more than $500,000 in revenue, property damage, and damage to their rare antiques inventory (Burbage, 1990). Andrew Slotin describes the scene that greeted him on his return to the family's store:

> We were in pure shock when we pushed open the front doors the day after the storm and saw, in quiet disbelief, what had happened. It was like it was raining inside our store, water dripping through the ceilings, through a hundred years of dust and dirt upstairs, splattering the inventory and covering the heart-pine floors. We have never felt so helpless. (Burbage, 1990)

The Slotins were able to move much of their salvageable inventory to a warehouse owned by a couple they met at the motel where the newly homeless family went for shelter. They spent the next three nights and days mopping and pushing water down the elevator shaft of their store to keep the ceilings from caving in. They considered moving their store out of the heavily damaged building but decided that, after 60 years in business, they would stay and restore the historic building. They were able to have a gala reopening 80 days after Hugo, and they dedicated that night to everyone who had helped them with the restoration (Burbage, 1990). Even their competitors sent them flowers and good wishes on their reopening.

The Lowcountry has many major industries that depend on natural resources, and these businesses were all severely affected by Hugo. David Gerhardt, forest manager for Westvaco Corporation, a paper products company that manages several area forests, said at the Heinz panel's March 1998 workshop that "Hugo was the number-one-ranked forest disaster in U.S. history. One billion dollars in stumpage was lost—more than hurricanes Andrew and Camille and the eruption of Mount St. Helens combined. That billion-dollar loss translates to $10 billion in value-added forest products." However, he went on to say that "the state and forest industry responded quickly. Three or four days after the storm they went to the governor and asked him to create a salvage task force." This task force helped pave the way for the salvage of approximately $150 million worth of downed timber.

Several other local businesspersons interviewed at the workshop stressed the importance of pre-disaster planning. Frank Brigman, owner of Brigman Foods in Charleston said his business sustained losses of $600,000 after Hugo. However, because his company had planned for the possibility of a hurricane, it had purchased business-interruption insurance. This policy made it possible for Mr. Brigman to provide assistance to his employees in the aftermath of Hugo and enabled his workers to remain productive throughout the cleanup. During his interview, Mr. Brigman emphasized that businesses need to have a disaster plan in place before a hurricane threatens, and that they should have disaster supplies on hand. He suggested that insurance companies could work with their customers in coastal hazard areas to develop disaster plans.

Paul Campbell of Alumax was also interviewed at the panel's workshop. His company's total loss from Hurricane Hugo was estimated at $29 million. The company sustained a deductible loss of $250,000 and $2 million in uninsured timber losses, in addition to the timber clean-up cost. Campbell credits Alumax's disaster insurance with cutting the company's recovery time in half. He explained: "It took 68 days to restart the facility, employee productivity did not suffer and we did not have to lay off workers—in fact we had improved morale." The company worked with its employees and assisted them with paid leave and interest-free loans.

Social Environment

In 1993, an extensive survey of Sullivan's Island residents was conducted to examine their perceptions of Hurricane Hugo's effect on their lives (Moore and Moore, 1993). The most common responses to the survey were statements reflecting apprehension that a similar event could recur. Many respondents replied that life after the hurricane seemed "less purposeful, less optimistic, and less satisfying" (Moore and Moore, 1993). Respondents recognized that the losses they experienced often could not be measured in dollars and cents. One wrote: "It destroyed the large trees. Everything else can be replaced." Another concurred, saying, "I would rather have lost my house than my trees." A young mother said she "lost the first year of my baby's life dealing with this. I neglected pictures, keepsakes, and other family members." One respondent seemed to sum up many other comments perfectly: "There is a tendency to deny how much one has suffered. The anger, frustration, grief, and sense of violation and of loss can be compared to the aftermath of an assault. The emotional stress seems to go on and on."

The sentiments expressed by the Sullivan's Island survey respondents were echoed by many others who had endured the hurricane's onslaught. Hugo both created new problems and exacerbated old ones. Homelessness was not a major problem for the Lowcountry prior to Hurricane Hugo, but afterward, countless residents lived in conditions that would horrify many people. Near Roseville, volunteers with Interfaith Outreach Ministries went to the aid of a man who, they heard, had lost his front porch. They discovered that the man was living alone in a one-room, 9- by 12-foot house with no electricity or running water (Brady, 1990). Sharron Christiano, a case worker with the ministry, explained that Hugo raised awareness of inadequate housing: "There are many, many people that have damage that never had electric, water, or bathrooms to begin with. Or they tell you they have a bathroom and it turns out to be a plastic garbage can. After we finish with Hugo, we hope to try to raise the quality of life of some of the people we have seen. There is more of a need in this county besides Hugo" (Brady, 1990).

The post-Hugo rebuilding process also had serious social impacts. Many laborers and construction workers came to the Lowcountry after the disaster because they thought there would be numerous jobs available. They arrived only to find no places to stay, because hotel rooms were fully booked with post-disaster workers from the Federal Emergency Management Agency and elsewhere, and the newcomers soon found that most of the reputable local contractors already had enough workers. Some of these workers had the misfortune of taking jobs with disreputable contractors, who got as much work as possible out of their employees and then left town without paying them.

Debby Waid, a social worker at Crisis Ministries tells of two men from South Florida who arrived at her shelter: "One of the men was sobbing. I could tell these were guys who worked regularly and had families waiting for them back home. They had not been paid by the unlicensed contractor they were working for, who had left town, and now they had no way to get home or to pay the bills they had run up. They were totally humiliated and ashamed, and this soon became a common story" (personal communication, Debby Waid, July 27, 1998). A number of disreputable contractors also bilked consumers by telling them they needed unnecessary repairs, beginning jobs and then leaving town with the unsuspecting homeowners' money, or simply by doing jobs in the quickest and most slipshod manner possible.

When Debby Waid was interviewed at the panel's March meeting, she told the panel that many of the people who most needed help after Hugo were unaware that help was available. One Charleston resident, a man whose wife had died the year before Hugo, was living with his two young children in an uninsured house that he owned. After Hugo hit, his house was completely uninhabitable. He did not have enough money to repair his home, so he asked relatives to take care of his children, and he eventually wound up in a homeless shelter. After a social worker heard his story, he was back with his children in his newly repaired home within one week. The man had been unaware of the many resources that would have helped him repair his home and keep his family together, and Ms. Waid speculated that his story is not uncommon. She was hopeful, however, that the situation would be much improved were a storm like Hugo to hit today: "I really feel like we know so much more now about what to do and what not to do. It was a very good education that I wish hadn't been so drastic."

Natural Environment

Hugo not only wreaked havoc on the buildings and homes of the Lowcountry, it also devastated much of the area's natural environment. Almost everyone's first priority after the disaster was to help the people whose lives had been destroyed by the storm. In fact, some efforts to ensure human safety made it difficult to assess the effects of the storm on the area's natural resources. David Whitaker, of the South Carolina Wildlife and Natural Resources Department (now called the Department of Natural Resources) said in a February 1990 statement to the South Carolina Fish and Wildlife Federation meeting "We were not able to get into the field until six days after the storm. We had to get special clearance to have a boat in the water since all waterways were closed to prevent looting of stranded boats and sea island homes" (Whitaker, 1990). What Whitaker eventually saw astounded him;

"Hurricane Hugo was the one that we all knew would come, and every year we hoped it wouldn't."

Whitaker told members of the Heinz panel that conditions were so bad that "one afternoon a couple of weeks after the storm, Larry DeLancey and Jimmy Jenkins, who work in the shrimp management program, came in and told me that they had seen shrimp jumping from anoxic water in Charleston Harbor and seabirds were eating them by the hundreds. The next morning I went out to see this for myself. Sure enough, in the area near the Charleston Coast Guard base, I found shrimp swimming near the surface and hundreds of gulls and terns feeding. . . . In a tidal creek that morning, I found hundreds of grass shrimp sitting very near the surface; I'd never seen this before."

Hugo took a toll on some of the area's best-known wildlife as well— its endangered species. The Atlantic Coast's largest population of the endangered red-cockaded woodpecker was located in Francis Marion National Forest prior to Hurricane Hugo (Glen Stapleton, Francis Marion National Forest, personal communication, March 25, 1998). Although only 10 woodpeckers were actually found dead after the storm, Hooper et al. (1990) estimated that 63 percent of the population in Francis Marion National Forest were killed or missing after Hugo. In addition, Derrick Hamrick (1991) vividly described a visit to the forest to photograph woodpeckers one year after the storm: "As I arrived, I had difficulty believing what my eyes were seeing! Uprooted trees with trunks thicker than my waist were lying flat on the ground. I had never seen such devastation by natural or manmade forces, and in every direction trees seemed as if they were matchsticks, one broken after another. The trees most severely affected were the mature pines, trees favored by the woodpeckers."

In the first months after the storm, Forest Service officials began to create artificial cavities to mitigate Hugo's effects. Although officials reported a dramatic increase in population numbers in the first few years after the storm, a cumulative 11.6 percent decline has been reported in the past three years due to multiple reasons, all directly related to the effects of Hurricane Hugo. In fact, the rate of decline has doubled each year. The decline is primarily attributed to the poor quality of habitat caused by the lack of prescribed burning and loss of critical nesting habitat. Glen Stapleton, the forest supervisor, told the Heinz panel that "50 percent of the Francis Marion workload is still related to Hugo."

Many other species, both common and endangered, were affected by Hugo. The ranges of five species of endangered or threatened sea turtles include South Carolina's beaches. Sea turtle nesting sites were damaged during the storm, and beach restoration activities after the storm further damaged many areas. Habitats for wading birds such as tricolored herons, glossy ibises, and white ibises were severely damaged; the numbers of white ibises on Pumpkinseed Island declined from 10,000 pairs in 1989 to zero in 1990 (Shepard et al., 1991). Fish also were affected adversely for several weeks after the hurricane. In freshwater areas, oxygen depletion caused fish kills for two weeks after the storm, resulting in an estimated loss of 5 million adult bream, catfish, largemouth bass, and other species (South Carolina Wildlife and Marine Resources Department, January 1990). Saltwater intrusion and sediment scouring caused by the storm surge following Hugo also had major negative effects on freshwater habitats. Conversely, marine habitats were disturbed by freshwater runoff, turbidity and siltation, and water quality degradation. Widespread invertebrate and fish kills were attributed to low dissolved-oxygen levels, clogging of gills by silt, and stranding when abnormally high tidal waters receded (South Carolina Wildlife and Marine Resources Department, 1990).

The Lowcountry's beaches and dune systems were battered by Hurricane Hugo. Prior to Hugo, 70 percent of the Lowcountry's developed beaches were classified as having one or more continuous, well-vegetated dune ridges

Figure 2.8. Hurricane Hugo Cut This Inlet through Pawleys Island. (*The News and Courier* and *The Evening Post,* 1989. Reprinted with permission of the *Post and Courier.*)

(Bush et al., 1996). After Hugo, only 15 percent of these beaches still had their dune ridges—the hurricane destroyed 17 miles of dunes (Bush et al., 1996). According to Lennon et al. (1996), "Hugo produced some of the greatest short-term erosion of modern times." Hugo's storm surge and storm-surge ebb also inflicted a great deal of damage; a study done shortly after Hugo in Folly Beach found 30 ebb-scour channels through the town, an average of three per city block (Lennon et al., 1996). Hugo also cut new inlets through many of the barrier islands of the Lowcountry, as shown in a photograph of Pawleys Island (figure 2.8) after Hugo.

The Lowcountry Looks Back

Perhaps the greatest lesson taught by Hurricane Hugo is that the costs to a community affected by a coastal hazard cannot be expressed fully in simple dollars and cents. This chapter introduced the reader to the myriad ways in which one community, the Carolina Lowcountry, was affected by one event, Hurricane Hugo. The full, or true, costs of Hugo are impossible to measure—the Heinz panel learned that the cost estimates of Hurricane Hugo's damages do not adequately address all of the quantifiable costs of the event, much less those costs that are more difficult to gauge. Cost information, even when related to quantifiable losses, is lost rapidly in the aftermath of a coastal hazard event. Hurricane Hugo taught the Carolina Lowcountry about costs not previously considered, such as costs to the environment, businesses, and social community. The next chapter discusses more fully the categories of costs associated with a major coastal hazard and presents a fuller range of these costs both for the Lowcountry and other coastal areas at risk.

Today, the residents of the Lowcountry are undoubtedly more prepared for a major hurricane than they were prior to Hurricane Hugo. Still, no matter how many good intentions a community has, how many disaster education campaigns are conducted, or how many more residents and visitors choose to evacuate, the effects of a mega-storm like Hugo cannot be predicted. Unless residents of coastal areas choose to leave their homes by the sea and the lives they have built there for other, safer regions, the threat of great losses will remain. The only question is how best to plan for the inevitable storm.

References

Baker, E. J. 1990. *Evacuation Decision Making and Public Response in Hurricane Hugo in South Caroline {sic}*. Quick Response Research Report, no. 39. Boulder, CO: Natural Hazards Center.

Baxley, C. 1994. Riders of the storm: Where are they now? *Charleston Post and Courier* online edition. (http://www.charleston.net/pcarchive/).

Brady, B. 1990. Homelessness still a problem in Dorchester after hurricane. *The News and Courier/The Evening Post* (March 18).

Burbage, J. 1990. Patience, endurance key to recovery: Family finds fortitude pays off for business. *The News and Courier/The Evening Post* (March 18).

Bush, D. M., O. H. Pilkey, and W. J. Neal. 1996. *Living by the Rules of the Sea*. Durham, NC: Duke University Press.

Charleston Metro Chamber of Commerce. 1998. Visitor Industry Impact. Charleston Metro Chamber of Commerce Web site (http://www.chamber.charleston.net/overview/visitor.htm).

Federal Emergency Management Agency Region IV Interagency Hazard Mitigation Team. 1989. *Hurricane Hugo*. FEMA 843-DR-SC. Washington, DC: Government Printing Office.

Frazier, H. 1994a. Diaries reveal hell behind storm. *Charleston Post and Courier* online edition. (http://www.charleston.net/pcarchive/).

Frazier, H. 1994b. Five years after hurricane. *Charleston Post and Courier* online edition. (http://www.charleston.net/pcarchive/).

Hamrick, D. 1991. Assisting homeless woodpeckers. *Birds Internat* 3(1):18–27.

Hewatt, A. 1779. *An Historical Account of the Rise and Progress of the Colonies of South Carolina and Georgia*. Vol. 2, pp. 181–182. London: A. Donaldson.

Hooper, R. G., J. C. Watson, and R. E. F. Escano. 1990. *Hurricane Hugo's Initial Effects on Red-Cockaded Woodpeckers in the Frances Marion National Forest*. Transactions 55th North American Wildlife and Natural Resources Conference, March 19–21. Washington, DC: Wildlife Management Institute.

Lennon, G., W. J. Neal, D. M. Bush, O. H. Pilkey, M. Stutz, and J. Bullock. 1996. *Living with the South Carolina Coast*. Durham, NC: Duke University Press

McDowell, E. 1994. The years ease but don't erase pain of Hugo. *Charleston Post and Courier* online edition. (http://www.charleston.net/pcarchive/).

Moore, J. W., and D. P. Moore. 1993. *Sullivan's Island, South Carolina—the Hurricane Hugo Experience: The First Nine Months*. Boulder, CO: The Natural Hazards Research and Applications Information Center.

The News and Courier and *The Evening Post*. 1989. *And Hugo Was His Name: Hurricane Hugo, a Diary of Destruction*. Sun City, AZ: C. F. Boone.

Parker, L., and W. Booth. 1989. Hurricane Hugo rips through South Carolina. *Washington Post* (http://www.weatherpost.com/hurricane/poststories/hugo-sc.htm).

Rubin, C. B., and R. Popkin. 1990. *Disaster Recovery after Hurricane Hugo in South Carolina*. Natural Hazard Research Working Paper, no. 69. Boulder, CO: The Natural Hazards Research and Applications Information Center.

Shepard, P., T. Crockett, T. L. DeSanto, and K. L. Bilstein. 1991. The impact of Hurricane Hugo on the breeding ecology of wading birds at Pumpkinseed Island, Hobcaw Barony, South Carolina. *Colonial Waterbirds* 14(2):150–157.

South Carolina Wildlife and Marine Resources Department. 1990. Summary of the impacts of Hurricane Hugo on South Carolina fisheries, nongame wildlife and game species. Internal report. (January).

Stauble, D. K., W. C. Seabergh, and L. Z. Hales. 1991. Effects of Hurricane Hugo on the South Carolina coast. *Journal of Coastal Research, Special Issue No. 8,* pp. 129–162.

Steiger, B. 1990. Valuable lessons from Hugo: Strand residents prepared. *Charleston Post and Courier* online edition (March 18). (www.charleston.net/pcarchive).

Whitaker, J. D. 1990. Effects of Hurricane Hugo on the state's crustacean resources. Paper presented at the South Carolina Fish and Wildlife Federation Annual Meeting, Myrtle Beach, South Carolina, February 8–9.

Chapter 3

Toward an Improved Understanding of the True Costs of Coastal Hazards and Disasters

Property damages from hurricanes, storms, and related wind, erosion, and flood hazards along the coasts of the United States have increased markedly in recent years. For hurricanes, the most dramatic and destructive of coastal hazards, more damage has been reported in the 1990s than in the previous two decades combined, even after adjusting for inflation (Pielke and Pielke 1997). Hurricane Andrew, a 145-mph storm when it hit southern Florida in 1992, is one of the major reasons for this increase. As of December 1998, Andrew was the costliest hurricane in U.S. history, with damage estimates exceeding $30 billion in 1992 dollars (Pielke and Pielke 1997). A little more than half of that total ($16.5 billion) was covered by insurance (Pielke and Pielke 1997). Just three years before Andrew, Hurricane Hugo's damage toll of $7 billion had topped the charts.

Population growth is often cited as one reason for the increased property losses, and census data support this view. Coastal county populations in the 18 eastern and Gulf Coast states vulnerable to hurricanes grew by 15 percent between 1980 and 1993—from 31.3 million to 36.1 million—compared to an overall growth rate of 12 percent for the United States as a whole (Insurance Institute for Property Loss Reduction and Insurance Research Council, 1995). Perhaps more significantly, the value of insured property in hurricane-prone areas is increasing at an even faster rate than population. Over the same period (1980–1993), for example, the value of insured property in coastal counties in the Atlantic and Gulf states exposed to hurricanes increased by 69 percent to $3.1 trillion. Residential exposures increased the most rapidly at 75 percent, and Florida and New York topped the list over-all with insured exposures of $872 billion and $596 billion, respectively (IIPLR and IRC, 1995). Yet, even while U.S. property damage increased dra-matically during the twentieth century, deaths from hurricanes have de-creased. The latter trend is attributed to improved forecasts and warning sys-tems, public education, and evacuation preparedness. However, the recent reversal of this trend may signal a new era of increasing vulnerability associ-ated with the continuing migration of people to coastal areas at risk from hurricanes. The loss of thousands of lives in Honduras and Nicaragua as a re-sult of Hurricane Mitch in 1998 provides a tragic illustration of the vulner-ability of developing countries, where warning systems are imperfect and it is difficult to evacuate potential victims.

Typically, damage estimates for natural disasters include insured property losses, federal disaster aid packages, public infrastructure repair costs, crop and timber losses, and similar quantifiable public and private costs. In recent years, however, researchers and professionals concerned with hazard reduc-tion have called attention to the fact that official loss statistics generally do not include a number of significant disaster-related costs. Examples include business interruptions and failures, psychological trauma and family and so-cial problems, disruption of governmental and private social services, and damage to natural resources and ecosystems. Sometimes these costs may find their way into the official loss statistics, but more often there is no mecha-nism for systematically identifying, evaluating, or reporting such costs. One consequence of this under-reporting is an inaccurate picture of the actual eco-nomic and social disruption caused by coastal hazards and disasters—what this book refers to as true costs.

Because of calls for increased accountability for public expenditures and heightened concern among private insurers, improvements are being made in data collection and reporting on disaster assistance and insured losses. One objective of this book is to contribute to this improvement by identifying the categories of hidden costs and suggesting ways in which they might be con-sidered.

True costs include both reported costs *and* hidden costs, which are often unreported or undocumented. Some costs of hazards are hidden simply be-cause they cannot be reported meaningfully in economic (i.e., dollar) terms. Professionals and volunteers who respond to disasters are intensely aware of some of these costs, particularly the personal trauma, uprooting, and pain ex-perienced by victims. But accounting for these and other hidden costs is ex-tremely challenging. The true costs of coastal hazards are difficult to sum up to a bottom-line figure because they are counted with different measures (e.g., lives lost versus property damaged), and over different time and spatial scales. Furthermore, there is a point when the marginal cost to collect and synthesize more data exceeds the potential benefit, although that point may vary from disaster to disaster. Rather than providing a single, precise bottom line, the concept of true costs provides a means to look differently at the complex tapestry of coastal hazards and disasters and gain insight into the scope and depth of their impacts and costs. This insight should lead to a better understanding of vulnerability and, in turn, to improved mitigation decisions and investments.

As the definition implies, the true costs of coastal hazards are difficult to identify and quantify; finding an accurate, useful way to report them is a very challenging problem. Pielke (1997) suggests four reasons why this is so. Multiple-order impacts are one reason; when storm surge and currents wipe out a key bridge, for example, the lack of access to homes and places of employment results in social and economic disruptions and losses—tracking these cascading, linked impacts is difficult.

A second problem has to do with the attribution of costs. A host of confounding variables make indirect impacts (and costs) difficult to attribute. For example, was a particular business failure attributable to the storm, or would it have been likely to occur in any event? Quantification is a third problem. How does one put a value on the loss of "community" associated with wholesale destruction of neighborhoods or of stress on families due to loss of homes? What is the value of an ecosystem's lost capacity to provide ecosystem services? A fourth problem is that of aggregation—how does one add things up? There are actually benefits to some economic sectors (e.g., construction and building supply) as insurance money and disaster assistance flow into a community. Inefficient equipment is replaced by new technologies, increasing productivity and competitiveness. Some losses to specific businesses whose activities are interrupted show up as benefits (i.e., increased revenues) to other firms less affected by the disaster. For example, resort communities that are undamaged become more attractive than they seemed before the storm.

Despite these difficulties and barriers, it is important that unreported or hidden costs be characterized and estimated as fully and accurately as possible. New cost categories need to be defined, appropriate metrics determined, monitoring and database protocols established, responsibilities divided among public and private entities, and the entire process institutionalized so that it is automatic after future disasters. In some instances, the best approach to understanding a category of costs might be to undertake a few very thorough case studies. In others, a new or improved database might be in order. These tasks will be no small undertaking. However, the results of such an endeavor will enable government, communities, businesses, and individuals to make mitigation investments that are more appropriate, cost-effective, and sustainable than past efforts have been.

This chapter characterizes and examines the true costs of coastal hazards, with a special emphasis on those that are unreported, undocumented, and hidden. The focus is on hurricanes, in part because many communities either have experienced one in recent history or are at risk. Although data and information are drawn from a number of events, Hurricane Hugo was selected for in-depth examination and was the subject of a Heinz panel workshop in Charleston, South Carolina, as discussed in chapter 2. This workshop included interviews with approximately 30 individuals who survived the storm or participated in preparation, response, and recovery efforts (see appendix A). Their knowledge and personal experience of that event provide the foundation for the discussion of Hurricane Hugo in this chapter.

It should be noted that disasters do create benefits to certain stakeholders. For example, the construction industry normally benefits from a disaster because there is an increased need for the rebuilding of damaged or destroyed structures. Regions unaffected by a particular hazard event may also experience hazard-driven benefits. For example, if a coastal community that is affected by a disaster cannot support its normal influx of tourists, then regions that have been spared can benefit economically from an unexpected influx of these displaced vacationers. Although this book focuses only on the costs associated with coastal hazards, a complete analysis of the problem needs to include benefits from disasters.

Methods of Analyzing the Costs of Coastal Hazards

There are a variety of ways to gather, organize, and analyze coastal hazards impact and cost data. The approach used depends on an organization's responsibilities, needs, interests, and specific objectives. Some of the ways in which impacts and costs might be examined are outlined here. The interrelationships among these methods and their potential utility, especially with respect to tabulating hidden costs, are also examined. Regardless of which approach or combination of approaches is used, it is important to capture all costs that are significant in assessing future vulnerability and determining the relative effectiveness of alternative mitigation strategies.

Direct versus Indirect Costs

When classified as direct or indirect, impacts and costs are differentiated by their linkage to the event and timing. This breakdown is especially useful for capturing cascading and linked impacts. Direct impacts and costs of a catastrophe are closely connected to the event, the associated hazards (e.g., storm surge, high winds, rain), and the resulting physical damage (Pielke, 1997). Examples of physical impacts of a hurricane include damage to homes, commercial and industrial structures, public buildings, water and waste treatment facilities, power generation or transmission facilities, communication facilities, automobiles, equipment of all types, bridges and highways, rail lines, port facilities and navigation aides, marinas and boats, agricultural crops, forests, fish and wildlife, recreational facilities, natural and renourished beaches and dunes, and natural water supplies. The public costs associated with such direct impacts include federal insurance payments, federal disaster aid, public infrastructure reconstruction, cost of debris removal, and state and local government expenses. Private-sector direct costs include insurance payments for damage to buildings and their contents, uninsured costs incurred by individuals and businesses, and costs incurred by charitable organizations such as the American Red Cross and Salvation Army.

Indirect or secondary costs are incurred in the days, weeks, or months following the event and are often linked to reported losses. They are generally more difficult to account for than are the direct costs and, hence, tend to be hidden. Indirect costs include losses due to business and industry interruptions, perhaps because of a loss of power, water, or physical access, or because employees are unavailable for their own personal reasons. Small businesses, often operating at the margin and uninsured for business interruption losses, may fail completely or migrate to other locations. Other indirect costs include a reduction in property values, loss or transfer of tourism revenues, and reduced availability of (or higher rates for) insurance. The interruption of critical human services to families, children, and the elderly is another indirect cost, as is the psychological trauma that accompanies the death of loved ones or loss of a home or workplace.

Nature is also affected indirectly. Fish and wildlife populations may be slow to recover, perhaps because of a loss of habitat or because pollution is released into the environment. The loss of, or damage to, critical habitat may result in the extinction of species previously threatened or endangered for other reasons. The loss of an erosion-buffering beach or wetland may alter a community's long-term vulnerability to coastal hazards. Post-storm debris removal and disposal operations may result in further loss of habitat and prematurely exhaust landfill capacity. At the same time, hurricanes are part of the natural disturbance regime for coastal ecosystems and, in fact, may have renewal benefits that are not yet fully understood. However, the natural ecosystems of today are generally mere fragments of their former sizes and, thus, are less resilient and more vulnerable. Endangered species are one symptom of this decreased ecosystem resiliency.

Short-Term versus Long-Term Costs

Short-term costs are associated with losses that occur at the time of the event and for which compensation is provided within a relatively short time period, such as a few days or weeks. Direct costs, by definition, are short term. They include the cost of tree and debris removal; the cost of setting up emergency shelters; and the cost of repairs to private, public, and commercial buildings. Long-term costs are incurred some time after the events, perhaps six months or more. They include some indirect impacts, such as a permanent loss of employment and loss of tax revenues, as well as some direct costs, such as additional living expenses for individuals.

Costs by Economic Sector

A breakdown of costs by economic sector is a useful way to summarize the costs of a disaster. Examples of economic sectors include housing, commercial and industrial property, agriculture, transportation infrastructure, and utilities. Appropriate economic categorization is a key to understanding reported versus unreported costs and reimbursed versus unreimbursed costs. For example, categories such as business interruptions, household and family costs, health costs, and natural ecosystem costs are not generally tallied and reported in official statistics, in part because they may be difficult to quantify. Accordingly, these costs tend to be hidden.

Breakdowns by Who Pays

The costs of disasters can be classified according to who pays. The categories include public-sector costs covered by federal, state, or local governments; and private-sector costs such as insurance payouts, uncompensated costs incurred by individuals and businesses, and humanitarian assistance provided by charitable organizations and individuals. This approach addresses questions about who pays and who benefits as response and recovery funds move within and among levels of government and between the government and private sector. Information of this type has important policy implications and is of interest to private insurers, taxpayers, governmental agencies, the Congress, and public interest groups.

Costs by Geographic Area or Political Entity

This sort of breakdown examines how costs, as well as the benefits, of response and recovery efforts are distributed over the area affected by a disaster. It may help examine issues of equity in aid to communities. For example, do oceanfront communities get more response and recovery attention than do equally affected inland communities? Are there differences between urban and rural areas? Between poor and affluent regions? Do chronic but less dramatic hazard problems get a fair share of funds and attention? Such breakdowns might also allow for comparison of communities that use different mitigation strategies. The practical issue of how data are recorded and managed—whether broken down by state, county, municipality, zip code, or other geographic boundary—determines whether and how fully these types of questions can be answered.

Other Approaches

There are also other ways to classify the costs of coastal hazards. For example, how are expenditures divided between reconstruction (i.e., bricks and mortar) and management (i.e., administration, mobilization, and demobilization)? What percentage of costs are associated with infrastructure and other construction and natural resource improvements versus response and recovery services? The costs of response and recovery versus expenditures to reduce future losses is another possible breakdown.

Heinz Panel Approach to Examining True Costs

As mentioned in prior chapters, the Heinz panel used four main categories or sectors for a detailed characterization and analysis of these costs: (1) the built environment, both public and private; (2) the business community, including interruptions, failures, and income transfers; (3) the social environment, including safety, health, families, and other human systems; and (4) natural resources and ecosystems, including the flow of nature's goods and services. Within these categories, costs are further divided into direct costs—the damage, destruction, and losses that are closely associated with the event—and indirect costs, the losses that are more distant from the event in

Table 3.1. Major Categories of Reported and Unreported Costs of Coastal Hazards

Costs Category	Examples	Direct or Indirect
Built environment	• insured/uninsured property loss: residential, commercial, industrial buildings; building contents; communications and transportation infrastructure • transportation stock: autos, trucks, rail cars, planes, boats, ships	mostly direct
Business community	• interruptions and failures: insured and uninsured • transfer of benefits and income (two-way)	mostly indirect
Social, health, and safety	• loss of human life • psychological trauma • disruption of social services • safety including preparation and response	direct and indirect costs
Natural resources and ecosystems	• loss of crops and forest resources • short- and long-term environmental degradation • temporary and permanent loss of ecosystem services	direct and indirect costs

both time and sequence and that may persist for many years. This relatively simple breakdown is summarized in table 3.1.

Several important patterns are evident in this approach to costs analysis. First, reported costs are mostly direct and fall into the built environment (e.g., buildings, infrastructure) and natural resource categories (e.g., loss of agricultural crops, commercial timber, and urban landscaping). Hidden costs, on the other hand, are mostly indirect and fall into the business, social, and natural resource and ecosystem categories. Second, many indirect impacts and costs flow from direct impacts and costs. Thus, it can be argued that increases in damage to the built environment or natural resources are accompanied by increases in indirect costs. The intuitive appeal of this argument becomes clear from examples—the increased psychological trauma associated with loss of an entire community of homes versus a few homes, or the increased threat of extinction for an endangered species whose last fragment of forest habitat is severely damaged. This relationship has important implications for mitigation that are examined in chapter 5. Finally, given the difficulties of hazard cost accounting discussed at the beginning of this chapter—sorting out multiple-order impacts, attribution of costs, quantification, and aggregation of costs—this work represents just a beginning.

Sources of Coastal Hazards Costs and Loss Data

Given the variety of loss categories, organizing schemes, quantitative and qualitative measures, time scales, geographic areas of interest, and different purposes individuals or organizations have for examining disaster costs, it is not surprising that there is no single, comprehensive natural hazard loss database available for the United States. It is fair to say that, in general, cost accounting for natural disaster losses is relatively chaotic. To compile loss data for a single disaster event or for a community affected by one or more disasters over time, consultations would be needed with a wide variety of state and federal agencies, private insurance organizations, nongovernmental organizations, and others. Some of these data would be useful for vulnerability analyses and mitigation decision making, but other desired data would not be accessible or would simply not exist. It is often difficult or impossible, for example, to get cost breakdowns by useful geographic subdivisions, such as counties, municipalities, or even states. This is particularly true for federal disaster expenditures.

In other cases, categories of costs may be mixed together, and loss data reported for one event might not be available for another event. For currently available loss data, it is often difficult to determine the cost estimation techniques used, the assumptions made, the quality of the data, and so on. Further, as detailed throughout this report, there are many important categories of disaster losses that are hidden or not accounted for; however, this is beginning to change. Calls for increased accountability for public expenditures and heightened concern among private insurers are driving significant improvements in data collection and reporting on disaster assistance costs and insured losses. One objective of this book is to contribute to this improvement by identifying hidden costs and suggesting ways in which they might be considered. Existing data sources are described next— some of the most useful and readily accessed are included in table 3.2. Other data suffer from the problems noted above or are not readily available.

Table 3.2. Key Databases Useful for Coastal Hazard Cost Accounting

Common Name of Information Source	Who Maintains	Type of Data	Principal Data Categories	Accessible to Whom
PCS Catastrophe History Database	Property Claim Services (PCS), a unit of Insurance Services Office, Inc.	Insured loss estimates based on reports from private insurers combined with damage information from post-event site inspections.	Estimates of total industry-wide insured losses by state and event; losses by line of business (e.g., personal, commercial, and vehicle).	Available to subscribers or by contacting PCS directly. Also see http://www.aisg.org
Catastrophe Paid Loss Database	Institute for Business and Home Safety (IBHS)	Proprietary claims data provided by a group of major insurers.	Building, contents, time element losses; personal losses, commercial losses; losses by line of business (e.g., automobile, home-owner's, commercial multi-peril); losses by state, county, and zip code.	Summary information available at http://www.ibhs.org. More-detailed information available on request for purposes consistent with IBHS mission.
Flood Loss Database	National Weather Service, Office of Hydrology	Loss of life and property losses.	Loss of life (numbers); property losses ($).	http://www.nws.noaa.gov/oh/hic/
Hurricane Data	National Hurricane Center, Tropical Prediction Center	Current and historical data on hurricanes and fatalities. Special hurricane reports.	Cost and fatalities; impacts and ground and satellite images of selected recent storms.	http://www.nhc.noaa.gov/
Normalized Hurricane Loss Database (Pielke and Landsea, 1998)	National Center for Atmospheric Research	Normalized loss data ($) based on GNP index of inflation, wealth factors, and population change factors.	Location and category of event; reported damage; 1995 population; population change; and normalized damage.	http://www.dir.ucar.edu/esig/HP_roger/hurr_norm.html

Private Insured Loss Data Sources

Historical information about the insured costs of natural hazards for 1949 to the present is available from Property Claim Services (PCS), a unit of the Insurance Services Office, Inc., in Rahway, New Jersey, and, since 1994, from the Institute for Business and Home Safety (IBHS) in Boston. Other potential sources for insured losses include insurance departments in individual states and databases maintained by the Insurance Services Office (ISO) in New York City.

Since 1949, the PCS Division has identified all natural disasters resulting in insured losses above a set threshold and assigned a catastrophe number to these events. This threshold was originally $1 million, but was raised to $5 million in 1982 and to $25 million in 1997. PCS also performs a vital service by providing estimates of industry-wide insured losses for each event. These estimates typically are issued shortly after the event occurs and are based on loss projections provided by private insurers combined with damage information from post-event site inspections performed by PCS representatives (Property Claim Services, 1995). The losses are not disaggregated below the state level; only recently have losses been broken down by line of business (e.g., personal, commercial, and vehicle). Since 1994, PCS has monitored and validated loss information for all events for which the preliminary estimate of insured damage exceeds $250 million. PCS then reports on changes in insured loss information every 60 days. This process continues until PCS believes that no further changes will occur in the loss figures. At that time, PCS issues its "final" estimates of insured property damage. The information provided by PCS has been a valuable resource to insurers, government agencies, and various types of research organizations.

More-detailed loss information for recent catastrophes is available from IBHS. The Catastrophe Paid Loss Database developed by IBHS includes insured loss information for all PCS-designated catastrophes since January 1994. This database uses actual claim payments as they are made over time to establish the ultimate insured cost of a catastrophe. In addition to providing a total insured loss estimate for each event, the database is designed to allow the losses to be broken down by annual statement line of business; by personal and commercial losses; by building, contents, and time element losses; and by state, county, and zip code.

The information compiled by IBHS is released quarterly by a group of major insurers. Because the companies contributing data are very large, their combined market share is sufficient to provide for reliable estimates of industry-wide losses for most catastrophes affecting the continental United States. To estimate the insured losses for each event, the data are aggregated for all data-contributing companies and the values are totaled using a weighted system based on the combined state market shares of all data-contributing companies. A description of this database is available in a report, *The Insured Cost of Natural Disasters: A Report on the IBHS Catastrophe Paid Loss Database,* which is available on the IBHS Web site (http://www.ibhs.org).

Data for individual events are normally available from departments of insurance in states affected by these events, but the level of detail varies across states. The ISO has a claims database, but it is not restricted to catastrophic events, so the losses corresponding to specific hurricanes or storms are not easy to determine.

Governmental Data Sources

A wide variety of federal, state, and local government agencies incur costs associated with hurricane response and recovery. Examples include the Federal Emergency Management Agency (FEMA), the federal agency responsible for coordinating overall response and recovery efforts for federally declared disasters. This agency maintains databases on National Flood Insurance Program (NFIP) loss reimbursements, disaster assistance, and administrative costs. Unfortunately, these data are not publicly available except in a highly aggregated form. Other federal agencies that keep loss data include: the Department of Agriculture, the U.S. Army Corps of Engineers and other military units such as the National Guard and the U.S. Coast Guard, the Small Business Administration (SBA), the Department of Housing and Urban Development (HUD), the Department of Transportation, and various units of the National Oceanic and Atmospheric Administration (NOAA).

As an example, NOAA's National Weather Service publishes *Storm Data,* a monthly publication that provides state-by-state damages from severe weather. The database is organized by individual events and provides information about deaths, injuries, property damage, crop damage, and other pertinent information. The losses from individual events may be caused by multiple perils such as wind, hail, tornadoes, and flooding. A breakdown of losses by peril would be difficult to achieve and is not available. Unfortunately, the quality of the data varies from state to state, and the loss per event is given in a range, rather than specific numbers. The use of ranges makes it difficult to aggregate losses and provide total loss estimates from multiple events or multiple years with any degree of confidence. For example, according to *Storm Data,* the losses from flooding in 1994 dollars over the time period 1975 to 1994 were between $19.6 and $196 billion, a wide range reflecting a high degree of uncertainty about these losses.

State and local government agencies, university researchers, and extension services also compile loss data after a disaster. However, there is little event-to-event or state-to-state consistency, and methods vary depending on the purpose of the survey. Much of the impetus for disaster-loss data collection at the state and local levels is to seek federal reimbursement for repair of infrastructure and other public facilities.

A noteworthy example of much-improved post-disaster impact and cost assessment was North Carolina's efforts following Hurricane Fran (North Carolina Disaster Recovery Task Force, 1997). The state established sector-specific action teams for business and employment, housing, human resources, and health and environment, each of which examined impacts and costs from their unique perspective. This process serves as an example of the type of post-disaster reporting structure that needs to be institutionalized in all coastal states.

Nongovernmental Organizations and University Research Centers

The American Red Cross (ARC) is one of a number of nongovernmental organizations (NGOs) that provide disaster assistance as an important mission. ARC disaster relief is free to victims and is provided primarily through the efforts of trained volunteers affiliated with local chapters nationwide. When a disaster is so large that it exceeds the capacity of a local chapter and its community to respond, the broader ARC network of people and resources is activated through the organization's Disaster Services Human Resources System. The Salvation Army is another important NGO involved in disaster response. Many other smaller NGOs respond to specific events or in specific locations. These privately supported organizations are extremely important to overall disaster relief efforts, because of both their financial contributions and the scope and quality of their services. For perspective on NGO costs, the ARC spent almost $67 million on Hurricane Hugo, with 78 percent for Caribbean response and 22 percent for South Carolina. In response to the devastation left in Central America by 1998's Hurricane Mitch, the ARC launched the largest international relief operation in its history. Its initial commitment of $6 million in assistance quickly grew to $18 million and will likely continue to increase, as the ARC continues to help meet the needs of the affected area's residents. Weekly shipments of critical relief supplies, including food, medicine, blankets, tents, and other essential materials, will continue for an indefinite period in 1999. Currently, there is no comprehensive accounting of NGO disaster response and recovery costs.

University research centers are also valuable sources of data on hazards and disasters. For example, the Natural Hazards Research and Applications

Center at the University of Colorado has assembled data on the U. S. costs of hazards and disasters of the past 20 years as part of the report *Disasters by Design: A Reassessment of Natural Hazards in the United States* (Mileti, 1999). The hazards studied include avalanches, droughts, dust storms, earthquakes, extreme cold, fires, floods, fog, heat, hurricanes, landslides, lightening, hail storms, ice/sleet events, blizzards, tornadoes, tropical storms, tsunamis, wind, and volcanoes. The information compiled is based in part on a careful review of the last 20 years of NOAA data, as well as data available from PCS, FEMA, and the Corps of Engineers.

Built Environment Costs of Coastal Hazards

For purposes of examining the costs of coastal hazards and disasters, the built environment is the aggregate human-constructed "physical plant," with all of its various elements. It includes the buildings where people live, work, learn, and play, and the infrastructure providing services to these structures. Other essential elements are the communication highways used to send information from one place to another, the pipes and transmission lines that carry vital supplies for use, or wastes to treatment. Very simply, the built environment comprises the substantive framework that enables human society to function in its many contexts—social, economic, political, and institutional (Geis and Kutzmark, 1995).

These built environment systems and facilities are divided into eight categories in table 3.3. Given the complex nature of communities, many of

Table 3.3. Elements of the Built Environment Vulnerable to Coastal Hazards

General Category	Specific Elements
Transportation infrastructure	• highways, streets, and roads, along with their support facilities—supply, storage, maintenance, fuel facilities, traffic signals and signs, etc. • public/mass transit and their support facilities—subways, railroads, airports, train and transit stations, storage, maintenance, supply, fuel facilities • aviation and related facilities • ports, marine storage, navigation aides, intermodal
Utility and power infrastructure	• electrical generation and transmission facilities—dams, fossil fuel, nuclear • gas production, storage, and distribution facilities • public and private water storage, treatment and distribution systems

General Category	Specific Elements
Utility and power infrastructure (*cont'd*)	• sewer and storm water collection, pumping, storage, and treatment facilities • communications infrastructure and networks—phone, data
Residential buildings	• single- and multi-family housing • apartment complexes and dormitories • retirement and nursing facilities • correctional and detention facilities
Economic enterprise	• commercial shopping districts and centers • banking, securities, and business services • office complexes • entertainment and recreation • natural resource extraction • manufacturing and industry • warehousing and distribution
Governmental service facilities and related private facilities	• city halls, county courthouses, local government buildings • state and federal public service and office buildings • police and fire stations • hospitals and clinics, emergency shelters, food and water storage areas • military bases and associated infrastructure • public squares, parks, youth centers, pools, etc.
Public and private education facilities	• pre-school, primary and secondary schools • colleges and universities • libraries
Interior property	• manufacturing and related business equipment • furniture, office equipment, supplies • lighting, plumbing, communication, electrical systems
Transportation stock	• cars, trucks, related equipment • railroad engines and cars • ships, port craft • commercial and recreational boats • aircraft—commercial, business, and recreational

these categories overlap. Schools, for example, are listed under education, but they often also serve as shelters and emergency facilities. Public transportation infrastructure, a separate category, is also related to the category of government functions. In fact, elements of the built environment in all of the categories are interrelated in terms of form and function, use, size, development pattern, location and configuration, and relationship to ecological systems.

Direct and Indirect Costs of Coastal Hazards to the Built Environment

Every hurricane that makes landfall is unique in terms of its size, speed of movement, winds, surge height, rainfall, timing with respect to tides, and impacts on the human-built environment. Hurricane Opal, an October 1995 storm that hit the Florida Panhandle, was mainly a "water storm" in that most of the damage was caused by a moderate storm surge and waves that destroyed many beachfront homes. Hurricane Andrew in 1992, on the other hand, was a more intense, compact storm in which wind was the main cause of direct physical damage. With Hurricane Hugo, both storm surge and high winds caused significant damage, although the most intense winds and highest surge came ashore in relatively lightly populated areas 20 miles north of Charleston. These impacts are discussed in greater detail later.

The hazard conditions leading to various potential direct and indirect costs to the built environment are summarized in table 3.4. Because buildings and infrastructure have assessed values or easily determined replacement costs, and because they are often insured, damages to the built environment are more easily tallied and account for the great majority of officially reported costs of hurricanes and other weather-related hazards.

Direct costs to the built environment are defined as the physical damage directly associated with the storm event—damage caused by storm surge, other causes of elevated water levels and flooding, wind and waves, saltwater inundation, and erosion. Examples include outright destruction of residential, commercial, industrial, and public buildings due to wind, surge, waves, and tornadoes; downed trees and other built environment debris that damages structures or interrupts transportation or power; building envelope failure (e.g., roof or window loss) caused by high winds that allows building contents to be damaged subsequently by rain and wind; damage to infrastructure, such as bridges, highways, and public and private utilities; damage to ports and harbor facilities, including deepwater shipping and commercial and recreational fishing ports, and vessels of all sorts; and damage to industrial facilities.

Indirect impacts and costs are those that are distant from the storm in both time and sequence. In table 3.4, a fine line is apparent between some direct and indirect impacts. Indirect impacts may follow very quickly after direct ones (e.g., building contents are damaged after a roof blows off). Here the direct–indirect linkage is more one of the sequence of the impacts, rather

Table 3.4. Impacts and Costs of Hurricanes and Other Coastal Hazards to the Built Environment[a]

Event or Condition[b]	Potential Direct Impacts and Costs	Potential Indirect Impacts and Costs
Wind speeds at and beyond structure design levels	Building damage and/or destruction (structural and nonstructural)	Loss of function, damage to and loss of furniture, personal effects, business records, business and industrial equipment; uninhabitable residences, health facilities; business interruption; social and family stress, homelessness; public service interruption (education, emergency response capability)
	Infrastructure failure and disruption—bridges, highway signs, traffic control devices, power substations, and utility lines	Transportation and utility disruption; navigation impeded; loss of safety/health services; business interruptions (loss of jobs); social and family stress
	Compromise of building envelope via loss of roof damage, broken doors, windows on residential, commercial, and industrial facilities; airborne debris	Damage and loss of furniture, personal effects, business records, business and industrial equipment; uninhabitable residences and business places; business failure or interruption (loss of jobs/tax base); social and family stress, homelessness
	Downed trees	Transportation disruption; power outages due to line breaks; building damage and compromised envelopes; subsequent contents damage; uninhabitable residences and business places; business failure or interruption; social and family stress, homelessness; natural resource damage
		Persistent and organic debris creation; Natural resource and ecosystem impacts of cleanup
Storm-surge flooding and wave action, with erosion and overwash	Building foundation/structural failure and collapse, mainly along ocean, but also inland; building envelope damage and destruction—windows, roofs; damaged equipment, vehicles	Personal/business property loss; public service interruption (education, emergency response capability); social and family stress; loss of rental and business income, loss of tourism; natural resource/ecosystem damage
	Industrial area, and deep and shallow water port facility inundation and foundation/structural damage	Interrupted trade and intermodal commerce at ports, fuel and other hazardous materials released from storage facilities; business interruptions; natural resource/ecosystem damage
	Waterborne debris	Persistent and organic debris creation; natural resource and ecosystem impacts of cleanup

(continues)

Table 3.4. Continued

Event or Condition[b]	Potential Direct Impacts and Costs	Potential Indirect Impacts and Costs
	Ship, boat, and other vehicle damage	Lost sea time and repair costs; commercial fishing interruptions; fuel and other hazardous materials released from boats; business interruptions; natural resource/ecosystem damage
	Infrastructure inundation, erosion, and failure—roads, railroads, bridges, highway signs, traffic control devices, power substations and lines	Transportation and utility disruption, loss of basic/daily community functioning; loss of health and safety services; business interruptions, loss of jobs and tax base; social and family stress and disruption; natural resource/ecosystem damage
	Saltwater intrusion into aquifers, lakes, reservoirs	Drinking water contamination (well and surface water)
Rain and induced flooding	Residential, commercial, and public building and equipment damage/destruction	Personal/business property loss, dislocation; loss of community functioning, health and safety needs and services, social and family stress and disruption, crime; loss of rental and business income; natural resource/ecosystem damage, fire
	Industrial area inundation and structural damage	Fuel and other hazardous materials release from storage facilities; business interruptions; natural resource/ecosystem damage
	Recreational moorage and boat/vehicle damage	Fuel and other hazardous materials release from boats; business interruptions; natural resource/ecosystem damage
	Infrastructure inundation, erosion, and failure—roads, railroads, bridges, traffic control devices, power substations and utility lines	Transportation and utility disruption; loss of community functioning and services, loss of power, water and sewerage function; business interruptions, tax base and job loss; social and family disruption and stress
	Inundation of freshwater lakes, reservoirs, and agricultural land	Drinking water contamination (well and surface water); natural resource/ecosystem impacts
		Debris creation; natural resource/ecosystem impacts of cleanup
Tornado	All of the same impacts as high winds, but more intense and localized	All of the same impacts as high winds, but more intense and localized

[a] Possible data sources are: private insurance databases, FEMA public and individual assistance, university/think tank research centers, local and state governments, and financial and mortgage institutions.

[b] Events or conditions may act in concert to exacerbate direct and indirect impacts (e.g., in the worst case, high winds, high winds, spawned tornadoes, large waves, high storm surge, intense rain, all occurring at predicted high tide).

than the timing, because they both may occur during the storm event. Other indirect impacts clearly follow some time after the storm; these are discussed in more detail in subsequent sections dealing with business interruptions and social and natural resource impacts and costs.

Hurricane Hugo—Built Environment Costs and Lessons Learned

When Hurricane Hugo made landfall just north of Charleston late on September 21, 1989, it was clear that the storm would have a devastating effect on the Carolina Lowcountry. Chapter 2 presented an overview of the characteristics and impacts of Hugo from the very personal perspective of local residents who participated in the March 1998 Charleston-region workshop. As part of that workshop, Heinz panel members met with a property developer and officials in state and local transportation, planning, building, historic preservation, and coastal zone management in an attempt to understand the full extent of built environment impacts and costs associated with what was, at the time, the largest single natural disaster in U.S. history. They offered the following insights:

- As evident from the better performance during the storm of the more recently built structures, modern building code provisions and improved enforcement had a positive impact on reducing vulnerability.
- Compromised building envelopes—loss of roof shingles or sheathing and panels, and broken doors and windows—caused by high winds led to greatly increased insured losses as storm and post-storm rains damaged building contents; much of this could have been avoided.[1]
- The lack of redundancy of key infrastructure and subsequent loss of those structures (e.g., bridge to Sullivan's Island) has very severe social impacts and costs in a community.
- The Charleston Public Works' emergency management plan and its effective implementation averted major sewage releases and treatment plant downtime, illustrating the value of advance planning and preparedness in minimizing indirect, post-storm impacts to other sectors.
- Poor or deferred building maintenance increased the vulnerability of many of the older and historic structures in the Charleston area; at the same time, many well-maintained older structures performed quite well in the storm.
- Opinions about present-day vulnerability compared to 1989 (when the hurricane struck) differed; some felt that improved building practices had increased the resiliency of the community, whereas others said the rapid growth of the area, particularly in hazard-prone areas on barrier islands and in the adjacent, low-lying communities of Mount Pleasant and James Island, made the area more vulnerable to future hurricanes.

Table 3.5. Reported Estimates of Net Built Environment[a] Damages from
Hurricane Hugo

Category	Reimbursements (millions of 1991 dollars)			
	Insurance Damage Total	Assistance	Public Loss	Unreimbursed
Residences	2,960	1,349	22	1,589
Commercial/Industrial	1,029	829	0	200
Federal flood insurance		365	0	365
Autos, misc.	215	182	0	33
Utilities	197	0	74	123
Ports authority	17	16	1	0
Agricultural structures[b]	294	0	0[b]	294
Charleston Naval Base	250	0	250	0
Shaw Air Force Base	50	0	50	0
Other government	142	0	142	0
TOTAL	$5,154[c]	$2,741	$539	$1,874

[a] In addition to reported built environment losses, the forest and agricultural sectors sustained
reported losses of $1.031 billion and $87 million, respectively.
[b] Farmers received some funds from FEMA. These funds are included under reimbursements for
residences.
[c] Built environment losses were 82 percent of total reported losses, estimated at $6,272 (1991 dollars).
Source: Modified from Guimaraes et al. (1993).

Reported losses to the built environment associated with Hurricane
Hugo in the Charleston region were estimated at $5.2 billion by the state
Budget and Control Board in 1991 (Guimaraes et al., 1993) (see table 3.5).
More recent overall estimates put total losses at more than $7 billion, but no
breakdowns are available for the total. Prior to Hugo, the insurance industry
had never suffered any loss of more than $1 billion from a single disaster.
Since that time, the industry has had 10 U.S. disasters that exceeded this
amount (Kunreuther and Roth, 1998).

Residences were particularly hard hit: more than 9,000 homes were destroyed, 27,000 sustained major damage, and 76,000 minor damage—
112,000 in all. Residential losses totaled approximately $2.9 billion. More
than half of that total was not covered by private insurance or public assistance, although most of the $365 million in federal flood insurance payments
went to offset residential and commercial structure losses (see table 3.5).
Roads, bridges, dams, harbors, marinas, and recreational areas incurred
nearly $19 million in uninsured damage that was reimbursed by federal pub-

lic assistance funds. Uninsured public building content losses amounted to $20 million, again reimbursed by federal public assistance. In all, just over half of Hugo's $7 billion costs were not reimbursed by either insurance or public or individual assistance. The extent of unreported or hidden costs is unknown; some of these costs may be associated with the built environment, but most of them likely were absorbed by the business community, social systems, and natural resources and ecosystems. These additional hidden costs are addressed in subsequent sections of this chapter.

Hurricane Andrew's Legacy—the Real Wake-up Call

Just three years after Hugo, in 1992, Hurricane Andrew caused substantially more insured property loss to South Florida than that which had resulted from the previous hurricane—$15.5 billion (IIPLR and IRC, 1995). Total economic damages for Andrew are estimated at $30 billion in 1992 dollars (Pielke and Pielke, 1997). Based on data compiled by IIPLR and IRC (1995), Andrew destroyed 28,000 homes and damaged an additional 107,000, leaving more than 180,000 residents temporarily homeless. For thousands more, life in "tent cities" lasted for months. A total of 82,000 businesses were damaged, 8,000 of them severely. More than 3,000 businesses closed their doors permanently. Thirty-one public schools were damaged, along with 59 health care facilities and hospitals. Some 9,500 traffic signs and signals were put out of order or destroyed, along with 3,000 water mains and 3,300 miles of power lines. More than 120,000 jobs were suspended temporarily, 1.4 million residents lost electricity, and 500,000 customers lost telephone service. Lost tourism income was estimated at $300 billion, as visitors rescheduled their vacations to other areas.

As of December 1998, Andrew was the most expensive natural disaster in U.S. history. Its impact and influence on the insurance industry has been particularly telling. Nine property insurance companies became insolvent in the wake of Andrew, adding to the burden of other insurers who picked up the pieces under the insurance industry's guaranty fund. Property insurance became more difficult to get as companies reevaluated their coverage portfolios in vulnerable coastal areas. As of 1998, the insurance market was still in turmoil in South Florida with respect to appropriate rates and available coverage in the area (Lecomte and Gahagan, 1998).

Linkages between the Built Environment and Business, Social, and Natural Resource Costs

There are strong connections between the built environment impacts and the costs outlined in table 3.4 and the vulnerability of a community's businesses and economy, social structure and institutions, and surrounding natural environment. In a community where the development siting is sensitive to the risks imposed by the physical environment (e.g., beach processes, periodic flooding), it is more likely that the public infrastructure and buildings will be more hazard-resistant and less vulnerable than in a community where development is less sensitive to these issues. Not only will the built environment be more resilient, but the economic, social, institutional, and natural resource and ecosystem functions will also be more resilient. This connection implies that a key to hazard mitigation lies in the sensitive siting, organization, and construction of the built environment (Geis, 1996). Table 3.4 shows some of the linkages between the built environment and other sectors.

LOSS OF LIFE AND INJURY. Among the most important costs usually resulting from damage and destruction of the built environment are those associated with the loss of life and injuries. But their impact does not stop there. The post-event impacts, such as complications from injuries, the terrible implications of a death for a family and a community, and the emotional and psychological stress that inevitably accompany such an event, can last for many years and even a lifetime. These indirect effects are often just as significant, or even more so, than the immediate effects of the storm.

LOSS OF PRODUCTIVITY AND COMMUNITY FUNCTIONING. When businesses, community facilities, and homes are damaged or destroyed, conveniences normally taken for granted are no longer available. Victims are temporarily homeless, businesses are closed. Gas stations cannot pump gas because there is no electricity. Banks and automatic teller machines are often closed or off-line, making cash on hand the only means of purchasing items. There is no place to cash checks or fill prescriptions. Post offices are often inoperable, and mail cannot be delivered. Doctors' and lawyers' offices can be closed for extended periods of time. Grocery stores, malls, schools, and daycare and health facilities may not be operating. All of these disruptions result in the loss of normal functioning, productivity, and jobs, representing great costs to families, businesses, and the community.

LOSS OF TOURISM. Tourism, an important industry for many communities, can be affected dramatically by disasters. The tourism industry needs a full range of physical facilities and infrastructure if it is to flourish—hotels, restaurants, transportation lines, utility systems, and an intact natural environment. Resort areas can be affected severely for years if tourists' perceptions of communities being "blown off the face of the map" must be overcome.

AFTER-EVENT RAINFALL LOSSES. Heavy rains after a hurricane can badly damage or destroy the furnishings of a residence with a partially missing roof, leading to the possible displacement of the family, accompanying emotional stress, and potential loss of property value, beyond the actual costs of repair. That same damage to a roof of a business facility can result in inoperable equipment, dislocation of the business, and the loss of jobs (with the accompanying ripple effect on employees), as well as the potential loss of taxes to the community.

INFRASTRUCTURE DISRUPTION. The damage to and destruction of the built environment infrastructure—transportation, utilities, and communication—often represents enormous economic, social, and general functional costs to a community, while also impeding emergency response and recovery activities. Many of these costs are not counted in the traditional accounting methods. More and more people live in the areas most vulnerable to hurricanes, within 50 miles of the Gulf of Mexico or the Atlantic Ocean. It is here where, for many coastal states, tremendous amounts of valuable infrastructure exist, especially transportation lifelines. A nonfunctional road can have major implications for the community: general loss of productivity; disruption of physical access, preventing residents from getting to work or other daily activities and preventing emergency vehicles from reaching their destinations, with the associated health and safety implications; and disruption of basic food supplies and other daily deliveries to the community.

A lack of dependable communications during and after a hurricane can be a critical problem. Cellular telephone towers are often nonfunctional because of a lack of electricity. Although each tower has a back-up battery supply, the batteries are not designed to operate for days without being recharged. As a result, cell phones are virtually useless in the affected area. In addition, other forms of communications are likely to be severely restricted. Police, firefighters, and emergency medical technicians can be slowed by equipment failures. Incompatible systems can be as serious a problem as the physical loss of the equipment. Different brands of radios and different operating frequencies can make cross-agency communications almost impossible, strangling the recovery efforts (Frank Koutnik, Florida Department of Emergency Management, personal communication, March 1998). A disruption of these functions represents a significant loss of productivity, poses serious safety and health problems, and can cause great emotional stress. All of these effects contribute to the true costs associated with an extreme natural event.

Damaged or destroyed utility lines and facilities—including electricity, computer and satellite links, gas, sewer, and water services—can cripple a region after a disaster. Power lines are often badly damaged or destroyed, resulting in the loss of power for days, weeks, or even months. This is particularly critical considering modern societies' dependence on electricity. Refrigerators, televisions, radios, lighting, heating, air conditioning, and a myriad of other automated appliances require electricity to function. Water supplies and use can also be affected. Electric pumps cannot pump drinking water into an area without power, and, even if they could, the water delivery system can be breached in many places. Even disaster victims who do get water may have to boil it to eliminate waterborne pathogens introduced to the supply in breached areas. A loss of elevated water tanks also results in a lack of safe drinking water, with all of its ramifications.

A nonfunctional sewer system also presents a unique set of problems. Most systems, even those that rely on gravity to flow, need pumps to deliver the effluent to sewage plants. If there is no power and many of the lines are broken, a very serious health problem can develop rapidly. This problem, combined with the unavailability of drinking water, can virtually cripple any recovery effort. All of these losses constitute the true indirect costs, accrued over time, associated with a hurricane or other significant weather-related event.

LOSS OF BUSINESSES, PROPERTY VALUES, AND TAX BASE. Another major indirect cost associated with damage to and destruction of the built environment is a substantial reduction in property values and a reduced tax base. Businesses and residences can be inoperational or unusable for significant periods of time, and many residents move out of the community permanently, resulting in a loss of jobs and a shrinking economy. For example, the southern portion of Dade County, Florida, experienced negative growth for the first time in its history after Hurricane Andrew.

Business Community Costs of Coastal Hazards

For purposes of examining the costs of hurricanes, coastal hazards, and disasters, the "business community" includes all types and sizes of business enterprises, ranging from large manufacturing plants to retail shops to service providers such as gas stations, motels, and restaurants. The focus in this chapter, however, is primarily on small businesses, generally defined as businesses with fewer than 50 employees. The rationale for this approach is that small businesses are deemed inherently more vulnerable to disaster-induced losses than are large businesses (Alesch and Holly, 1996). This is, in part, because smaller firms may be less likely to have business interruption protection and other types of insurance. Smaller firms also tend to be less diversified in their products and services, situated in just one geographic location, and dependent on a walk-in customer base—all factors that may render these firms more vulnerable to disasters (Alesch and Holly, 1996).

Direct and Indirect Costs of Coastal Hazards to the Business Community

The existing research on disaster-related costs incurred by the business community is quite limited, and, for the reasons noted earlier, focuses primarily on small businesses. The available literature on the subject is reviewed briefly below. The categories of impacts and costs that are incurred by businesses are summarized in table 3.6 and discussed in the text, as well as in the business community overview of the panel's Hurricane Hugo case study that follows.

It is no great surprise that business disruption, and even business failure after disasters, is correlated with the extent of damage to structures that house businesses. Both Bolin (1994) and Kroll et al. (1991) found that businesses that experienced greater disaster-related building damage were less likely to recover than were their less affected counterparts. But even if business-related buildings are not seriously damaged, indirect disaster impacts, such as utility outages and other lifeline interruptions, can seriously impede the resumption of business. For example, research found that utility loss resulting from the 1993 Midwest floods was a much more important cause of business closure in the city of Des Moines than was direct flood damage (Tierney, 1994, 1997; Tierney et al., 1996). More frequently, businesses in Des Moines had to suspend operations because of a loss of electricity, water, and sewer and wastewater services rather than a lack of customers or employee access to the business. By contrast, the physical damage to building structures, rather than lifeline service interruption, was the dominant problem after the 1994 earthquake in Northridge, California (Tierney, 1995).

Interruptions in utility and other lifeline services have ripple effects on businesses. Those forced to close have immediate cash-flow problems. Employees lose work, and customers who must go elsewhere for goods and services may not return when the business reopens. Other businesses require a certain amount of overall commercial activity in their geographic area if they are to prosper. If a disaster occurs in the area, then the operations and recovery of these individual businesses will be affected. A lack of employees and customer access may hamper the ability of businesses to function or recover. Potential problems include employees who are unable to get to work, damage to the business owner's home or other properties, loss of customers, difficulties getting supplies and materials, difficulties delivering products or services, and difficulty paying employees (Durkin, 1984; Kroll et al., 1991).

Loss containment is another issue for businesses. The ability of a business

Table 3.6. Business Community Costs of Coastal Hazards and Disasters

Event or Condition	Possible Impacts/Costs	Possible Data Sources
Direct damage to building, equipment, or other components of physical plant[a]	Debris removal and disposal, building repair, equipment repair/replacement, closure and loss of business,[b] permanent loss of customers	IBHS/Insurance industry data, American Red Cross, State Departments of Commerce, Industry
Direct damage to public infrastructure (transportation, power, phone, sewer and water, gas, etc.)	Interruption of distribution and supply networks, inability to produce or provide retail services, closure and loss of business,[b] permanent loss of customers	FEMA data on public infrastructure costs
Release of hazardous or toxic materials at business site	Hazardous material disposal, start-up impeded by government regulations, closure and loss of business,[b] permanent loss of customers	State environmental agency data, EPA databases
Employee impacts (personal loss/injury, loss or damage to home, loss of vehicle and/or public transport)	Increased absenteeism, increased stress and loss of job focus, loss of personal transportation, stress on personal finances, increased family strife/abuse, closure and loss of business,[b] permanent loss of customers	State workman's compensation databases, U.S. Department of Commerce and Small Business Administration business failure data
Damage to complementary businesses and services (fuel, restaurants, motels; office services)	Inability to support normal business functions, permanent loss of customers dependent on complementary businesses, tourism-dependent business decline	University of Delaware Disaster Research Center, ongoing research projects
Natural resource loss (crops and timber), ecosystem damage, beach erosion	Debris removal and disposal, loss of food and fiber processing businesses and jobs (may be permanent), loss of tourism linked to beaches or natural environmental amenities	NOAA's coastal resources centers
Loss of insurability or increased insurance costs	Increased future vulnerability	IBHS and other insurance industry databases

[a] This damage often covered through hazards insurance.
[b] This damage may be covered in part by business interruption insurance.

to obtain funding to cover the costs associated with the disaster affects its ability to recover. The types of business aid currently available include insurance, loans from the SBA, bank loans, and help from relatives or other individuals. Previous disaster experience may lead businesses to develop recovery plans and arrangements for relocation in the event of building damage or take other steps to cope with disaster-related problems. Owners who suffered previous disaster losses, perhaps because they are more familiar with how to obtain various sources of recovery aid, are more likely to recover (Drabek, 1994; Dahlhamer and D'Souza, 1997).

Another significant category of business costs are payments from one sector of the economy that benefit other sectors. These transfers, which can be quite large, are likely to have impacts on specific firms (e.g., claims payments by the insurance industry to disaster victims), but normally represent a negligible net loss to society as a whole. In fact, as noted earlier in this chapter, a disaster can have positive short-term effects, such as an increase in construction activity with the creation of new jobs to implement the recovery process (Guimaraes et al., 1993).

Hurricane Hugo: Impacts On and Costs To the Business Community

The Heinz panel discussed business losses in the Charleston region with business community organization leaders and owners and operators of large and small businesses that "survived" Hurricane Hugo. According to Mary Graham of the Charleston Chamber of Commerce, only about 12 percent of businesses remained "in trouble" a month after the hurricane, despite a prediction that about 30 percent of businesses would fail (personal communication, March 25, 1998). All of the interviewees had some insurance, consisting of a mix of commercial, state, and, in some cases, federal insurance, and some were able to tap sources such as the SBA disaster loan program to cover uninsured business losses.

Many of the impacts and costs listed in table 3.6 were significant for Charleston-area businesses in the wake of Hurricane Hugo. These impacts included direct damages to the physical plant, equipment, and supply networks; indirect impacts due to the interruption of public services; and losses associated with reductions in employee productivity. Many of these costs were insured, but some were not. The available data suggest that the total commercial and industrial claims associated with Hurricane Hugo totaled about $1 billion and represented 33,000 to 40,000 property claims, each averaging $20,000 to $30,000. The estimated nonreimbursable business loss was on the order of $200 million, the third-largest category of insured losses after residential and forest damages.

Additional costs included the loss of complementary businesses; for example, decreased tourism led to the shutdown of hotels or restaurants. Damage to the roadways and bridges adversely affected businesses. Extensive damage to commercially valuable timber in the Francis Marion National Forest significantly reduced the supply of wood to the processing sector in coastal Carolina, resulting in layoffs and labor migration into other sectors (Glen Stapleton, U.S. Forest Service, Francis Marion National Forest, personal communication, March 25, 1998). Secondary hazards, such as the release of toxic substances, were another environmental issue for businesses. Finally, the purchase of insurance decreased after Hugo, in part because of increased premiums and a lack of available coverage. The overall results of the Heinz panel's March 25, 1998, interviews of Charleston-area business leaders are summarized in the following text.

INSURED AND UNINSURED BUSINESS LOSSES ASSOCIATED WITH HURRICANE HUGO. Although there may be a widespread perception that most business losses are insurable, the panel learned that most of the businesses in the Charleston area incurred some uninsured damages beyond insurance deductibles. Among our interviewees, these losses ranged from $600,000 to $2 million. The uninsured losses included not only short-term business interruptions of a month or so, but also some longer-term losses.

EFFECTS ATTRIBUTABLE TO INTERDEPENDENCIES IN THE LOCAL ECONOMY. Perhaps most notable among business losses were the chain effects created by dependencies inherent in the local economy. For instance, many employers could not resume business until road networks were reopened. Some employees could not report to work even though roads were passable, because schools were not yet open and families had no daycare alternatives. As another example of these chain effects, businesses such as island ferry boats, which depend on tourism, restarted operations only with the resumed operation of related establishments, such as restaurants and hotels.

EFFECTS ASSOCIATED WITH BUSINESS RELATIONS WITH THE FEDERAL GOVERNMENT. In at least two cases, relationships with the federal government were prominent factors affecting the magnitude of business loss. One business derived much of its revenue from servicing a national park. Because this asset is publicly owned, business interruption insurance was unavailable. In another case, business losses were affected by closures prolonged by the requirement for federal inspections of pollution control equipment before certain plant operations could be restarted.

POST-EVENT ACTIONS TO MITIGATE IMMEDIATE AND FUTURE LOSSES. Interviewees at the March workshop described numerous short-term actions taken in the aftermath of the hurricane. Many businesses offered small cash grants, interest-free loans, and other assistance (such as liberal leave) to employees adversely affected by the disaster. Other interviewees noted that some practical post-event needs were hard to meet but could be part of their disaster planning in the future. Examples include stocking up on bottled water, ice, and paper plates, and making tools such as chain saws available for loan.

Also notable was the sense of community spirit championed by the businesses and their employees. For instance, "accountants wielded jackhammers" at one manufacturing facility. And the interviewees reported that, after the hurricane, their employees nearly fully repaid their loans. The fundamental cost structures of business operations did not change significantly, although some firms installed back-up facilities (such as generators). In general, most businesses in the Charleston area reported some modest increases in insurance premiums.

RESOURCE TRANSFERS AMONG AFFECTED SECTORS. The Hurricane Hugo interviews confirmed that significant resource transfers can occur after extreme events. As insurance money poured into the area, bank deposits increased significantly and industries such as building and construction prospered for approximately 18 months. In addition, immediately after the hurricane, an influx of claims adjusters and other outside experts flooded local hotels, pouring additional short-term revenues into the area's economy. Other establishments that prospered in the aftermath included appliance stores and car dealerships, where sales were boosted for about nine months.

Social, Health, and Safety Costs of Coastal Hazards

Most of the social costs associated with coastal hazard events go unrecognized in official assessments, in part because they are difficult to define and quantify. To estimate the social costs of any major disaster event, it is necessary to examine the effects on the social institutions, such as a community's families, schools, and places of worship, as well as the social networks connecting groups and people. At the individual, household, and community levels, profound social disruption is likely to occur. The extent to which this results in lasting social change, as well as the expected direction of that change, continues to be the subject of debate among disaster researchers (Morrow and Peacock, 1997).

The health-related effects of a storm usually are thought of in terms of the deaths and injuries that occur during the event. But these costs also include the medical expenses and loss of productive work associated with premature births and deaths, persistent illnesses, physical injuries, and psychological problems that continue to occur throughout the recovery period. The health problems resulting from a major disaster, and the concomitant human suffering, are likely to have profound sociological effects on the community and its institutions. For this reason, they are considered together.

Safety costs include the expenses that households are likely to encounter in preparing for and responding to coastal storms. The most obvious costs are associated with the protective actions taken well in advance to safeguard lives and property; these actions include purchasing flood, wind, and homeowner's or renter's insurance. Mitigation initiatives, such as shutters and retrofitting to make homes more storm resistant, require substantial financial resources. Household preparation may involve major expenditures for generators and pumps, as well as the purchasing of emergency supplies, such as food and water, radios, and flashlights. Evacuation is likely to result in substantial household expenses, including the costs of transportation, private lodging, and food. Time, and therefore productivity, is likely to be lost from work, school, and regular activities. The inconveniences associated with evacuating, including staying in shelters, can be quite stressful and can have serious implications for the ill or frail elderly.

Some household expenditures can be estimated by collecting data on insurance premiums, costs of shutters and other mitigation actions, and emergency supplies, as well as through assorted marketplace analyses. However, many, if not most, of these extra household-level expenses can best be captured through household surveys. In general, household expenses related to storm protection remain an important, but largely unreported, cost category.

Evacuation is also an expensive matter for a community. Shelters have to be opened and staffed. Food, water, and medical supplies must be provided. Extra police and other government personnel are required to manage the evacuation. Evacuations in response to storm warnings are also very expensive for local businesses in terms of lost trade. Of course, the costs of not evacuating from a dangerous area can be even greater.

Direct and Indirect Social, Health, and Safety Impacts and Costs

Although it is impossible to capture all of the expenditures associated with the social, health, and safety costs of a coastal storm, table 3.7 provides some examples of the consequences of specific disaster-related events or conditions

Table 3.7. Social, Health, and Safety Costs of Coastal Hazards

Event or Condition	Possible Impacts and Costs	Possible Data Sources
Household mitigation and preparation	Purchase of various types of insurance; shutters and home retrofitting; purchase of emergency supplies	Insurance company records; market analyses; household surveys
Evacuation	Extra expenses for gas, lodging, and food; loss of work time; inconvenience; health problems for ill and frail elderly; operation of shelters; extra police and other personnel	Market analysis; employer and household surveys; hospital and medical records; sheltering agencies reports; local government reports
Direct impact on population	Injuries and/or deaths; premature births and deaths; pain and suffering; grief; loss of income due to deaths and injuries; cost of fire and police response; medical and funeral expenses	CDC[a] and hospital records; surveys; actuarial tables; government agency reports; medical insurance, hospital and funeral records
Damaged homes and communities	Stress and illnesses from living in damaged homes; injuries and deaths associated with cleanup and repairs; temporary or permanent dislocation; storage and moving expenses; home repair costs; replacement of personal property; contractor fraud; provision of temporary housing for homeless; absenteeism and inefficiency at work and school	Surveys of individuals and caregivers; hospital and medical records; analysis of population movement patterns; market analysis of related goods and services; insurance payouts; household surveys; increases in sales tax revenues; police records; records for shelters, tent cities, trailers; employer and school surveys
Loss of public and private transportations	Inability to get to work or to services; inability to access relief and other vital services (e.g., health care)	Absenteeism; underutilization of services; unemployment; patterns of underutilization of services
Disrupted or overburdened social support networks	Less kin assistance; loss of friends and support systems; greater reliance on public assistance	Surveys, self-reports; community services; unemployment; patterns of underutilization of services
Loss of neighborhoods	Loss of assistance; loss of businesses and services; loss of property value; loss of community pride	Community surveys; changes in assessments; level of civic participation
Individual stress	Decreased ability to function; premature aging and dependency; increased incidence of suicide; lost human potential; increased alcohol and drug use	Employer and school surveys; CMHS[b]; vital statistics, medical records; loss of income and productivity; alcohol sales; police records

(continues)

Table 3.7. Continued

Event or Condition	Possible Impacts and Costs	Possible Data Sources
Family stress	Increased family conflict; increased domestic violence; increased desertion and divorce; child abuse and abandonment; inadequate parenting	Police and agency records; reports from shelters, police, courts, CMHS[b]; increased use of family services; survey of churches
Loss of local community services (e.g., child care, schools, churches, libraries, parks and recreation programs, police and fire protection, medical facilities	Loss of employment (i.e., productivity); work absenteeism or inefficiency; reduced education, increase in school dropouts; child depression and behavior problems; untreated illnesses and injuries; increased crime, looting; increased reliance on external service providers	Community and household surveys; employer surveys; school records; teacher surveys; surveys of service agencies; surveys and self-reports; police records; federal reimbursements to local governments
Temporary loss of local volunteers and funding	Greater dependency on outside services	Reports of local agencies, charities, churches
Overburdened responders	Worker burnout; high turnover rates; caregiver stress; political instability; scapegoating	Agency and household surveys; cost of counseling services, retreats, workshops; changes in office political climate
Potential of secondary hazards (debris removal, toxic wastes, etc.)	Fear, insecurity; health problems, such as allergies	Self-reports; medical records

[a] Centers for Disease Control and Prevention.
[b] Center for Mental Health and Substance Abuse (formerly National Institute of Mental Health and Prevention).

and suggests possible data sources for estimating their true costs. In some cases, household economic costs are included because they have direct implications for emotional and social well-being. The emphasis is at the household level, but some examples of the use of community resources to respond to the needs of individuals and households are also mentioned. When a major storm hits a coastal community, all of its social institutions are affected. Indeed, the entire social fabric that defines a population as a community is likely to be weakened greatly by changes brought on by the storm. Residents relocate (some permanently), neighborhoods are destroyed, friendships severed, support networks broken. The community will probably never be the same.

Social Impacts and Costs

Probably the most profound social costs are paid by families. Family roles and responsibilities can undergo considerable change associated with household and employment disruption, economic hardship, poor living conditions, and reliance on agencies to provide for basic needs. Life patterns are disrupted, family relationships are changed, and role frustration likely occurs (Bates et al., 1963). Increased family conflict has been documented (Bolin, 1985; Morrow, 1997). Family desertion and divorce may increase (Morrow, 1992, 1997; Enarson and Morrow, 1997). Within the family, relations between adults and children and among children become more stressful, as do relations with kin outside the household (Erikson, 1976; Morrow, 1997). Parenting can become extremely difficult when neighborhoods are unsafe to play in, child care is unavailable, and recreational facilities are nonexistent.

Similarly, social networks are weakened or broken by relocation or by the stresses of rebuilding lives and homes in depressing and shattered environments. Although neighborhoods often come together in the immediate aftermath in an altruistic "community of sufferers" (Fritz, 1961), as the days turn into months, relentless physical and emotional burdens are likely to damage social bonds, resulting instead in what Erikson (1994) describes as "corrosive communities." Post-disaster social support will also vary within communities, and not necessarily according to need. For example, in a study that measured emotional, informational, and tangible support after Hurricane Hugo, major patterns of neglect were found among black and less educated victims, regardless of degree of disaster loss (Kaniasty and Norris, 1995).

At the community level, churches and community agencies experience a loss of members, reduced donations, and fewer local volunteers as people leave the community or become absorbed in their own recovery efforts. Schools are likely to be closed temporarily, relocated to a new building, or forced to operate under difficult circumstances. Students at Homestead High School in Florida, for example, were without a library in either their school or their community for an entire school year after Hurricane Andrew. Recreational facilities and programs may be curtailed for months, even years.

Inadequate response, whether real or perceived, to critical community needs on the part of government agencies or officials often results in political change or instability after a disaster (Morrow and Peacock, 1997; Olson, 1997). It is not uncommon for one particular official to bear the brunt of citizens' pent-up frustration and anger and, as a scapegoat, be maligned, dismissed, or even prosecuted (Morrow, 1992; Averch and Dluhy, 1997).

Social impacts can increase the costs of a coastal storm to the business sector, as discussed previously. Many business costs, such as absenteeism and reduced employee efficiency, can be traced in large part to health and family problems resulting from the stresses of recovery. The time-consuming and emotionally draining process of applying for assistance programs, settling insurance claims, and rebuilding or repairing homes also makes for distracted employees.

Some indirect family costs may be reflected in increases in divorces, police domestic calls, and other social indicators. However, most disruptions are evident only in the intimacy of private homes and thus are difficult to assess adequately. At the community level, the expenses related to increased demands on law enforcement agencies, the courts, and social services should be obtainable. Some indirect social costs, such as the loss of church membership and charity donations, are also measurable. However, the adverse impact on the development of children whose schools were damaged or destroyed, for example, would be very difficult to assess.

Clearly, the development of even rough estimates of the direct and indirect health and social costs of coastal storms will require considerable effort. Future research projects need to focus on mechanisms to capture more complete data, verify their accuracy, compare and aggregate data from a variety of sources, and analyze these databases appropriately.

Health and Safety Impacts and Costs

The most obvious effects on the residents of coastal areas hit by storms are the lives lost and the injuries resulting from the wind, water, and chaos of the event. Less apparent are the premature births, heart attacks, strokes, and other medical problems, even deaths, precipitated by fear and stress before, during, or immediately after an event. Those who are already ill or infirm are at heightened risk when emergency and intensive care services are disrupted temporarily. Typically, external medical resources arrive quickly in a heavily damaged community; however, as reported in the Hugo case study, their arrival does not necessarily result in quality medical care by qualified personnel.

The cost of feeding and sheltering displaced storm victims is a major expense incurred by government and NGOs, such as the American Red Cross and the Salvation Army. As discussed later in this chapter, the poor are particularly vulnerable to disasters, and in the case of major events, the government and NGOs can spend large sums to supply temporary housing and relief supplies, such as emergency water and food, food stamps, and other essentials.

Major indirect costs are imposed by health problems resulting from poor environmental conditions caused by damaged homes and disrupted utilities; these conditions include extreme temperatures, contaminated food, polluted water, bacteria-carrying mud and debris, and mildew and mold in the air. Unsafe roads and heavy traffic can lead to increased rates of automobile and pedestrian accidents. Much of the clean-up and recovery work occurs under unsafe conditions and is performed by unskilled labor or residents inexperienced with home repair. This results in many injuries, and even deaths, from falls off of roofs or out of trees, chain saw accidents, generator fires, and so on.

The stress of coping with daily needs and activities while trying to rebuild homes and lives under distressed conditions can take a heavy emotional toll on both adults and children (Vernberg et al., 1996; Grant et al., 1997). Increased use of alcohol and drugs is common, especially by males (Enarson and Morrow, 1997), and a recent study of several major natural disasters documented increased suicide rates (Krug et al., 1998). It is not unusual for conflict and violence to increase after a major storm. The disturbances can range from community lawlessness and looting in the immediate aftermath of the event to increased incidents of child abuse and domestic violence (Santa Cruz Commission for the Prevention of Violence against Women, 1990; Wilson et al., 1998).

Accounting for health-related costs is not as straightforward as might be assumed. Official reports of deaths and injuries from storm impacts typically are available within hours, but counts of delayed deaths and injuries, if reported at all, are usually limited to those occurring during the first few days. After that, no systematic attempt is made to identify the extent to which an injury, illness, or death is disaster related. Some estimates could be made by aggregating the expenses of emergency medical responders, medical insurance payments, invoices for hospital and other medical services, and funeral expenses. This would not be an easy task, however, because, even if the data were forthcoming, confidentiality laws might block attempts to check for duplications and gaps at the individual level.

A full accounting of the economic costs of lost or diminished lives would require estimates of the economic productivity losses they represent. Potential income losses in the formal (i.e., tax reported) sector can be estimated using actuarial tables, average salaries, and other economic indicators, as is usually done in legal cases involving loss of potential income. However, in the case of disasters, this is not done. Methods are also needed for tallying the loss of productivity and income in the informal (i.e., non–tax reported, e.g., "under the table," employment) sector, perhaps similar to those used in estimating the market value of homemakers' services. According to Odum (1992), at market rates a full-time homemaker's services were estimated to be $16,000–$17,000 annually (1991 dollars).

The costs associated with feeding and sheltering evacuated and dislocated storm victims are seldom, if ever, systematically collected and aggregated. There is a great deal of variation in the extent to which NGOs, as well as government agencies, are forthcoming with data. Expenses associated with increased community services, such as police and fire response to protect health and safety, as well as agency costs associated with family and social problems, should be available through local agencies, but they may be difficult to sort out. Some of these costs will be reflected in federal reimbursements to local governments.

The bottom line is that an accurate accounting of most long-term indirect health and social costs is extremely difficult to achieve. The accounting process can begin only with the establishment of systematic data collection procedures as part of federal and local planning for disasters and long-term recovery.

Safety, Health, and Social Costs: The Case of Hugo

To better understand the costs related to safety, health, and the social environment, the Heinz panel interviewed several key persons who were involved heavily with the South Carolina response to Hurricane Hugo. Although there were some glitches, in general the interviewees felt that the preparation and emergency phases of the response went fairly well, particularly in the Charleston area. Communities farther inland were not expecting the amount of wind and water they received and were less prepared.

By most accounts, the emergency response phase generally went well, with the exception of reports of tension related to the National Guard delaying some island residents from returning to their homes. There was also one case of an unauthorized emergency clinic being set up by unqualified medical personnel. As a result of the significant and pervasive scope and magnitude of the damage caused by Hugo, the services of NGOs, such as the Salvation Army and American Red Cross, were not well coordinated in the beginning, resulting in some duplication and gaps. Early health problems included insect and snake bites, but most of the serious injuries were from cleanup and repair activities, such as chain saw accidents or falls from roofs. Newspaper reports in the first five days after the storm indicated that 20 South Carolinians died as a direct result of Hurricane Hugo (Greer, 1989).

The local food stamp program was greatly expanded, distributing stamps worth $62.5 million in 10 days following the storm. Although many families living on the economic margin were in dire need, there were reports of less needy residents taking advantage of the program. Rescue personnel, governmental officials, and contractors converged on the Charleston area, often taking housing and other resources sorely needed by residents. All interviewees emphasized the lack of planning for recovery; most of the major problems occurred months, even years, later as the lengthy recovery process continued. The plight of many in need of help did not come quickly to the attention of authorities, resulting in unnecessary suffering and emotional trauma. This was particularly true for the frail elderly, the illiterate, and those living in isolated areas. Schools were closed for more than three weeks, adding to the disruption of children's and parents' lives. Many regular social services were likewise unavailable; for example, a women's shelter was closed for three weeks—at a time when family violence is likely to increase.

Many of those left homeless by the hurricane were already living on the economic margin. All but two of the 275 public housing units in Charleston County were damaged, affecting about 1,300 families. Most were able to return to their homes within a few days, but some had to be housed temporarily elsewhere. Eventually, their uninsured household property losses were covered by the FEMA Individual and Family Grants Program or by HUD, but recovery was a lengthy, and sometimes confusing, process. Some private landlords took advantage of the market by raising rents; price gouging was observed throughout the area. Fraud by "contractors" and other workers was reported widely. The number of homeless was increased by transients, and it remained inflated for four years after Hurricane Hugo.

The emotional and psychological problems encountered by individuals and families trying to cope with the stress of the post-storm environment strained social service agencies, particularly as the recovery process dragged into months, even years. Many problems did not come to the attention of responders soon enough, sometimes resulting in serious psychiatric problems. Worker burnout was common among social service providers. Several interviewees mentioned unaddressed problems among the middle class, where disagreements and even violence occurred within households and between neighbors.

The aim of the Heinz panel was not to identify all of the issues, but rather to collect examples that illustrate some of the problems encountered after a coastal storm, particularly those not commonly addressed. This objective was amply satisfied, in that during the panel's March 1998 workshop the interviews served to highlight many of the direct and indirect costs related to the safety, health, and social environment of those caught in the path of a coastal storm.

Natural Resource and Ecosystem Costs of Coastal Hazards

Some of the nation's most valued natural resources and resource-based activities are in the coastal zone. Hundreds of large and small estuaries and nearshore coastal waters rich in fish and shellfish support commercial fisheries that had a dockside value of $3.5 billion in 1996 (National Marine Fisheries Service, 1997). Marine fish and shellfish also supported 64 million marine recreational fishing trips that year (National Marine Fisheries Service, 1997), translating to additional billions of dollars in economic impacts on coastal marinas, charter operators, boat manufacturers, retail suppliers, and other marine trade businesses. These coastal waters, wetlands, and reefs, together with beaches, barrier islands, and rocky shores, provide sunbathing, swimming, diving, boating, and nature-based recreational experiences to many millions of coastal visitors each year, an industry that provides an estimated 28 million jobs and more than $50 billion in goods and services annually for the U.S. economy (Environmental News Network, 1998).

Productive, high-value coastal agriculture and forestry also depend on coastal natural resources and are among the industries most vulnerable to natural disasters. Nonrenewable resources, such as oil, gas, and minerals, are often abundant in coastal lands and waters, especially along the Gulf Coast. These are the highly visible economic contributions of coastal natural resources. But coastal ecosystems also provide a variety of "free" services that are used and valued by human society, but are often hidden in an economic analysis—storm buffering provided by beaches and dunes, for example, and flood water storage and conveyance by wetlands and streams. In addition, nutrient cycling and waste treatment in wetlands and sediments help clean coastal waters. The critical habitat, food, shelter, and spawning and nesting support for valued fish, birds, and other wildlife are perhaps more appreciated functions, but they, too, are often neglected in cost accounting.

What is the value of these ecosystem services? The very high economic estimates found in a recent study by Costanza et al. (1997) are controversial, but few dispute the vital contributions of coastal ecosystems to the sustainability of modern society. Much more attention needs to be given to the impacts and potential costs of hazards and disasters to these natural resources and services, as well as how they are affected by flood mitigation activities.

Direct and Indirect Costs of Coastal Hazards to Natural Resources and Ecosystems

Each hurricane, storm, or other weather-related hazard event that strikes the coast has unique impacts on natural resources and ecosystems. Differences in storm size, speed of movement, wind speeds, storm surge heights, timing with respect to tides, and landfall location relative to vulnerable natural resources make for high variability in impacts and costs. However, one can identify the range of potential impacts and how these impacts might be altered by both development and mitigation activities. Possible direct and indirect hazard impacts to natural resources and ecosystems are summarized in table 3.8; the potential vulnerability of any given location varies and needs to be estimated for that location. Examples of mitigation tactics to protect natural resources from the impacts of hurricanes and other severe storms will be addressed in chapter 5.

Direct costs to natural resources and ecosystems are defined as the physical damage directly associated with the storm event—storm surge, other causes of elevated water levels and flooding, wind and waves, saltwater inundation, erosion, and so on. Examples of costs include the erosion of recreational beaches; loss of buffering dunes and upland property; destruction of agricultural crops due to flooding, winds, and salt water; and loss of urban landscaping and industrial forests due to high winds and water damage.

As mentioned earlier in this chapter, indirect costs to natural resources and ecosystems are linked to damage and impacts to the built environment. Examples include the widespread distribution of persistent debris; accidental spills of fuel, sewage, industrial waste, household chemicals, or other contaminants onto the land or into the marine environment; and environmental damage associated with storm debris or material cleanup, including illegal filling of wetlands in low-lying areas and loss of landfill capacity.

With the exception of agricultural crop and commercial forestry losses, natural disaster costs to natural resources and ecosystems are largely unreported and hidden. They are missing from present methods of calculating

Table 3.8. Natural Resource and Ecosystem Costs of Coastal Hazards and Disasters

Event or Condition	Potential Direct Impacts and Costs	Potential Indirect Impacts and Costs	Possible Data Sources
Wind, surge, and flood damage or destruction of plants and animals	Loss of commercially viable natural resources/crops—forestry, agriculture, fisheries; other plant and animal mortality	Decline of commercial resources: forestry, agriculture, fisheries; increased risk of fire from damaged forest resources; increased vulnerability to pest invasions	USDA, USFS, state DNRs, USFWS, national and state park services (within park boundaries), local chambers of commerce
	Loss of residential trees	Increased power demand for additional heating or cooling needs; psychological effects	Municipal department of public works, utility company sales reports, community surveys, media reports
	Spread of invasive/exotic plants and animals	Loss of native vegetation; alteration of habitat; increased vulnerability to pest invasions	USGS (Biological Resources Division), state GAPs, local university biology departments
Damage or destruction to landscape	Habitat loss	Loss of biodiversity; increase in number of threatened and endangered plant and animal species	State GAPs, USFWS, national and state park services (within park boundaries), state natural heritage programs
	Soil and riverbank erosion and land loss	Degradation of water quality: sedimentation of tributaries, loss of tree cover, increased water temperatures, increased turbidity, and decrease of dissolved oxygen; nonpoint-source pollution (pest and herbicides, fertilizers, failed septic systems, etc.)	USGS (Water and Biological Resources Division), USACE, USEPA (Office of Oceans and Coastal Protection), state coastal zone management programs (NOAA), state DNRs, FEMA and state disaster assessments, NFIP claims, insurance industry sources
	Beach, dune, and wetland erosion	Loss of shoreline habitat (dunes, beaches, wetlands, etc.); destabilization of building foundations (damage and risk of future deterioration); increased demand for coastal fortification, (seawalls, etc.) with potential adverse environmental effects; loss of recreational beaches and related recreational opportunities; loss of tourism and jobs	USGS (Water and Biological Resources Division), USACE, USEPA (Office of Oceans and Coastal Protection), state coastal zone management programs (NOAA), state DNRs, FEMA and state disaster assessments, NFIP claims, insurance industry sources

Disturbance of natural ecosystems	Loss of old-growth and unique protected forests, dune, swamp, and other coastal ecosystems	Future habitat loss or permanent alteration; increase in number of endangered and threatened species; species extirpation or extinction; increased vulnerability of coastal ecosystem to subsequent events; loss of resiliency; overwhelming of assimilative capacity	USGS (Biological Resources Division), USFWS, state DNRs, NMFS, other natural resource agencies, private land trusts and other NGOs
	Sediment loading of coastal rivers, tributaries, and estuaries	Increase in turbidity; decrease in dissolved oxygen; loss of aquatic vegetation, vertebrates, and invertebrates; decreased capacity of tributaries/streambed channels; loss of navigable waterways; increase in dredging costs; increase of subsequent flood risk; decline of commercial and recreational fisheries	USGS (Water Resources Division), EMTC, USEPA (Office of Water), USACE, state coastal zone management programs
	Saltwater intrusion into surface and groundwater	Loss of water supply for humans and animals; loss of freshwater species; alteration of habitat	USGS (Water Resources Division), EMTC, USFWS, local water management and supply agencies
	Increased freshwater flow into estuaries	Decline of marine and estuarine species; decline of commercial fisheries	USGS (Water Resources Division), USFWS, NMFS, state DNRs
	Breaching of barrier islands	Habitat loss; loss of private and public property; damage to or loss of infrastructure	USGS (Geologic Division), USFWS, FEMA, state DNRs, NMFS
	Long-term habitat contamination from toxic releases, saltwater inundation	Prevention of wildlife recovery; habitat loss; increase in number of endangered and threatened species	USEPA, USFWS, state DNRs, NMFS, state natural heritage programs, NGOs
	Increased vulnerability of coastal ecosystem to subsequent events; loss of resiliency; overwhelming of assimilative capacity	Future habitat loss or permanent alteration; increase in number of endangered and threatened species; species extirpation or extinction	USGS (Biological Resources Division), USFWS, state DNRs, NMFS

(continues)

Table 3.8. Continued

Event or Condition	Potential Direct Impacts and Costs	Potential Indirect Impacts and Costs	Possible Data Sources
Wind, surge, flood damage to the built environment	Point-source pollution discharges into air and waterways (chemical releases, sewage, hazardous, or toxic materials)	Loss of aquatic resources; decline of commercial and recreational fisheries; health and safety impacts	USEPA (Office of Emergency Response), USFWS, NMFS, local fishery reports, state DNRs
	Nonpoint-source pollution discharges into waterways (pesticides, herbicides, fertilizers, urban runoff, failed septic systems, etc.)	Loss of aquatic resources; decline of commercial and recreational fisheries; health and safety impacts	USEPA (Office of Emergency Response), USFWS, NMFS, local fishery reports, state DNRs
	Release of debris into the environment, through event or through cleanup efforts	Water quality degradation; loss of land due to filling of landfill space; air quality degradation due to burning of refuse; decreased aesthetic appeal of landscape	USEPA (Office of Emergency Response, Office of Water), USFWS, state DNRs state coastal zone management programs (NOAA), community surveys, media reports, state solid-waste management agencies
	Loss of access to shore (damage to piers, docks, roads)	Decline in recreational activities, fishing, and boating; loss of tourism, economic impacts	Local chambers of commerce, tourism promotion organizations
	Rebuilding efforts	Unregulated filling of wetlands and other sensitive habitats (loss of habitat); suburban/exurban land consumption due to post-event planning practices (sprawl)	FEMA, HUD, building permit records, USEPA, municipal planning offices, USACE
	Long-term damage to machines and vehicles due to inundation, sediment intrusion, or similar mechanical damage	Decreased agency budget and resources for mitigation and environmental restoration	Long-term agency cost reports and records of mechanical replacement and repair in years following event

the overall costs of natural hazards and disasters. As a consequence, they are likely to be overlooked during response and recovery efforts and are not factored into decision making regarding investments in long-term mitigation. Also, they may be regional in nature and not easily addressed by communities.

Hurricane Hugo—Natural Environment Impacts and Costs

As part of the Heinz panel's March 1998 Hurricane Hugo workshop, panel members met with natural resource scientists and professionals in an attempt to understand the actual natural resource impacts and costs associated with what was, at the time, the largest single natural disaster in U.S. history. The panel focused on four impact and cost areas: forestry, beaches and dunes, water quality, and fish and wildlife. The results of the interviews are summarized here to illustrate the range and types of natural resource and ecosystem impacts caused by a major storm or hurricane. Other disasters may have very different impacts, depending on the resources at risk and the character of the storm. Although the impacts and costs of Hugo to natural resources and ecosystem services cannot be extrapolated to other events, the information collected does serve to increase understanding of the relationship of costs to both the risk and the extent of vulnerability, and to mitigation investments.

COASTAL FOREST IMPACTS AND COSTS. Timberland covers 40 percent or more of the land area in most coastal states. Just as these forests provide many societal benefits associated with the production and use of wood products, they also play a vital role in the cultural and economic life of people living in the coastal region. For example, forest industries were the second leading employers in Mississippi and Alabama in 1997, employing almost 106,000 people in the two states. In North Carolina, Oregon, Virginia, and Georgia, forest products industries ranked among the top four manufacturing employers, with an associated annual payroll exceeding $1 billion in each state (American Forest and Paper Association, 1998).

Standing timber can be damaged in a number of ways by coastal storms. Wind damage ranges from light defoliation to the uprooting and downing of trees during a storm. Longer-term, chronic impacts associated with saltwater inundation and stress-related disease and insect infestation can vary greatly between storms and between stands. The impact of a storm on a coastal forest is determined by a combination of wind speed and duration, storm surge, precipitation, and stand-dependent variables such as forest type, species mixture, size class, and canopy structure. Hardwoods were generally more vulnerable than were pines in Hurricane Hugo; and tall, larger trees suffered more damage than smaller trees. Lowland hardwoods sustained the highest incidence of damage owing to their large crowns and shallow root systems (Sheffield and Thompson, 1992).

Although catastrophic losses of timber caused by hurricanes are uncommon, averages mean little to a forest owner, logger, or mill worker after a hurricane has eliminated the source of his or her livelihood. Hurricane Hugo, considered the nation's most serious storm-related forest disaster, damaged more than 4.5 million acres (37 percent) of South Carolina's timberland (Sheffield and Thompson, 1992). Direct losses in standing timber exceeded $1 billion in value. Even though salvage operations commenced quickly after the storm, the amount of timber damaged exceeded the normal annual timber harvest in South Carolina by roughly 300 percent (Straka and Baker, 1991). This phenomenon resulted in a surplus of timber to be harvested and a shortage of loggers, harvesting equipment, mill capacity, seedlings for reforestation, and tree planters.

No state or federal funds were provided to private forest industries to aid in salvage operations after Hurricane Hugo. The South Carolina Foresters Council met during the week following the storm and asked the governor to create a "salvage task force" to aid forest managers in the massive job of removing the damaged but usable timber (David Gearhardt, Westvaco Corporation, personal communication, March 25, 1998). There was no state or local disaster plan for the forest industry, however, that would have facilitated the granting of permits to remove trees that were not salvaged. The debris left in public and private forests after Hugo was, and still is, a serious problem for forest managers in South Carolina. Because there is so much downed timber still left form Hurricane Hugo, forest managers cannot use prescribed burns to maintain or improve habitat for the red-cockaded woodpeckers or other wildlife.

Timber generally is considered South Carolina's largest cash crop. In the years following Hurricane Hugo, the competition for timber intensified, resulting in rising prices and declining wood quality. Manufacturers of solid-wood products were most affected, and a few have gone out of business (Syme and Saucier, 1992). The ripple effects of widespread forest damage on the economy of the coastal region extend beyond the forest industry. In Berkeley County, timber harvests from federal lands had generated more than $1 million annually in the five years prior to Hugo, money that was dedicated to schools and roads. After Hugo, new taxes were passed to make up for the shortfall in public funds for these purposes (J. Scarborough, economic development director, Berkeley County, SC, personal communication, December 21, 1998).

Another long-term cost related to hurricanes is an increase in flood damage potential. After hurricanes Hugo and Fran, a great deal of debris from fallen trees was removed; however, debris remained in many areas that were not easily visible or where short-run, debris-related problems were not considered significant enough to warrant spending limited funds for removal. Today, some of that remaining debris has led to decreased capacity for rivers and swamps to contain flood waters, leading to costly flood damage. An example of this is a flood inundation problem associated with Camp Branch in Lake City, South Carolina. Because this problem was not addressed immediately following either hurricane, the area has experienced repeated flood-related costs. In addition, a current U.S. Army Corps of Engineers study of the flood inundation problem has cost $100,000 thus far, and potentially may lead to further investments by the federal and local governments. This example reinforces that the long-term costs associated with a hazard event are very hard to quantify, since, historically, many costs have not been associated with the events that actually caused them.

BEACH AND DUNE IMPACTS AND COSTS. Hurricanes, nor'easters, West Coast winter storms (particularly during El Niños), and chronic erosion can, and often do, cause extreme damage along the shoreline, including a loss of beach sand offshore or downdrift, undermining or overwashing of the dunes that protect uplands, or, in extreme cases, the cutting of new ocean inlets. Where beaches are backed by bluffs, such as along the West Coast, beach erosion leads to bluff undermining, slumping, and upland property loss. Once a beach or dune is lost, its capacity to buffer the next storm is reduced dramatically. Following major erosion events, the recreational value of beaches declines sharply, because of both reduced beach area and loss of aesthetic appeal. Local tourist dollars are lost altogether or transferred elsewhere.

Topsail Island, North Carolina, is a good example of this scenario. After Hurricane Bertha, Topsail Island's built environment suffered very little storm-related erosion damage. However, the beach and dune system, which serve as buffers in storm events, experienced significant damage. A couple of months later when Hurricane Fran struck Topsail Island, significant erosion damage to the built environment occurred because the natural buffering capacity of the beach and dune system had been so damaged by Hurricane Bertha.

Many of these beach and dune impacts and costs were also experienced during Hurricane Hugo. The storm caused serious beach and dune erosion along 65 miles of South Carolina's coast—from Folly Beach, just south of Charleston, to the North Carolina state line (Kana et al., 1991). The height

of the surge (ranging from 10 to 20 feet), intensity of the storm, and relatively low dune elevations resulted in the destruction of every foredune and
the redistribution of sand offshore or in washover fans. As a result of this flat-
tening, the beach was nearly 500 feet wide in some locations, more than
twice the normal width. With such a flat profile and lack of dunes, many
properties that were not destroyed by Hugo were considered at high risk
after the storm. This situation provided the impetus for an emergency beach
and dune restoration program to provide immediate protection for threatened upland properties and, eventually, efforts to restore the recreational
beach to pre-Hugo conditions.

Following the storm, the state of South Carolina and the federal government joined in a beach and dune system restoration with three phases: beach
scraping and dune shaping, beach nourishment, and dune revegetation.
Eventually, this effort cost $9.8 million, comparable to the cost of all South
Carolina beach nourishment projects combined between 1980 and 1988
(Kana, 1990). The state covered approximately 60 percent of these costs,
with the federal government—FEMA and the Corps of Engineers (i.e., taxpayers nationally)—picking up the rest. By comparison, the annual benefits
of coastal tourism in South Carolina are estimated at nearly $5 billion annu-
ally (Kana, 1990), and beaches are one of the principal attractions.

In 1989, the U.S. Army Corps of Engineers had recently completed a feasibility study of beach nourishment in the Grand Strand (Myrtle Beach) region of South Carolina. Hurricane Hugo significantly changed the beach
profile of the area. Therefore, federal, state, and local agencies had to reevaluate the study to ensure that their actions would be beneficial in light of the
changes caused by Hugo. The reevaluation costs exceeded several million
dollars. The reevaluation also revealed that the change in beach profile led to
the need for a much more expensive project requiring more sand deposition
than had originally been anticipated. The need for a greater amount of sand
may have also led to increased sea turtle mortality during the construction of
the project.

A number of lessons can be derived from South Carolina's experience with
Hugo-induced beach and dune erosion and subsequent restoration. Some of
these lessons relate to beach processes. Major storms such as Hugo are rare,
but they intensify or accelerate normal processes, sometimes causing permanent coastal change. However, much of the erosion observed after storms reflects a temporary shift of sand to offshore bars. Most of that sand likely will
return to the beaches, although some may be lost permanently either downdrift or offshore. With respect to shoreline development, the lesson from
Hugo (as well as chronic, less powerful storms) is that judicious construction

setbacks, elevation of buildings above expected storm surge heights, and soft stabilization can protect upland property while preserving options for beach and dune protection and post-storm restoration (Kana, 1990).

Indirect effects of Hugo's damage to beaches and dunes and of post-storm restoration efforts included adverse impacts on endangered and threatened sea turtles. This example illustrates how natural processes and human responses to them can result in unexpected and unwanted outcomes. Sea turtle nesting sites were damaged heavily by Hugo and by beach scraping performed as part of dune rebuilding after the storm. The beaches from North Island to Folly Beach were "completely flattened" by Hugo, destroying 54 percent of the historical loggerhead sea turtle nesting sites in the state (South Carolina Wildlife and Marine Resources Department, 1990a). Approximately 25 percent of all 1989 sea turtle nests in South Carolina had not yet hatched at the time of Hugo, and all of these were destroyed (Cely, 1991).

Sea turtles and other "charismatic megafauna" get some public attention when their habitats are destroyed or damaged, even by natural processes. But damage to more obscure plant and animal life may be overlooked. The impacts of disasters on hundreds or even thousands of species that occupy nearshore dune, beach, and benthic habitats—clams, crab, shrimp, and worms are examples—are little understood or even recognized. Are there cascading effects on the food chain that adversely affect commercial fish, shellfish, shore and wading birds, and many other species? Scientists do not know. Recolonization may be rapid on natural beaches, but there are no data available to explain why this occurs or whether beach nourishment contributes to it.

The costs of beach nourishment, both to the taxpayer and to natural ecosystems onshore and offshore from which sediments are "borrowed," are a controversial issue nationally. More than $3 billion has been spent on artificial beach nourishment since World War II (Congressional Quarterly Researcher, 1998), much of it in recent years as this "soft" shore protection option has gained favor over hardening the shoreline with groins, seawalls, and revetments. As relative sea level continues to rise and shorelines retreat overall, especially along the Gulf and Atlantic coasts, the use of beach nourishment as a means to protect coastal shoreline investments is likely to increase.

WATER QUALITY AND OTHER POLLUTION IMPACTS AND COSTS. Hurricanes and other major storms have the potential to affect water quality in a number of ways and, thus, also affect human and ecosystem health. For example, saltwater inundation associated with storm surge can contaminate wells, particularly shallow ones. This was only a minor problem in the case of Hurri-

cane Hugo because most water in the affected area is drawn from deep arte-
sian wells or treated surface sources (Wayne Fanning, South Carolina
Department of Environmental Health and Natural Resources, personal communication, March 25, 1998). All municipal surface wells were closed permanently after the storm. Nevertheless, drinking water did taste bad after
the storm, in part because phenols leached into the system from pine needles
and other vegetation downed by high winds. Surge-driven salt water spreading inland also killed vegetation.

The loss of dissolved oxygen in streams and estuaries can result in fish
and shellfish mortality. Following Hurricane Hugo, dissolved oxygen levels
decreased with increasing distance toward and up into the three major rivers
(i.e., Wando, Ashley, and Cooper Rivers) that flow into the Charleston Harbor estuary, and dissolved oxygen in surface waters of the estuary was lower
than the levels in bottom waters. Not all hurricanes, of course, affect estuarine water quality in the same manner as Hugo did, because of differences in
storm track, wind direction, and rainfall. After Hurricane Donna struck the
Florida coast in 1960, the storm surge increased salinity in North Florida
Bay for two months. Massive kills of fish and invertebrates after Hurricane
Donna were attributed to oxygen depletion (Tabb and Jones, 1962). Charbreck and Palmisano (1973) found increased salinity in the tidal creeks and
marshes of the Mississippi Delta after Hurricane Camille made landfall in
Mississippi in 1969.

Accidental spills of sewage and outright failures of treatment plants and
household septic systems are other major water-quality and health concerns
associated with coastal storm disasters. In the case of Hugo, the Charleston
area fared relatively well, in part because of well-executed, effective emergency management procedures developed far in advance of the storm (John
Cook, Charleston Commissioner of Public Works, personal communication,
March 25, 1998). In 1989, plants in Charleston and North Charleston were
responsible for more than 90 percent of the region's wastewater treatment.
Charleston's plant was affected by storm surge that led to a 10-hour shutdown; backup of the system was avoided by an emergency evacuation. Although this no doubt resulted in some waterway contamination, it allowed
the plant to be brought online again relatively quickly, operating primary
treatment facilities for eight days on emergency generators. Although many
pumps sustained damage, the use of alternate routing and bypass pumps prevented significant spills.

Since the storm, Charleston's wastewater treatment contingency plan
often has been cited as a national model, and it continues to be improved.
However, more than 100 small sewage treatment plants did not recover as

quickly. These were mostly small private systems and municipal systems in harder-hit areas to the north that had no emergency generators, contingency plans, or qualified staff (Wayne Fanning, South Carolina Department of Environmental Health and Natural Resources, personal communication, March 25, 1998). Recovery was problematic, spills were significant, and many systems never resumed operation.

Hazardous materials discharges to standing water bodies and groundwater are another threat during disasters. As part of pre-Hugo preparations, state officials visited storage sites and moved hazardous materials to high ground or into safe storage. After the storm, the Coast Guard focused on the condition of larger facilities, such as storage tanks. Flights were made to locate stray drums and other possible hazardous wastes. Numerous small releases occurred, especially fuel from boats and underground tanks, some of which floated to the surface, but state officials said adverse impacts were minimal. No data on the numbers, types, or amounts of releases were available. With respect to hazardous waste management in the face of disaster, the region is judged no better off today than prior to Hugo.

Post-storm debris management was another problem with Hugo, when vast amounts of vegetation, including potentially toxic, treated building materials from destroyed buildings, as well as other materials were burned at different sites with little management. Even with the burning, some 17 years of landfill capacity was used up with storm debris, meaning new sites would need to be developed at significant expense (Wayne Fanning, South Carolina Department of Environmental Health and Natural Resources, personal communication, March 25, 1998).

FISH AND WILDLIFE IMPACTS AND COSTS. Hurricane Hugo dramatically altered the coastal forests, beaches, wetlands, and estuaries of South Carolina. Some changes were relatively short-lived, such as lowered salinity and increased freshwater flows into estuaries. Other changes in fish and wildlife habitat were more permanent and resulted in dramatic losses of local flora and fauna. Populations of many species, such as the wild turkey and red-cockaded woodpecker, have not fully recovered from the storm, principally because of continuing human alteration of coastal and forest ecosystems. These and other impacts, both ecological and economic, to fish and wildlife resources are among the best-documented stories about the hurricane.

The hurricane's effects on wildlife and fishery resources adversely affected the economy of South Carolina by impeding several forms of outdoor recreation. Access to fishing, boating, and hunting sites was eliminated in some areas for years after the storm, and target resources were diminished by mortality and destruction of the habitat needed for species recovery. Turkey observations and spring harvests generally correlate with population size (Baumann et al., 1991). The loss of revenues associated with the decline in turkey and deer hunting, canceled fishing tournaments, and damaged fishing piers generally was uninsured. Virtually no information was available to describe the additional economic losses associated with impacts on nonconsumptive wildlife uses, such as bird watching and nature tours. Hurricane Hugo was an economic disaster for most of South Carolina's commercial fish and shellfish operations. The losses included vessels; port facilities; seafood in cold storage; seafood processing plants; and the season's harvest of shrimp, oysters, and clams. The high value of these assets suggests that damages may have exceeded $25 million, much of which was uninsured.

A systematic, quantitative survey of wildlife mortality was not possible immediately after Hugo, because most personnel efforts were directed toward search and rescue missions, protection of property from looters, and restoring basic services (Cely, 1991). Longer-term effects on management were evident, including adverse impacts on the South Carolina Wildlife and Marine Resources Department's fiscal situation and capability to perform many natural resource management and protection functions.

Harm to endangered species, such as the loggerhead turtles discussed earlier, were among the most significant wildlife impacts of the storm. For example, as noted earlier, South Carolina's endangered red-cockaded woodpecker population was reduced dramatically by the timber losses associated with Hugo. Hurricane impacts on the woodpecker may be representative of those on other forest-dependent birds, particularly species that require older, open stands of pine. Several other birds and small mammals use the woodpecker's tree cavities, as do several species of reptiles and amphibians. In addition to the red-cockaded woodpecker, 27 other endangered species live in the old-growth pine forests of this region. Quantitative information is not available on the impacts of Hurricane Hugo on most of these forest-dependent species.

The eye of Hugo passed about 80 kilometers south of Pumpkinseed Island, the home of South Carolina's largest wading-bird colony. Habitat damage took its greatest toll on white ibises, whose numbers declined from 10,000 pairs in 1989 to 0 in 1990 (Shepard et al., 1991). Twenty-five of the 54 bald eagle breeding sites in South Carolina were affected by Hurricane Hugo, with all nests destroyed, accounting for a 46 percent loss statewide (Murphy, 1994).

Hugo's damage to hardwood trees was significant and was expected to reduce the long-term value of habitats for deer, turkey, squirrel, and raccoon

(South Carolina Wildlife and Marine Resources Department, 1990a). State biologists predicted that, in the short term, the increase in sunlight on the forest floor would have a positive impact on coastal white-tailed deer populations by creating a highly suitable growing environment for the herbaceous plants and shrubs preferred by this species. Nine years after the storm, the predicted longer-term impacts are evident. The early-successional habitat that served as tender browse for deer in the first few years after the hurricane has reached a height that is not attractive to deer, and the forest openings are now densely populated with larger trees and shrubs. Deer hunting is still impeded by the "impenetrable thicket" and debris created by the hurricane (Bill Mahan, South Carolina Department of Natural Resources, personal communication, April 8, 1998).

Marine and freshwater fisheries were also affected seriously by Hurricane Hugo. After the storm, field sampling was conducted by the Wildlife and Marine Resources Department to determine impacts on shellfish and finfish resources. Marine fishery resources were damaged by excessive freshwater runoff, storm surge, turbidity and siltation, and water quality degradation. Fish and invertebrate kills were reported and attributed to low dissolved oxygen, clogging of gills by silt, and stranding when abnormally high tidal waters receded (South Carolina Wildlife and Marine Resources Department, 1990a). Low salinity and dissolved-oxygen levels affected the movement of shrimp, blue crabs, and finfish, displacing many species seaward.

During the first two days after Hurricane Hugo, South Carolina marine resources personnel reported dead white shrimp and blue crab in trawls taken in the Ashley River. The catch rates for white shrimp in lower Charleston Harbor increased initially after the storm, but then declined dramatically over the next three weeks, suggesting that the larger shrimp moved seaward. Commercial shrimpers moved farther offshore to trawl for shrimp during the first weeks following Hugo, with some reporting very high catch rates (Whitaker et al., 1989).

The impacts of Hurricane Hugo on South Carolina's commercial crab fishery appear to have been minimal, but fishermen reported larger than usual catches of female crabs offshore, and male crabs, which normally favor the more inland reaches of an estuary, were found in the lower estuary (Whitaker, 1990). This temporary shift in the population was attributed to the low salinity levels associated with intense rainfall during Hugo and a second major rainstorm that occurred six days after the hurricane.

The most serious impact of Hurricane Hugo on freshwater fishery resources was dissolved-oxygen depletion, which caused fish kills in coastal streams and ponds for two weeks after the storm, resulting in the loss of an estimated 5 million adult bream, catfish, largemouth bass, and other species. In an attempt to mitigate the impacts of the hurricane on recreational fishery resources, officials began to restock redbreast, bluegill, and shellcrocker in November 1989 (South Carolina Wildlife and Marine Resources Department, 1990a). The effectiveness of these restocking efforts has not been evaluated.

Boat travel was obstructed in many freshwater streams by riparian trees downed during the hurricane. To restore navigation, the state fish and wildlife agency cleared 98 miles of stream channel in the Little Pee Dee River, Lynches River, and Edisto River (South Carolina Wildlife and Marine Resources Department, 1990a). Shortly after the storm, a fisheries impact assessment was initiated by state marine resources personnel, who were assigned to gather information on losses and damage to vessels, equipment, docks, marinas, boat ramps, and other property utilized by fisheries interests. The commercial fisheries fleet in the coastal area from Johns Island and Folly Beach northward to Murrells Inlet incurred the most severe damage. Fifty-one shrimp trawlers were damaged badly or sunk in this area alone, and five commercial seafood buildings were destroyed completely (South Carolina Wildlife and Marine Resources Department, 1990a). Boat docks, fuel and ice vendors, and many other shore-based support facilities were destroyed or damaged.

The storm affected an estimated 1,404 commercial fishermen, 236 oystermen and clammers, and approximately 387 dock personnel at wholesale seafood dealers (South Carolina Wildlife and Marine Resources Department, 1989). A coastwide total of approximately 70 commercial fishing vessels were stranded in marshes, mudflats, and town streets. Two commercial shrimp fishermen working on the Wando River were killed. Substantial losses of inventory of fresh and frozen seafood and bait were reported at some docks (Sandifer, 1989).

Although many vessels were damaged, the shrimp fishery quickly resumed operations after the storm, but many vessels came into the area from Beaufort, Georgetown, and parts of North Carolina. One report from the South Carolina Wildlife and Marine Resources Department (1989) stated that much of the shrimp harvested after Hugo was taken to ports where these other vessels were based and "resulted in further economic losses to the wounded communities." A five-week delay in South Carolina's fall oyster season resulted in severe economic losses for many individual harvesters (Sandifer, 1989). The clam industry was also affected; six of ten clam dredges in South Carolina were seriously damaged, and three could not be repaired (Sandifer, 1989).

The disruption of recreational fishing activity also affected South Carolina's coastal economy. All of the state's ocean fishing piers in the vicinity of Charleston and northward were destroyed by the hurricane. Hammond and Cupka (1977) conducted an economic evaluation of the state's fishing piers and reported that pier anglers contributed $2.4 million directly into the local economy and that October was the month with the second-highest pier fishing activity. Tackle stores in the Charleston area reported sales down as much as 80 percent during the month following Hurricane Hugo. Three fishing tournaments were canceled. Participation in the Arthur Smith King Mackerel Tournament, which had been postponed for three weeks, declined by nearly 50 percent. This tournament has been credited with generating local economic benefits in excess of $15 million annually during prior years (South Carolina Wildlife and Marine Resources Department, 1990b).

In summary, South Carolina's natural resources, and the ecosystem goods and services derived from them, were hit hard by Hurricane Hugo. Although some of the costs have been quantified, few are included in the official loss totals compiled by the federal government or insurance company organizations. Many natural resource impacts and costs are documented poorly, if at all, leading to a significant underestimation of storm impacts. A better understanding of these unreported, hidden costs could have significant implications for local, state, and federal decisions regarding mitigation investments. Communities could also benefit from contingency plans to minimize natural resource impacts and costs in all high-risk regions of the country, including general plans for post-storm assessments of natural resource damage and loss (see chapter 5).

Conclusions and Recommendations

Accounting for the true costs of coastal hazards and disasters—reported losses as well as unreported, undocumented, or otherwise hidden costs—presents the coastal hazards community with both a challenge and an opportunity. It is a challenge to undertake more accurate risk assessments and an opportunity for wiser investment of limited mitigation dollars. In this chapter, the Heinz panel attempted to characterize the true costs of coastal hazards and disasters using quantitative estimates when data are available or through qualitative descriptions when they are not. Some of these costs have been illustrated with graphic examples from panelists' own experience, from the literature, and from interviews with local business and government leaders who endured Hurricane Hugo. It is clear from the analysis that, while the typically reported costs of coastal hazards and disasters capture the largest categories of economic impacts, they leave out other societally important concerns. Many costs are unaccounted for—costs to the built environment; the business community; individuals; families; neighborhoods; public and private social institutions; natural resources and the environment; and even people far from the disaster, who give directly to private relief efforts and indirectly through their tax contributions to the national treasury.

Significant improvements can be made in coastal hazard and disaster cost accounting. Some of these advances can be achieved with a modest effort and investment. Others will require significant resources, improved intergovernmental and public–private cooperation, and political support and will. In considering needed changes, the Heinz panel makes the following recommendations.

- The Federal Emergency Management Agency, the National Emergency Management Association, the Institute for Business and Home Safety, and the American Red Cross and other voluntary disaster relief organizations should collectively convene a task force of their governmental and nongovernmental counterparts to identify ways to improve and coordinate disaster-cost data collection, reporting, and accessibility.
  —An important objective for such a task force would be to find ways to better incorporate the hidden costs of coastal hazards and disasters as identified in this report.
  —Cost data of all types should be made more accessible by being located at or linked to a single World Wide Web site.
- Current methodologies and databases used by federal and federally mandated disaster response agencies to report expenditures associated with a given event should be expanded to include a more complete range of costs, consistent with the business, social, and natural resources categories recommended in this report.
  —Protocols should be developed to promote consistency among diverse databases with respect to geographical scale, reporting period (e.g., fiscal year), and purpose.
  —Where it is inappropriate for existing databases to incorporate these data, new record keeping and reporting mechanisms should be established.
  —New information collected should, at a minimum, include type of loss, location, cause of loss, and actual or estimated dollar amounts in all four categories: business, social, natural resources, and built environment.
- Existing and new databases should record the geographic location of losses down to at least the zip code level. This would be especially valuable to

municipal, county, and state officials who need these data to analyze risk and decide on appropriate mitigation strategies and investments. These data, when displayed using a geographic information system (GIS), would also be useful for public education and guidance of mitigation at all levels.

—The Institute for Business and Home Safety database of paid insured catastrophe losses provides information about insured losses by zip code for post-1994 events. If such information were available from FEMA and other sources, results might be combined into a single estimate of losses by zip code, thereby providing an improved picture of the geographic distribution of losses.

- Post-disaster reports for hurricanes and other disasters, currently written by state agencies and others, should be expanded to address the business, social, health, and natural resource and ecosystem impacts and costs.

—To implement this new structure, state emergency managers, in cooperation with federal agencies and private-sector representatives, should enhance their existing stakeholder network from each of these categories in advance. Then, when a disaster strikes, post-disaster teams can be mobilized quickly.

—A periodic update procedure should provide for a more complete accounting of the long-term and often unreported costs that accrue in the years following a disaster.

—Sector-specific post-disaster teams for business and employment, housing, human resources, and health and environment should be assembled following a disaster. The North Carolina Disaster Recovery Task Force on Hurricane Fran serves as a possible state-level model.

- Individual communities should consider implementing community-based post-disaster damage and loss reporting. A comprehensive pre-disaster assessment of the full range of potential costs at the community level would provide a basis for establishing such a reporting process.

- An intensive, intergovernmental research effort is needed to identify federal, state, and local public policies that directly or indirectly promote growth and development that increase the vulnerability of communities to coastal disasters.

—The policies so identified and the programs that flow from them should be changed to include "natural hazard vulnerability and mitigation needs" as key criteria in decision-making processes.

—At the federal level, NOAA and FEMA should take the lead in this research; at the state level, coastal zone management programs, in alliance with economic development and emergency management agencies, should lead the way.

Note

1. This observation is supported by research on Hurricanes Hugo and Andrew that showed that insurance losses increase linearly with wind speed until the gradient speed reaches 70 meters per second (157 miles per hour), after which insured losses increase much more rapidly. The rapid loss was associated with the loss of roof sheathing, doors, and windows (Sparks and Bhinderwala, 1993; Sparks et al., 1994).

References

Alesch, D. J., and J. N. Holly. 1996. How to survive the next natural disaster: Lessons for small business from Northridge victims and survivors. Paper presented at the Pan Pacific Hazards 96 meeting, July 29–August 2, Vancouver, British Columbia, Canada.

American Forest and Paper Association. 1998. Forest and paper industry state economic impact statements (8 September). (http://www.afandpa.org/congressional/eis/index/html).

Averch, H., and M. Dluhy. 1997. Crisis decision-making and management. In W. G. Peacock, B. H. Morrow, and H. Gladwin (eds.), *Hurricane Andrew: Ethnicity, Gender, and the Sociology of Disaster.* London: Routledge, pp. 75–91.

Bates, F. L., C. Fogleman, V. Parenton, R. Pittman, and G. Tracy. 1963. *The Social and Psychological Consequences of a Natural Disaster: A Longitudinal Study of Hurricane Audrey.* Washington, DC: National Research Council.

Baumann, D. P., W. E. Mahan, and W. E. Rhodes. 1991. Effects of Hurricane Hugo on the Francis Marion National Forest wild turkey population. Proceedings of the National Wild Turkey Symposium 7:55–60.

Baumann, D. P., L. D. Vangilder, C. I. Taylor, R. Engel-Wilson, R. O. Kimmel, and G. A. Wunz. 1990. Expenditures for wild turkey hunting. Proceedings of the National Wild Turkey Symposium 6:157–166.

Bernd-Cohen, T., and M. Gordon. (forthcoming, 1999). State coastal program effectiveness in protecting beaches, dunes, bluffs, and rocky shores. *Coastal Management* 27(2).

Bolin, R. C. 1985. Disasters and long-term recovery policy: A focus on housing and families. *Policy Studies Review* 4(4): 709–715.

Bolin, R. C. 1994. *Household and Community Recovery after Earthquakes.* Boulder: Institute of Behavioral Science, University of Colorado.

Cely, J. E. 1991. Wildlife effects of Hurricane Hugo. *Journal Coastal Research* 8:319–326.

Charbreck, R. H., and A. W. Palmisano. 1973. The effects of Hurricane Camille on the marshes of the Mississippi River Delta. *Ecology* 54(5):1119–1123.

Congressional Quarterly Researcher. 1998. Coastal development: Does it put precious lands at risk? *Congressional Quarterly Researcher* 8(31):721–729.

Costanza, R., R. d'Auge, R. de Groot, S. Faber, M. Grasso, B. Hammond, K. Limburg, S. Naeem, R. V. O'Neill, J. Paruelo, R.G. Raskin, P. Sutton, and M. Van den Belt. 1997. The value of the world's ecosystem services and natural capital. *Nature* 357:253–260.

Dahlhamer, J. M., and M. J. D'Souza. 1997. Determinants of business disaster preparedness in two U.S. metropolitan areas. *International Journal of Mass Emergencies and Disasters* 15(2):265–281.

Drabek, T. E. 1994. *Disaster Evacuation and the Tourist Industry.* Boulder: Institute of Behavioral Science, University of Colorado.

Durkin, M. E. 1984. The economic recovery of small businesses after earthquakes: The Coalinga experience. Paper presented at the International Conference on Natural Hazards Mitigation Research and Practice, New Delhi, India, October 6–8.

Enarson, E., and B. H. Morrow. 1997. A gendered perspective: The voices of women. In W. G. Peacock, B. H. Morrow, and H. Gladwin (eds.), *Hurricane Andrew: Ethnicity, Gender, and a New Sociology of Disaster.* London: Routledge, pp. 116–140.

Environmental News Network. 1998. Year of the Ocean–Recreation. (http://www.yoto.com/industry/recreation/index.asp).

Erikson, K. T. 1976. *Everything in Its Path: Destruction of Community in the Buffalo Creek Flood.* New York: Simon & Schuster.

Erikson, K. T. 1994. *A New Species of Trouble: Explorations in Disaster, Trauma, and Community.* New York: W. W. Norton.

Fritz, G. E. 1961. "Disaster." In R. K. Merton R. A. Nisbet (eds.), *Contemporary Social Problems.* New York: Harcourt Brace, pp. 651–694.

Geis, D. E. 1996. *Creating Sustainable and Disaster Resistant Communities.* Aspen, CO: The Aspen Global Change Institute.

Geis, D. E., and T. Kutzmark. 1995. Developing sustainable communities: The future is now. *Public Management* (22 August):4–13.

Grant, S. M., S. B. Hardin, D. J. Pesut, and T. Hardin. 1997. Psychological evaluations, referrals, and follow-up of adolescents after their exposure to Hurricane Hugo. *Journal of Child and Adolescent Psychiatric Nursing* 10(1):7–17.

Greer, R. 1989. Two deaths raise Hugo's S.C. toll to 20. *State Newspaper* (September 27), Metro/Region p. 11A.

Guimaraes, P., F. L. Hefner, and D. P. Woodward. 1993. Wealth and income effects of natural disasters: An econometric analysis of Hurricane Hugo. *Review of Regional Studies* 2:97–114.

Hammond, D. L., and D. M. Cupka. 1977. *An Economic and Biological Evaluation of the South Carolina Pier Fishery.* Technical Report, no. 20. Columbia: South Carolina Wildlife and Marine Resources Department.

Insurance Institute for Property Loss Reduction and Insurance Research Council (IIPLR and IRC). 1995. Community Exposure and Community Protection: Hurricane Andrew's Legacy. Wheaton, IL, and Boston: IIPLR and IRC.

Kana, T. W. 1990. Conserving South Carolina's beaches through the 1990s: A case for beach nourishment. Report prepared for the South Carolina Coastal Council. 30 pp.

Kana, T. W., F. D. Stevens, and G. Lennon. 1991. Post-Hugo beach restoration in

South Carolina. In T. W. Kana (ed.), *Proceedings, Coastal Sediments '91*. Seattle: American Society of Civil Engineers, pp. 1697–1711.

Kaniasty, K., and F. H. Norris. 1995. In search of altruistic community: Patterns of social support mobilization following Hurricane Hugo. *American Journal of Community Psychology* 23(4):447–478.

Kroll, C. A., J. D. Landis, Q. Shen, and S. Stryker. 1991. Economic impacts of the Loma Prieta earthquake: A focus on small business. Working Paper No.91-187. Berkeley: University of California, Transportation Center and the Center for Real Estate and Economics.

Krug, E. G., M. Kresnow, J. P. Peddicord, L. L. Dahlberg, K. E. Powell, A. E. Crosby, and J. L. Annest. 1998. Suicide after natural disaster. *New England Journal of Medicine* 338(6):373–378.

Kunreuther, H., and R. Roth Sr., eds. 1998. *Paying the Price: The Status and Role of Insurance against Natural Disasters in the United States*. Washington, DC: Joseph Henry Press.

Lecomte, E., and H. Gahagan. 1998. Hurricane protection in Florida. In H. Kunreuther and R. Roth Sr. (eds.), *Paying the Price: The Status and Role of Insurance against Natural Disasters in the United States*. Washington, DC: Joseph Henry Press, chap. 5.

Mileti, D. S. 1999. *Disasters by Design: A Reassessment of Natural Hazards in the United States*. Washington, DC: Joseph Henry Press.

Morrow, B. H. 1992. The aftermath of Hugo: Social effects on St. Croix [May]. St. George's, Grenada: Caribbean Studies Association.

Morrow, B.H. 1997. Stretching the bonds: The families of Andrew. In W. G. Peacock, B. H. Morrow, and H. Gladwin (eds.), *Hurricane Andrew: Ethnicity, Gender, and the Sociology of Disaster*. London: Routledge, pp. 141–170.

Morrow, B. H., and W. G. Peacock. 1997. Disasters and social change: Hurricane Andrew and the reshaping of Miami? In W. G. Peacock, B. H. Morrow, and H. Gladwin (eds.), *Hurricane Andrew: Ethnicity, Gender, and the Sociology of Disaster*. London: Routledge, pp. 226–242.

Morrow, B. H. 1999. Identifying and mapping community vulnerability. *Disasters: The Journal of Disaster Studies, Policy and Management* 23(1):1–18.

Murphy, T. M. 1994. Hurricane Hugo and bald eagles–management implications of nature's experiment in habitat alteration. *Journal of Raptor Research* 28(1):62–63.

National Marine Fisheries Service (NMFS). 1997. *Fisheries of the United States—1996*. Current Fishery Statistics, no. 9600. Washington, DC: National Oceanic and Atmospheric Administration, NMFS, Office of Science and Technology/Fisheries Statistics and Economics Division.

North Carolina Disaster Recovery Task Force. 1997. *Recommendations for Action* [February 14]. Raleigh, NC: Office of Lieutenant Governor.

Odum, M. 1992. If the GNP counted housework, would women count for more? *New York Times* (April 5).

Olson, R. S. 1997. Un-therapeutic communities: A cross-national analysis of post-disaster political unrest. *International Journal of Mass Emergencies and Disasters* 15(2):221–238.

Pielke, R. A., Jr. 1997. Reframing the U.S. hurricane problem. *Society and Natural Resources* 10:485–499.

Pielke, R. A. Jr., and C. W. Landsea. 1998. Normalized hurricane losses in the United States, 1925–1995. *Weather and Forecasting* 10:621–631.

Pielke, R. A. Jr., and R. A. Pielke Sr. 1997. *Hurricanes: Their Nature and Impacts on Society.* London: John Wiley and Sons.

Property Claim Services. 1995. *Property Claim Services Report, Catastrophe Report for 1994.* Rahway, NJ: American Insurance Service Group.

Sandifer, P. 1989. Report to the Governor's Economic Recovery Commission Subcommittee on Agriculture, Forestry and Marine Resources. Preliminary report from the South Carolina Department of Wildlife and Marine Resources, Columbia, SC, December 27, 1989. 7 pp.

Santa Cruz Commission for the Prevention of Violence against Women. 1990. Violence against women in the aftermath of the October 17, 1989, earthquake [Report to the mayor and city council of the City of Santa Cruz]. Santa Cruz, CA.

Sheffield, R. M., and M. T. Thompson. 1992. Hurricane Hugo effects on South Carolina's forest resource. Res. Pap. SE-284. Asheville, NC, U.S. Forest Service, Southeastern Forest Experiment Station. 51 pp.

Shepard, P., T. Crockett, T. L. DeSanto, and K. L. Bilstein. 1991. The impact of Hurricane Hugo on the breeding ecology of wading birds at Pumpkinseed Island, Hobcaw Barony, South Carolina. *Colonial Waterbirds* 14(2):150–157.

South Carolina Wildlife and Marine Resources Department. 1989. Impact of Hurricane Hugo on South Carolina's commercial fisheries. Internal report. 3 pp. Unpublished.

South Carolina Wildlife and Marine Resources Department. 1990a. Summary of the impacts of Hurricane Hugo on South Carolina fisheries, nongame wildlife and game species. Internal report dated January 1990. 25 pp. Unpublished.

South Carolina Wildlife and Marine Resources Department. 1990b. Preliminary effects of Hurricane Hugo on South Carolina's marine recreational fisheries. Internal report. 14 pp. Unpublished.

Sparks, P. R., and S. A. Bhinderwala. 1993. Relationship between residential insurance losses and wind conditions in Hurricane Andrew. In R. A. Cook and M. Soltani (eds.), *Hurricanes of 1992: Lessons learned and implications for the future.* Proceedings December 1–3, 1993.

Sparks, P. R., S. D. Schiff, and T. A. Reingold. 1994. Wind damage to envelopes of houses and consequent insurance losses. *Journal of Wind Engineering and Industrial Aerodynamics* 5:145–155.

Straka, T. J., and J. B. Baker. 1991. A financial assessment of capital-extensive management alternatives for storm-damaged timber. *Southern Journal of Applied Forestry* 15(4):208–212.

Syme, J. H., and J. R. Saucier. 1992. Impacts of Hugo timber damage on primary wood manufacturers in South Carolina. Clemson University, Department of Forest Resources, and Southeastern Forest Experiment Station, USDA Forest Service, Clemson, SC, General Technical Report No. SE-80. 28 pp.

Tabb, D. C., and A. C. Jones. 1962. Effect of Hurricane Donna on the aquatic fauna of North Florida Bay. *Transactions of the American Fisheries Society* 91(4):375–378.

Tierney, K. J. 1994. Business vulnerability and disruption: Data from the 1993 Midwest floods. Paper presented at the 41st North American Meetings of the Regional Science Association International, Niagara Falls, Ontario, November 16–20.

Tierney, K. J. 1995. Impacts of recent U.S. disasters on businesses: The 1993 Midwest floods and the 1994 Northridge earthquake. University of Delaware, Disaster Research Center, Preliminary Paper no. 230.

Tierney, K. J. 1997. Impacts of recent disasters on businesses: The 1993 Midwest floods and the 1994 Northridge earthquake. In Barclay G. Jones (ed.), *Economic Consequences of Earthquakes: Preparing for the Unexpected.* Buffalo, NY: National Center for Earthquake Engineering Research, pp. 189–222.

Tierney, K. J., J. M. Nigg, and J. M. Dahlhamer. 1996. The impact of the 1993 Midwest floods: Business vulnerability and disruption in Des Moines. In Richard T. Sylves and William L. Waugh Jr. (eds.), *Disaster Management in the United States and Canada,* 2nd edition. Springfield, IL: Charles C. Thomas, pp. 214–233.

Vernberg, E., A. LaGreca, W. Silverman, and M. Prinstein. 1996. Prediction of post-traumatic stress symptoms in children after Hurricane Andrew. *Journal of Consulting and Clinical Psychology* 64: 712–723.

Whitaker, J. D. 1990. Effects of Hurricane Hugo on the state's crustacean resources. Paper presented at the South Carolina Fish and Wildlife Federation Annual Meeting, February 8–9, Myrtle Beach, SC. 22 pp.

Whitaker, J. D., L. B. DeLancy, and J. E. Jenkins. 1989. An assessment of the effects of Hurricane Hugo on the commercial crustacean resources of South Carolina. South Carolina Wildlife and Marine Resources Department, Division of Marine Fisheries, internal report. 20 pp.

Wilson, J., B. Phillips, and D. Neal. 1998. Domestic violence after disaster. In E. Enarson and B. H. Morrow (eds.), *The Gendered Terrain of Disaster: Through the Eyes of Women.* Westport, CT: Praeger, pp. 115–122.

Chapter 4

Risk and Vulnerability Assessment of Coastal Hazards

What is measured is not all that matters, and what matters is not always measured.

—R. Pielke Jr.

Society measures the impacts of coastal hazards in terms of the costs as defined in detail in the previous chapter. The potential for future costs is defined in terms of risk and vulnerability. In this report, "risk" refers to losses associated with a triggering event, such as a hurricane, and "vulnerability" refers to the characteristics of the society or environment affected by the event that lead to costs. How society views risk and vulnerability is a central factor in decision making regarding which mitigation actions to take. Coastal hazard costs and judgments concerning risk and vulnerability are two sides of the same coin—the former reflects a measure of what matters to society in the aftermath of a hazardous event, and the latter reflects a measure of what matters to society in advance of a hazardous event. Costs, risks, and vulnerability underlie coastal hazards policies, which are the result of a long time series of impacts and periodic adjustments based on what is learned during a disaster.

The assessment of risk and vulnerability is important because it is tied directly to the decisions made to reduce societal and environmental exposure to coastal hazard impacts. Ideally, everything that matters to society with respect to coastal hazards would be measured in terms of true costs, and these costs would serve as the basis for actions to reduce societal and environmental risk and vulnerability. Of course, in practice, not all costs are identified, measured, or even measurable. To the extent that measures of costs do not incorporate important aspects of impacts, decision making in advance of future events could be less than optimal.

During the last several decades there has been an observed decrease in intense hurricanes (Landsea et al., 1996). Over the past century, a Category 4 storm has hit the United States, on average, about every six years (Hebert et al., 1993). Hurricanes Andrew and Hugo are the only Category 4 storms to make landfall on the U.S. coast since 1969. In addition, on average two hurricanes strike the U.S. coast each year, with two intense hurricanes (Category 3, 4, and 5 which cause more than 85 percent of damages) striking the U.S. coast every three years (Hebert et al., 1993). Other statistical information related to landfall frequency observed since 1900 includes: (a) 35 percent of all hurricanes hit Florida, (b) 70 percent of Category 4 or 5 storms hit Florida and Texas, and (c) along the middle Gulf Coast, southern Florida, and southern New England 50 percent of all landfalling hurricanes are Category 3 and higher (Jarrell et al., 1992). While a hurricane landfall at any particular coastal location is relatively rare, for the U.S. Gulf and Atlantic coasts as a whole, hurricane landfalls are almost certain every year.

Decision making about mitigation does not always effectively incorporate considerations of true risks and vulnerabilities. The risks and vulnerabilities in an area can be overestimated, hidden, or unreported, thus leading to incorrect estimates of the expected costs and benefits of different mitigation measures. Consider the following three examples of errors in conclusions or decisions that stem from a lack of understanding of the risks and vulnerabilities (see Pielke and Pielke 1997 for additional discussion).

First, decision makers sometimes overestimate risks and damage. For instance, trends in U.S. economic losses and loss of life from hurricanes are shown in figure 4.1. The figure shows two distinct trends: a dramatic increase in economic damages in recent decades, and decreasing loss of life since the 1950s. Based on these trends, several incorrect conclusions have been drawn by policymakers and the media. A 1995 U.S. Senate report asserted incorrectly that hurricanes "have become increasingly frequent and severe over the last four decades as climatic conditions have changed in the tropics" (Bipartisan Task Force on Funding Disaster Relief, 1995). In fact, the past several decades have seen a *decrease* in the frequency of severe storms, and the period 1991 to 1994 was the quietest in at least 50 years (Landsea et al., 1996). In addition, the decrease in hurricane deaths has led some to conclude that "great killer hurricanes, like those seen in decades past, appear to be gone forever from the shores of the United States because of early warning systems" (Reuters News Service, 1996). Yet, in 1995, the director of the U.S. National Hurricane Center wrote that "a large loss of life is possible unless significant mitigation

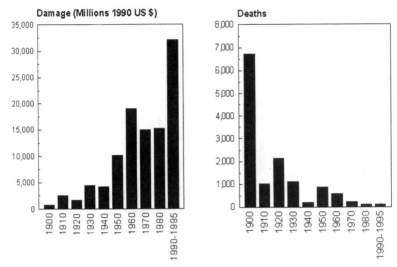

Figure 4.1. Hurricane Damage and Deaths in the Twentieth Century. (Pielke 1997 as adapted from Hebert et al. 1993).

activities are undertaken" (Sheets, 1995). These misinterpretations illustrate how risks and vulnerability can be incorrectly estimated. Figure 4.2 shows a more representative view of trends in hurricane-related economic losses, one that suggests what the impacts of past storms would have been had they made landfall in 1996 (Pielke and Landsea, 1998).

Second, vulnerability can be hidden from decision makers. Figure 4.3 shows, in a highly simplified form, a comparison of wind speeds of Hurricane Andrew in different areas of South Florida and the resulting property damage. Although the patterns of winds were much more complex than are shown here, the underlying point is sound: greater damage than expected occurred in many places. This was particularly troubling because the South Florida building code was among the strongest in the nation. Investigations conducted following Andrew found that the unexpected patterns of damage resulted from inadequate enforcement of the existing codes and changes in styles of homes to those less capable of withstanding high winds. Some in the insurance industry suggested that $4 to $6 billion in property damages could have been avoided had the existing code been followed. With hindsight, it is clear that Andrew's passage served as a large-scale "assessment" of vulnerabilities. It revealed places where mitigation efforts were lacking or additional effort could have reduced costs. Prior to Andrew, these vulnerabilities were hidden, in the sense that decision makers were largely unaware of the poten-

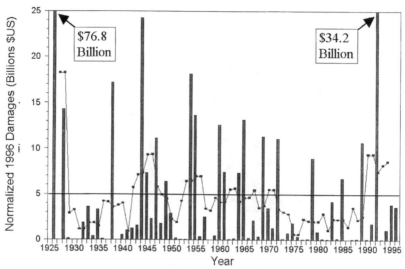

Figure 4.2. U.S. Normalized Hurricane Damage (1925–1996).

tial true costs of a storm like Andrew. One role that risk and vulnerability assessment can play in the policy process is to identify vulnerabilities before an event occurs. For instance, the information in the map shown in figure 4.3 could have been produced through an assessment—before the community experienced the tremendous impacts of Andrew.

Third, vulnerability can be underestimated. Although economic costs are often well documented, the health and social costs resulting from a major disaster such as Hurricane Andrew can be enormous yet escape notice by decision makers. During the year after the storm, life in the southern part of Dade County, Florida, was extremely difficult. Deaths from direct impact were few, but many serious injuries and deaths occurred in the prolonged aftermath because of accidents and hazardous environmental conditions. Thousands had to endure months, even years, of disrupted lives, both at home and at work; endure physical surroundings that could only be called miserable; and struggle to rebuild their homes and communities under very difficult circumstances. Social service agencies reported widespread depression among both clients and workers. Alcohol sales increased. Absenteeism rates were high at both work and school, and productivity declined. Teachers struggled to reach distracted students, and there were untold lags in educational development. All recreational facilities, including movie theaters, bowling alleys, skating rinks and parks programs, were closed, most for a year or more. Not surprisingly, family relationships were strained and incidents of domes-

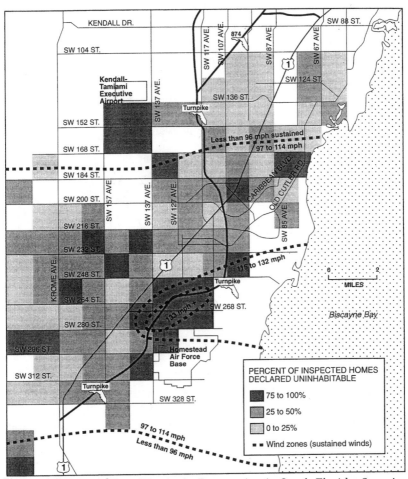

Figure 4.3. Map of Post-Hurricane Destruction in South Florida, Superimposed on a Map of Hurricane Andrew's Wind Speed. (Pielke and Pielke, 1997. Copyright John Wiley & Sons Ltd. Reproduced with permission.)

tic violence, child abuse, desertion, and divorce increased. To the extent that these costs are unreported, they will likely be left out of future risk and vulnerability analyses, setting the stage to repeat the past (Peacock et al., 1997).

In these three examples, improved risk and vulnerability assessment might have provided information about the true costs relevant to decision making about mitigation. Of course, even with better information about true costs, the same outcomes might have occurred, because decision making involves much more than information. Nonetheless, one of the important motivations for seeking to better understand the true costs of coastal hazards is to improve risk and vulnerability assessment in order to reduce societal and environmental exposure to coastal hazard impacts. Improved accounting will be a hollow victory if it is not used by policymakers to make informed judgments of the state of preparedness for future impacts. This chapter examines the notions of risk and vulnerability, and then discusses conventional approaches to risk assessment and the emerging area of vulnerability assessment. Practical applications of these methods are presented.

Risk and Vulnerability Assessment Methods

Risk assessment is the determination of the likelihood of adverse impacts associated with specific coastal hazards to the built, natural, business, and social environments. Vulnerability assessment is concerned with the qualitative or quantitative examination of the exposure of some component of society or the environment to coastal hazards. Vulnerability also depends on both geography and time. The location of an individual, structure, or ecosystem is critical to its safety at the time of a potentially catastrophic event. Furthermore, the relationship between community development and vulnerability grows closer over time, as there is increasing vulnerability and risk due to societal or natural processes. However, the extent of a community's vulnerability to coastal hazards depends on how the community develops and whether protective measures are put in place to reduce future vulnerability to disasters. A combination risk and vulnerability assessment is a systematic approach to organizing and analyzing scientific knowledge and information for potentially hazardous activities that could pose risks under specified conditions (National Research Council, 1994). Risk and vulnerability assessment includes data gathering, scientific testing, and evaluation of a potential hazard and exposure.

Risk management is the process by which the results of an assessment are integrated with political, economic, and engineering information to arrive at programs and policies for reducing future losses and dealing with the damage after it occurs. This process involves various approaches to reducing vulnerability, including modifying the event itself, if possible. Alternative mitigation strategies and actions to reduce vulnerability can be compared using some form of benefit–cost analysis, in which costs and benefits are defined broadly as indicated in chapter 3. Too often, benefit–cost analysis is reduced to a narrow economic exercise in which many costs are hidden or ignored. The purpose of comparing expected costs with expected benefits is to evaluate the trade-offs at the margin about reaching goals concerned with protection of the built and natural environments. A common criticism of benefit–cost analysis is that it fails to accommodate the full range of factors that decision makers implicitly must take into account (Railton, 1990). In other words, lacking knowledge of the true costs of coastal hazards, how can risk and vulnerability assessment methods be anything other than incomplete?

The following sections seek to broaden understanding of risk and vulnerability assessment in the context of the four true-cost categories discussed throughout this report. With a broader sense of true costs, it might be possible to place benefit–cost methodologies on a more solid foundation that better represents everything that truly matters to decision makers.

Vulnerability of the Built Environment

How vulnerable is the built environment to weather-related coastal hazards such as hurricanes? The answer depends in part on *natural conditions* over which humans have little control—risk of exposure to storms (e.g., landfall frequency, intensity), or specific storm-related hazards such as storm surge, high winds, rainfall, and flooding. The character and resilience of the environment are also important natural conditions; for example, the types of landforms and land elevations available for building in a community influence vulnerability. But *societal conditions* are paramount to the question of built environment vulnerability. Some important questions that a community must consider in assessing its vulnerability to coastal hazards and disasters include the following:

- Where are population and residential, commercial, and industrial development concentrated in relation to each type of coastal hazard risk, and in what direction is the community growing with respect to these risks?
- What is the value of property exposed to these risks and what proportion of it is insured?
- What is the present layout for sewer, water, and drainage systems with respect to hazard risks and what does the community's capital improvement plan say about expanding services into areas subject to natural hazards?
- What "green infrastructure" services do natural ecosystems provide to the community? What is their value and how are these services being protected and enhanced?
- How well have existing buildings been constructed with respect to potential coastal hazard forces?
- How resilient are transportation, utility, and communications links and facilities?
- What are past, present, and likely future coastal hazard mitigation strategies and measures? Is there effective land-use planning? Are coastal haz-

ards fully considered in the process of development siting? Are there strong and well-enforced building codes?

Answers to these questions help define the vulnerability of the built environment today and, after factoring in population and development trends, suggest its future vulnerability.

Coastal Demographic and Development Trends

A variety of data are available that provide a national picture of the vulnerability of the built environment to coastal hazards as well as vulnerability trends. Demographic data show, for example, that coastal county populations in the 18 East Coast and Gulf Coast states vulnerable to hurricanes grew 15 percent between 1980 and 1993—from 31.3 million to 36.1 million—compared to the national growth rate of 12 percent (Insurance Institute for Property Loss Reduction and Insurance Research Council, 1995). Over the same time period, the value of insured property in coastal counties increased by 69 percent to $3.1 trillion, with residential exposures to hurricanes increasing most rapidly at 75 percent, and with Florida and New York topping the state list with $872 billion and $596 billion, respectively, in insured exposures (Insurance Institute for Property Loss Reduction and Insurance Research Council, 1995). Figure 4.4 shows populations in 168 coastal counties from

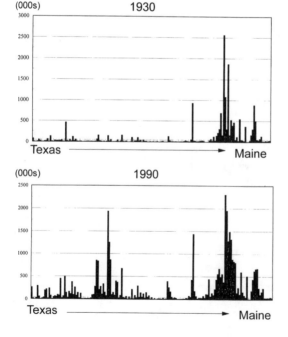

Figure 4.4. Coastal Population by County. (Pielke and Pielke 1997.)

Texas to Maine for 1930 and 1990, demonstrating the tremendous growth in the Southeast.

As recently as 1988, most insurers and scientists believed that it would be unlikely for any one U.S. hurricane to result in more than $7 billion of insured damages (Insurance Research Council, 1986). Hurricane Andrew in 1992 proved otherwise, with insured property losses of $15.5 billion concentrated in a relatively small, suburban area (Lecomte and Gahagan, 1998). Insurance industry research organizations project potential losses for Category 4 and 5 hurricanes in some locations at more than $50 billion. Further, for hurricanes Andrew and Hugo, insured losses accounted for just 60 percent of reported losses (Pielke and Landsea, 1998).

The vulnerability of the built environment to hazards striking coastal counties, combined with trends in population growth and the value of insured property, suggest there is a problem of first-order magnitude. Individual communities, however, exhibit significant variability in actual vulnerability, owing mainly to differences in local hazard awareness and investment in effective mitigation. Some communities are highly vulnerable simply because the forces accompanying an extreme hazard—wind, storm surge, and flooding—are so powerful that, no matter how well the community was designed and built, significant damage and destruction will occur. Much coastal hazard vulnerability, however, can be attributed simply to inappropriately designed and built communities—the result of not using the best available knowledge and practices. Almost every planning and development decision made at the local level has implications for the vulnerability to, and thus the impact of, an extreme natural event. This effect applies to all development, both existing and new.

Relationship of the Built Environment to Business, Social, and Natural Resource Costs

There are clear links between the degree of built environment vulnerability and the community's vulnerability to hazard-related business interruptions, disruptions of social structure and institutions, and damage to the natural environment and the flow of ecosystem goods and services. A built environment that is sensitive to the natural risk conditions with respect to development siting, provision of services, and design and construction is more hazard resistant and less vulnerable than one that is not (Geis, 1996). Not only will the built environment be more resilient, but also economic, social, institutional, and natural resource and ecosystem functions will be more resilient. Although built-environment mitigation strategies are emphasized, many additional strategies and tactics can be used by individuals, families, businesses, and communities to reduce social, economic, and environmental vulnerability to coastal hazards. These approaches are addressed in the following sections.

Social, Health, and Safety Vulnerability

In one sense, it is social vulnerability that turns a coastal storm into a disaster. Any given disaster can be thought of as a failure of the social systems constituting a community to mitigate or adapt to an environmental event (Bates and Pelanda, 1994). As researchers have observed: "The disruption of networks of social interaction and the inability of social actors to operate on the basis of normative information are what define the disaster as a social event" (Peacock and Ragsdale, 1997). It is the patterns of development and social organization in a community that determine the extent to which it is able to withstand a coastal storm.

This social perspective does not presume that all residents of a community affected by a storm share equal vulnerability. Some will be able to withstand high winds and water and continue meeting daily needs virtually uninterrupted, whereas others will be displaced or rendered dependent on outside assistance and resources. This variability in impact is not random, but rather develops out of everyday patterns of social interaction and organization, particularly the stratification patterns that determine access to resources (Oliver-Smith, 1986; Maskey, 1989).

Pre-impact social factors determine to a great extent the vulnerability of certain categories of people and social institutions, and, thus, how they will be affected (Anderson, 1995; Morrow, 1999). In other words, there is unequal access to opportunities leading to unequal exposures to risks, which are a consequence of the socioeconomic system. Accordingly, it is more important to discern how human systems place individuals in relation to each other and to the environment than it is to interpret natural systems (Cannon, 1994). An essential first step to effective mitigation and safer communities is to improve understanding of the processes by which storm vulnerability is socially created, and for whom.

Effects of Income Level

Although the United States is affluent by international standards, poverty remains a fact of life for nearly 38 million Americans, or approximately 14.5 percent of the population (Bureau of the Census, 1996a). Over the past 50 years, disparity between the rich and poor has been growing, and the poorest have become increasingly isolated in inner cities and remote rural areas. Poverty-level households are more likely to live in poorly built and inadequately maintained housing, making them particularly vulnerable to storms (Bolin and Stanford, 1991; Phillips, 1993). Most often renters, they have little control over the conditions and storm-worthiness of the structures in which they live. Many low-income households find affordable housing in mobile or modular homes offering little protection. Furthermore, the dwellings of the poor are often located in floodplains and other vulnerable locations.

Unlike the affluent who build large homes in coastal floodplains because of the ambiance, workers with livelihoods tied to fishing, tourism, and other coastal enterprises have little choice. And nearly every coastal community has some "residents" who are totally vulnerable—the homeless, who can be found living in cardboard shacks, under expressways, or in other flimsy hovels (Phillips, 1996). Poor households are less likely than are other residents to have the financial reserves to purchase supplies in preparation for a storm or to buy needed services and materials to secure their home in the aftermath. Low-income residents are less likely to have access to transportation that would enable them to heed storm warnings and evacuate effectively, or visit relief supply depots and disaster assistance centers after an event. Their low-paying jobs are likely to be lost when businesses close or move after a disaster. Jobs servicing individual households—housecleaning, yard work, and child care—disappear when employers lose their homes or leave the affected area (Morrow and Enarson, 1996). From a community standpoint, the poor are likely to require substantial government assistance during response and recovery. They are most apt to be left homeless, become the inhabitants of temporary housing, and remain so for a long time (Phillips, 1993; Peacock et al., 1997).

Effects of Age, Skills, and Experience

Households caught in the path of storms possess differing amounts of human or personal resources, such as health and physical ability, relevant experience, education, time, and skills. The vulnerability to disaster of elderly-only households varies significantly with age, health, extended family, and economic resources. However, it can be expected that many older community residents as a group lack the physical and economic resources necessary for effective disaster response, are more likely to suffer health-related consequences, and will recover more slowly (Phillips, 1991; Tobin and Ollenburger, 1992). While the U.S. total population has tripled during this century, the proportion over 65 years of age has increased elevenfold and was estimated at 33.2 million in 1994 (Bureau of the Census, 1996b). The senior citizen population is expected to more than double by 2050 to approximately

80 million, and the fastest growth rate is expected for the group over 85 years of age. At the other end of the spectrum, the physical vulnerability of children is obvious. However, children in the United States generally live in households with at least one able-bodied adult.

In addition to dependency associated with age, some community residents have physical and mental limitations that can influence their disaster response. As a result of improved medical care and rising survival rates for persons affected by birth defects, life-threatening and chronic diseases, and accidents, more Americans than ever before live with disabilities of some kind (Tierney et al., 1988). According to the 1990 U.S. Census, approximately 10.4 percent of the population between the ages of 16 and 64, or some 16.5 million people, are classified as having a work disability, mobility disability, or self-care limitation (Bureau of the Census, 1996c).

Household living arrangements also have consequences in disasters. The resources available to any household are affected significantly by its ratio of healthy, productive adults to dependents. The proportion of U.S. housing units occupied by married couples with minor children has been decreasing and in 1990 accounted for only 26.3 percent of all households (Bureau of the Census, 1992). About 9.1 percent of all families are headed by a single parent, usually female, whereas 30 percent consist of non-family households, that is, persons living alone or with unrelated adults (Bureau of the Census, 1996d). The trend is toward smaller households; the average size in 1997 was projected to be 2.6 persons. Although smaller households can be highly mobile, they may lack sufficient economic and human resources with which to prepare and respond effectively. In an era of two-wage-earner families, single-parent families, particularly when headed by women, are likely to be living on the economic margin. Conversely, the rising costs of raising children has placed extra burdens on large families. Families with many dependents—children or dependent adults, such as elderly and disabled members—face greater economic difficulties.

The personal experience, education, and skills possessed by the resident adults can influence significantly a household's ability to respond effectively. Scant attention has been paid to the relationship between personal qualities and effectiveness in negotiating the many processes necessary to respond to, and recover from, a disaster. The disadvantages posed by illiteracy or lack of language proficiency when seeking information and filling out application forms are obvious. Problems arising from cultural differences between response agency workers and victims have been reported (Phillips, 1993; Morrow and Enarson, 1996). Less is known about the relationship between education and impact and recovery, but it can be expected that, at a minimum, higher education levels are associated with better employment opportunities, even in a depressed post-disaster economy, as well as greater proficiency in dealing with bureaucracies, resulting in greater access to resources.

There is information about the relationship between a person's prior disaster experience and the appropriateness of their response, which depends on the nature and timing of that experience. The positive effect of having experienced a hurricane predisposing the person to start preparing earlier is mentioned frequently in the literature on hurricane preparation (Baker, 1991; Gladwin and Peacock, 1997). However, certain circumstances, such as a person's having easily survived a mild hurricane or near miss, can actually contribute to complacency. Although knowledge of appropriate mitigation and safety practices is important, it is insufficient to predict appropriate behavior reliably, because many other factors, such as money and access, affect household decisions and actions (Watts, 1983; Varley, 1994).

During the response to a major storm, a lack of family and social networks can be a critical factor influencing the outcome for individual households. Although relatives are unlikely to be the primary source of assistance in the United States, they nevertheless provide an important base of disaster-related help for many (Nigg and Perry, 1988; Morrow, 1997).

Fast-growing communities with many new residents are more likely than older areas to contain isolated households with limited social and family networks. Similarly, recent immigrants may not have strong connections to the larger community and may be hesitant to seek assistance outside their ethnic group for a variety of reasons, including fear of government officials based on past experiences with repressive regimes in their home countries. Likewise, migrant agricultural workers are unlikely to be well integrated into community institutions and, therefore are easily overlooked in disaster planning. Resorts tend to be located in aesthetically pleasing but highly vulnerable areas, such as beaches and barrier islands, and tourists and other transients can be highly vulnerable when a storm strikes (Drabek, 1994, 1995).

An important factor in storm mitigation is the extent to which individuals have control over their circumstances. Resiliency depends not only on their economic situation, but also on their relationship to decision makers. The social and political structure is far from objective or impartial, promoting the interests of some over others. At the household level, renters have little, if any, control over the buildings in which they live, including whether they are structurally sound, have shutters or wind protection, are insured, or get repaired after a storm. Neighborhood or community recovery is an important external factor affecting how well individuals and households rebound. In many respects, the recovery of a neighborhood is tied directly to the political power of its residents. Unincorporated or rural areas may have difficulty getting attention in the highly politicized environment surrounding a storm or other disaster (Morrow and Peacock, 1997). Politically marginalized or disenfranchised groups and communities have difficulty competing for resources (Dash et al., 1997).

The effects of many vulnerability factors are compounded by being a member of social categories devalued by the dominant forces in society. There are many ways in which membership in a racial or ethnic minority can result in social and economic marginality and, thus, influence disaster impact, resiliency, and outcome (Phillips, 1993; Girard and Peacock, 1997). Although the data are sometimes contradictory, mortality rates tend to be higher among minorities (Bates et al., 1963; Bolin and Bolton, 1986). Marginalized minority groups often are excluded from community disaster planning and preparation activities (Faupel et al., 1992; Phillips, 1993), including mitigation initiatives (Tierney, 1989).

Effects of Gender

Disaster planning, management, impact, response, and even research are largely social processes, and, as such, unfold in social systems that are often divided by gender (Enarson and Morrow, 1998). The result is that gender-specific responsibilities, constraints, and resource limitations serve to accentuate the vulnerability of women, who are likely to suffer disproportionately at all stages of a disaster (e.g., Khondker, 1996; Enarson and Morrow, 1997). The different sets of response and recovery needs of women have yet to be adequately addressed in disaster work (Fothergill, 1996).

The most obvious gender effects are associated with poverty. Largely as a result of the economic inequality stemming from fewer economic opportunities, households headed by women are much more likely to be poor. In 1994, for example, 34.6 percent of female-headed households in the United States were below the poverty threshold compared to 14.5 percent of the general population, as were 24.9 percent of women living alone compared to 17.8 percent of men living alone (Bureau of the Census, 1996d). The disadvantages faced by poor women are compounded when these women are marginalized further by race, ethnicity, or old age.

There are many additional ways in which women's disaster experiences differ from those of men. Sex-role stereotypes and expectations profoundly influence the daily lives of women and men and are likely to be accentuated in times of crisis (Drabek, 1986; Hoffman, 1993). One way in which gender differences affect disaster phenomena is in the assessment of risk and subsequent activities associated with household preparation and evacuation (Cutter et al., 1992; Flynn et al., 1994), including the use of social and family networks (Drabek et al., 1975). It is important to consider the heavy care-giving responsibilities that fall to women, both within households (Finch and Groves, 1983; Abel and Nelson, 1990) and in responding agencies and groups (Neal and Phillips, 1990; Reskin and Padavic, 1994).

Women are more apt to be working in low-status jobs, which are subject to fluctuation in the best of times and are likely to disappear after an event, often unnoticed by authorities. There are likely to be fewer job opportunities for women in post-disaster economies (Enarson and Morrow, 1997). There is some evidence that women-owned businesses have a particularly difficult time surviving a community disaster, and that women applicants are less likely to be approved for small business loans (Nigg and Tierney, 1990).

Business Vulnerability

The vulnerability of businesses to weather-related coastal hazards is clearly linked to the built environment, in that the location and structure of a par-ticular business or industry determines, in large part, the impact. Business vulnerability is also linked to the social costs of storms because these firms employ people. As mentioned in the previous chapter, the existing research on coastal hazard–related costs incurred by the business community is quite limited. The literature focuses on small businesses, generally defined as busi-nesses with fewer than 50 employees, because it is assumed that these busi-nesses will have a particularly difficult time recovering after a disaster. At the Heinz panel's March 1998 workshop, several business owners were inter-viewed and offered insights they had gained through enduring Hurricane Hugo. Some of the lessons learned by these owners assisted them in recover-ing from this disaster and may be useful to others in assessing the vulnera-bility of their own businesses to coastal hazards. These lessons include the following:

- have a disaster plan and update it annually;
- support strong and well-enforced building codes;
- maintain proper disaster supplies and the capability to deliver them (transportation, emergency lighting);
- ask your insurance company to work with your business on a disaster plan;
- try to get employees back to work as soon as possible;
- obtain business-interruption insurance;
- support greater disaster coordination among city, county, and local gov-ernments;
- ensure that both insurers and reinsurers do business in your state;

- discuss the problems of business recovery with environmental regulators prior to a disaster;
- pay attention to weather forecasts; and
- work with employees who suffered losses during a disaster (give them time off; interest-free loans) so that business productivity and employment is maintained and morale is improved.

Vulnerability of Natural Resources and Ecosystems to Coastal Hazards

Leatherman et al. (1995) characterize the coast as a "movable boundary" that is in a continuous state of flux in response to storms, sea-level rise, and deltaic, fluvial, and other natural processes. Geology and hydrology determine the types of coastal landforms in a region; define the size of bays, tidal regimes, and relative sea-level changes; and influence shoreline migration. Seasonal changes in storm waves, currents, and depositional patterns often create broad summer beaches, which annually erode to narrow beaches in winter (Williams et al., 1991). Climate variability associated with periodic El Niño events has a dramatic impact on storm and erosion cycles on the West Coast. On the East Coast and Gulf Coast, barrier islands generally migrate landward in the face of relative sea-level rise and along the coast in the direction of prevailing waves and longshore currents. In many areas, coastal wetlands that fringe bays, estuaries, and leeward island margins have migrated inland as sea level has risen. But in Louisiana, sea-level rise, coupled with rapid land subsidence, has resulted in the conversion of roughly 1 million acres of coastal marshes to open water since 1900, as well as a net loss of over 33 percent of the land mass associated with Louisiana's seven barrier island chains.

Human development activities often interrupt the natural processes that maintain coastal shorelines and wetlands. Roads and other hard structures serve as barriers to the inland migration of wetlands, and jetties block longshore sediment transport and deposition on many sandy shorelines. Thus, the vulnerability of natural resources and ecosystems to coastal hazards, particularly major storms and hurricanes, needs to be considered in terms of the unique physical and geologic processes of a location. For example, when estimating the vulnerability of a given area to hurricanes, the risk of exposure with respect to storm intensity, occurrence, and landfall frequency can be defined in terms of probabilities but not changed. Equally important risk factors are the likelihood of exposure to storm surge, waves, wind, and inland flooding, and the extent and distribution of debris. Hazard risks, in turn, are related to the character and resilience of the natural environment—the land configuration, elevation, and topography; the buffering capacity of beaches and dunes, reefs, or undeveloped barrier islands; the degree of human manipulation and resulting ecosystem fragmentation; and the health of species that inhabit the area. Climate variability at different scales is another important physical variable; an example is global climate change and associated sea-level rise, estimated at 1.5 to 2 mm per year (about one-half foot) over the last 100 years, a rate that is projected to increase in the next century. Other climate processes operating at shorter-term scales are also important considerations in risk assessment. Examples are seasonal storm patterns; interannual patterns in El Niño and La Niña; and interdecadal patterns, such as the Pacific decadal oscillation that strongly influences storm patterns and intensity along the U.S. West Coast.

Human settlement patterns—their type, intensity, and geographic distribution—are additional factors determining the vulnerability of natural resources and ecosystem services to coastal hazards. From the perspective of modern industrial society, coastal lands and waters have long been considered natural resources in the development context because they are "something that lies ready for use" (DuBay et al., 1999). As a result, barrier islands, mainland shorelines, and lowlands that fringe coastal bays and estuaries— areas cited for their immense natural value—are also locations for many of the nation's largest concentrations of people and development. Extensive land transportation networks, ports and harbors, resource extraction industries, other shoreline business and commerce, residential development, and recreational development and activity have dramatically, and, in some cases, irreversibly, changed the coastal environment.

Under normal circumstances, coastal natural resources are under high and continual stress from interactions with the built environment. Coastal hazards—particularly hurricanes and large storms—are important natural phenomena in the maintenance of some ecosystems. However, extensive development-related fragmentation of natural environments has lowered ecosystem resiliency, such that direct and indirect impacts of storms can have significantly larger, more costly, and long-lasting impacts on coastal natural resources than might otherwise be expected. Many coastal lands that have been set aside as protected natural areas are vulnerable to damage from large storm events. Because these lands may be among the few remaining (and isolated) examples of that ecosystem type, these sites become more important to protect. Such sites may require major restoration expenditures and extended time periods to recover functional baseline levels, if they ever do.

Historical patterns that contribute to increased hazard vulnerability are particularly difficult to address, whereas development in new areas is, theoretically, more manageable from a hazards perspective. However, demographic, political, and economic pressures contribute to barely restrained development in some coastal areas that are both ecologically important and at high risk of natural hazards. Pressures on coastal ecosystems have never been greater, and, given upward trends in population and development, these pressures are likely to grow further. Just as scientists and others are learning about the immense value of coastal ecosystems and the resources and services they provide, these assets are at increasing risk of loss.

Another aspect of natural resource vulnerability arises in the period following weather-related disasters, when there is often a substantial, temporary relaxation of environmental and pollution-related controls in an effort to facilitate recovery. As a result, during the period after a disaster, many recovery activities can exacerbate the adverse impacts on the natural and human environment and further impede the ability to manage and protect coastal ecosystems.

Interactions of Development and the Environment

Coastal barrier islands, with their natural dune systems and bay-side marshes; coastal wetlands; floodplains of coastal rivers; and coastal forests all play important roles in absorbing, and thus reducing in other locations, the winds and floodwaters of major coastal storm events. Natural dune systems, with their deep root mats, are highly stable and resist erosion, in contrast to human-engineered dunes. Coastal wetlands and upland forests provide resistance to high winds. Coastal wetlands and riverine floodplains absorb and reduce the energy of storm-induced flood waters. Through breaches and overwashes, storms introduce sediments into bays and create new shallow water habitats, which are important both ecologically and for coastal stability.

Unless it is designed and situated carefully, coastal development can have a deleterious impact on natural coastal resource features that perform important storm mitigation and other ecological functions (Geis, 1988). This, in turn, can exacerbate damages to coastal communities during major storm events and compromise the capability of these natural systems to recover all of their natural ecological functions following major coastal storms (National Research Council, 1998). The harmful effects of poorly planned development fall into two categories.

First, coastal development that involves direct building on, or taking sand from, barrier dunes; bulk-heading; filling in of wetlands and shallow water habitat; restricting floodplain capacity; or clearing of coastal forests directly harms these natural systems. Second, the destruction and fragmentation of natural features that moderate the effects of storms, winds, and flooding increase the potential for damage to coastal development both directly along the coast and further inland, and, thus, inflate the costs of recovery. As naturally vegetated dune systems, wetlands, floodplains, and forests are destroyed or compromised, their ability to absorb wind and water energy is lowered. Insurance risk assessment models recognize the role that coastal forests play in moderating storm wind impacts further inland.

Coastal development that adversely affects the integrity of natural features of coastal systems can induce injury to these systems during and after major storm events and interfere with the ability of these systems to recover ecological function. Development that takes place too close to natural dunes or wetlands can interfere with the ability of these resources to migrate and rebuild themselves following major coastal storms. Efforts to prevent barrier breaches and overwashes, as well as construction of bay-side channels, can prevent the formation of new shallow-water habitat. Fragmentation of coastal wetlands, floodplains, and forests interferes with and retards the recovery of fishery and wildlife habitats. In addition, nutrient-rich sewage discharges and run-off from roads, agricultural lands, and animal feedlots leads to a buildup of nutrients in coastal sediments that will be released during major storm events, resulting in or intensifying anoxic conditions. Oil products also may be released, interfering with the recovery of biological communities, if oil storage facilities are designed and located improperly.

Examples of Risk and Vulnerability Assessments

With the foregoing overview of vulnerabilities as background, it is instructive to examine how risk and vulnerability assessments are used by the insurance industry, by the Federal Emergency Management Agency (FEMA), in environmental protection programs, and by communities seeking to develop a vulnerability inventory. In all cases, considerations of risk and vulnerability are important components in estimates of the potential for future costs. However, as the following four examples show, there is no precedent for a comprehensive approach that allows for full consideration of costs. There is clearly a need for community decision makers to incorporate considerations of all aspects of risk and vulnerability assessment into their decision processes.

Case Example 1: How Insurers Assess Risk and Vulnerability

Technical risk assessment is used in many financial and engineering contexts to assess a priori the risks faced by a venture or structure. It has been applied extensively by the nuclear power industry to earthquake risks, and it underlies current efforts within the insurance and reinsurance industries to assess the risks posed by tropical cyclones. This approach recently has been modified for application to the assessment of natural hazard risks.

Advances in information technology have led to the development of catastrophe models, which have proven very useful for quantifying risks based on estimated probabilities and expected damage. The development of faster and more powerful computers now makes it possible to examine extremely complex phenomena in ways that were impossible even five years ago. Large databases can now be stored and manipulated so that large-scale simulations of different disaster scenarios under various policy alternatives can be easily undertaken.

A catastrophe model is the set of databases and computer programs designed to analyze the impact of different scenarios on hazard-prone areas. The model combines scientific risk assessments of the hazard with historical records to estimate the probabilities of disasters of different magnitudes and the resulting damage to affected structures and infrastructure (Bipartisan Task Force on Funding Disaster Relief, 1995). The information can be presented in the form of expected annual losses or the probability that, in a given year, the claims will exceed a certain amount. The models can also be used to calculate estimated insured losses from specific hypothesized events (e.g., a Hurricane Andrew–level storm hitting downtown Miami and Miami Beach).

More specifically, catastrophe models combine the characteristics of the disaster with characteristics of the property in the affected region to determine a "damageability" matrix, which provides information on the potential losses from disasters of different magnitudes to the structures at risk. The occurrence of Hurricane Andrew and the 1994 Northridge, California, earthquake stimulated the insurance industry to pay more attention to output from these models indicating what could happen in hurricane- and earthquake-prone areas over 10 years, 100 years, or even 1,000 or 10,000 years. The models provide the insurer with an opportunity to determine how much coverage it should provide, what premiums it should charge, and in what areas it should (or should not) offer policies to reduce the probability of severe financial losses to an acceptable level (Kunreuther, 1998).

The technical assessment of risk usually relies on a software model with four components: hazard, exposure, damage, and loss. The hazard component is a software representation of physical events, such as tropical cyclones, earthquakes, tornadoes, and floods. It includes estimates of the likelihood of each event for each area of interest to allow for the determination of risk. The exposure component describes the specific geographical and structural attributes of a property. This module translates the broad forces that define a hazard into the specific forces (e.g., wind speed, ground motion) that act on an individual structure such as a house or building. The damage component contains an engineering description that translates the force on the structure into an estimate of the physical damage, combined with an estimate of the cost to repair the damage. This translation is usually performed through the application of empirically determined damage functions. The insured-loss component is then derived from the estimate of structural damage by applying algorithms that reflect the specific coverage terms. These algorithms reflect provisions such as deductibles, building contents, loss-of-use coverage, and coverage exclusions (e.g., in the United States, wave and flood damage from storms is excluded from the typical homeowners and commercial property policies).

The key issue for insurance firms is to avoid aggregating risk in a geographic area subject to a single hurricane or storm so that the chance of insolvency is reduced to an acceptably low level. Thus, catastrophe models do not usually model policies individually, but rather aggregate insured property values in each zip code area. If a company insures large numbers of properties in areas that can be affected by a single tropical cyclone, then the models show that the insurer has the potential for a much larger catastrophe loss than would an insurer with a more geographically diversified portfolio. Models must be designed to take these aggregations into account by modeling the spatial extent of each event, rather than just the individual probability distribution for each property.

At present, the insurance industry relies on proprietary models (appendix B) to assess the exposure of their portfolios to risk. The tropical cyclone risk models currently used by the insurance industry create a simulated climatology of storm events based on the historical record.

These storm-set models attempt to extrapolate from the short historical record an accurate representation of the frequency and intensity of storms that could make landfall at any location. Each one is designed to capture details of storm size and structure that can be used to indicate the wind field at a particular property. These local wind data then are combined with empirical damage functions to yield property damage estimates. These functions are based on observed damages to structures by winds of known speed.

The simulated storm sets in the current generation of models define storms in an operational manner using a number of characteristics. These include the following:

- *Probability.* Landfall probabilities are estimated based on historical data sets by a variety of statistical and operational techniques. Because the historical data set contains few storms of high intensity or within restricted geographic areas, generating these probabilities necessarily involves numerous assumptions for both interpolation and extrapolation.
- *Minimum central pressure.* Pressure data for existing storms are part of the public storm data set and are a key indicator of storm strength. The distribution of central pressures can be used to create a distribution of intensity in the simulated storm set.
- *Radius of maximum wind.* Modelers typically use equations to calculate this parameter and the shape of the storm. Radius data are collected routinely on reconnaissance flights but have not routinely been incorporated into the widely available public archive. The radius of maximum wind also is inferred from measurements of central pressure, but this relationship has little scientific basis.
- *Forward speed and direction.* The forward speed of the storm at landfall is determined from reconnaissance flights recording the successive positions of the storm center. This measurement is used in some models to help constrain the distance that the storm travels inland and the likely path that the storm will take.
- *Filling rate.* This is a measure of the rate at which a storm weakens after it makes landfall, as the low pressure center of the storm "fills" in. It is usually determined from the empirical study of a subset of the storms in the data set and is highly parameterized in the models.
- *Maximum sustained wind.* The maximum sustained wind has various definitions within the public data set and is used differently in the models. It is a key indicator of storm intensity and damage likelihood. Like central pressure, it can be used to create an intensity distribution in the simulated storm set.
- *Peak wind gust.* Some of the damage models use the peak wind gust as an indicator of the damage likelihood. This parameter poses extrapolation issues similar to those raised when using sustained wind and central pressure.

For most areas that experience tropical cyclones, historical observations of storms span only 50 to 100 years, and the accuracy of the observations decreases as one looks back in time. Thus, serious questions exist as to how well the historical record represents the actual occurrence of storms, particularly for the rarest and largest events. This is an area of active research in which several new techniques are being used to improve estimates of historical patterns.

Disregarding possible human effects on the global climate, the climate system obviously changes from year to year and decade to decade. These changes affect the number of tropical cyclones that occur and the number that make landfall. Thus, future activity, on all time scales, will not equal the average activity of a short historical period. However, research into the climate system soon may allow researchers to forecast future activity in a way that will allow insurers to better understand their expected catastrophe risk.

Case Example 2: The Federal Emergency Management Agency

The Federal Emergency Management Agency (FEMA), through a cooperative agreement with the National Institute of Building Sciences (NIBS) and a contract with Risk Management Solutions in California, has developed a loss estimation software tool called HAZUS (Hazards U.S.). It is PC-based and runs through an integrated geographic information system (GIS) platform. Currently, HAZUS has the capability to perform loss estimates for earthquakes. Work is now under way to expand HAZUS for application to coastal and riverine floods and wind (i.e., hurricane) hazards. As part of this work, surge inundation will be examined. The goal of the HAZUS project is to create a nationally applicable, state-of-the-art product that can be used by state and local entities to determine their risks. Once a community understands its risks, officials will have the knowledge to improve planning for a future event, be better able to mitigate against future damages, and become more prepared to respond following an event.

HAZUS can also be used by those involved in response and recovery to perform quick situation assessments following an event. Because loss estimates are based on user-supplied magnitude and location information, it is possible to input data for an event soon after it occurs and run an analysis to estimate the impact. This tool provides responders with a variety of information, including which areas are likely to have incurred the most damage and which lifelines may be inoperable.

HAZUS was designed in a modular format to take advantage of similarities in the analysis of different hazards. For instance, the same inventory can be applied to all of the hazards (earthquake, hurricane, flood) to produce a loss estimate. It is anticipated that the HAZUS analysis will follow the same basic process for all hazards. HAZUS uses event data to develop estimates of the social and economic losses that are likely to occur with that event. HAZUS analyzes the residential, commercial, and industrial building stock; the lifeline inventory (roads, bridges, railroads, power lines, sewer systems, etc.); essential facilities (including hospitals and schools); and high-potential-loss facilities (dams, levees, etc.). In addition to estimating the damage to and cost of replacing or repairing the built environment, HAZUS also analyzes secondary effects, such as fires, that may result from the event and whether and how many people may require shelter.

HAZUS comes equipped with a large amount of default data that were gathered on a national scale. However, state and local users are encouraged to examine this data set and update it as appropriate, because this will result in improved loss estimates. A strength of the HAZUS model is its flexibility. Any of the parameters used in the analysis can be examined and changed by the user. This allows someone with an in-depth knowledge of the construction practices or site composition for a particular part of the country to customize the model so that it more accurately represents actual conditions. Additionally, the inventory and hazard databases can be updated or replaced if improved information becomes available.

In addition to the inventory data and default earthquake hazard data that are provided with the program, a large amount of supplemental multihazard data is included, such as historical hurricane tracks, digital floodplain boundaries, digital information about land use, digital representations of storm surge, a wind decay model, the complete Census Bureau street files, and digital elevation data. Although it is not currently possible to perform "full scale" loss estimates for these hazards, it is possible to conduct gross-exposure analyses using the multihazard data overlaid by the HAZUS inventory information.

Case Example 3: Risk and Vulnerability Assessment for Environmental Protection

Natural resources risk and vulnerability assessments are common components of many environmental protection programs. Among the most widely used databases and approaches for these assessments are environmental sensitivity analyses, "GAP" analyses, and state Natural Heritage Program rankings of ecological features and their vulnerability.

Natural resource sensitivity analyses can be based on empirical or qualitative observations. For many coastal states, the most intensive assessments of natural resources risk and vulnerability (i.e., sensitivity) have been conducted to support oil spill contingency planning. Oil spill coordination offices in Texas, Louisiana, and Florida, for example, maintain access to maps of shellfish beds, bird rookeries, bald eagle nests, and other important ecological features to guide oil spill prevention and response activities. All Gulf states are working with the U.S. Minerals Management Service to develop a database of environmentally sensitive areas to support the review of spill contingency plans submitted by oil producers. This collective effort is called the Gulf-Wide Information System (Norman Froomer, US Minerals Management Service, New Orleans, personal communication, July 23, 1998). The natural resources identified in these sensitivity analyses are considered vulnerable because (1) they are damaged by exposure to oil or oil spill response measures, such as the use of dispersants, scrapers, or burns; (2) they are considered rare or threatened and therefore merit priority in contingency planning; or (3) they have important economic or social value that would be diminished by a spill.

The National Gap Analysis Program (GAP) has been undertaken to identify biological resources and the level of protection afforded these resources through various conservation programs in each state. The GAP is a vulnerability analysis based on the degree to which native animal species and natural communities are represented in the present-day mix of conservation lands. Those species and communities not adequately represented in the existing network of conservation lands constitute conservation "gaps," which otherwise could be identified as a state's least-protected biological resources. The principal objective of the GAP is to provide broad geographic information on the status of ordinary species (those not threatened with extinction or that are naturally rare) and their habitats so that land managers, planners, scientists, and policymakers have the information needed to make more-informed decisions (Scott et al., 1993). The state GAP programs produce, at a minimum, the following mapped information:

- existing natural vegetation to the level of dominant or co-dominant plant species;
- predicted distribution of native vertebrate species;
- public land ownership and private conservation lands; and
- distribution of any native vertebrate species, group of species, or vegetation communities of interest or priority within the network of conservation lands.

In the early 1970s, The Nature Conservancy developed the Natural Heritage Program concept as a means of providing detailed, objective information on the nation's biological and ecological features. Since its inception, the program has grown to cover all 50 states, which generally manage their Natural Heritage databases in collaboration with The Nature Conservancy. Natural Heritage data centers are staffed by botanists, zoologists, and ecologists who piece together facts on the location and status of rare and endangered species and ecological communities in each state. They gather evidence from the literature, expert references, specimen collections, satellite imagery, aerial photographs, and field surveys. They maintain this information in manual files, maps, computer databases, and computerized mapping systems. They also use this information to rank species and ecological communities according to their biological status and degree of vulnerability (The Nature Conservancy, 1998). State Natural Heritage programs are among the most widely used sources of information for planning and regulating coastal development activities. These programs also often guide the acquisition, protection, and restoration of lands in both coastal and inland areas. Other programs that commonly involve coastal resources risk and vulnerability analysis are the 28 National Estuary programs, funded by the U.S. Environmental Protection Agency, and the state Coastal Zone Management programs, which are supported by the U.S. Department of Commerce.

Case Example 4: Community-Level Vulnerability Maps

Effective storm mitigation at the community level begins with the development of a community vulnerability inventory (Cutter, 1998), sometimes referred to as a community hazard and risk assessment (Geis, 1997), or access profile (Blaikie et al., 1994; Morrow et al., 1994). One common practice is to register disabled persons who are likely to need special attention in an emergency or evacuation. Although it is unrealistic to attempt to collect other vulnerability data for individual households, it is entirely feasible for planners to maintain databases reflecting the extent to which highly vulnerable groups are represented in each neighborhood.

A community vulnerability inventory would reflect where at-risk categories of residents are concentrated. Those at risk include:

- poor households;
- elderly, particularly frail elderly;
- physically or mentally disabled;
- children and youth;
- woman-headed households;
- large households;
- ethnic minorities (by language spoken);
- renters;
- recent residents, immigrants, migrants;
- the homeless; and
- tourists and transients

Maintaining up-to-date information on the most vulnerable categories of residents is a major step toward effective mitigation and local response (see Morrow, 1999). Ideally, the geographical locations of these concentrations of high-risk categories are mapped. The resulting community vulnerability map provides an invaluable tool for emergency managers and disaster responders from both the public and the nonprofit sectors, allowing informed estimates of anticipated community needs at all levels of response. The next step is to link educational and other mitigation programs, evacuation plans, distribution of relief supplies, and other response services directly to local neighborhood needs. These maps can also reflect neighborhood storm-related resources, such as shelters, community centers, parks, local service groups, and storm response networks. Community planners can then merge this vulnerability information with other point-specific community and housing data suitable for spatial analysis, as well as flood, surge, and other storm-related databases or risk assessment models, such as HAZUS. The resultant GIS allows planners "to integrate social and geographic data in order to understand disaster as a social phenomena" (Dash et al. 1997). It is a powerful tool, not only for predicting impact, but also for anticipating community needs before, during, and after a storm, pinpointing risk and relating it to existing neighborhood resources as well as weaknesses.

An example of integrated community vulnerability mapping is the "Hazards of Place" project currently under way for Georgetown County, South Carolina (Cutter, 1998). This project tests a conceptual model of vulnerability that incorporates both biophysical and social indicators. A GIS was used to establish areas of vulnerability based on twelve environmental threats and eight social characteristics. The results suggest that the most biophysically vulnerable places do not always intersect with the most vulnerable populations. This finding reflects the likely "social costs" of hazards on the region. While economic losses could be severe in areas of high biophysical risk, in Georgetown County these areas tend to be economically resilient and may recover relatively quickly. Conversely, it would take only a moderate hazard event to disrupt the well-being of most county residents and retard their longer-term recovery from disasters. The research provides relevant data to emergency management planners for effective future mitigation and expands current understanding of what makes people and places vulnerable to hazards.

Conclusions and Recommendations

Risk and vulnerability are defined in a social process based on explicit or implicit decisions about what matters. Value judgments are intrinsic to the definition of what is at risk or vulnerable with respect to coastal hazards. How risk and vulnerability are defined is a reflection of what matters in terms of expected costs associated with coastal hazards. What is measured is not all that matters, and what matters is not always measured.

Conventional risk assessment has tended to emphasize that which has been (or can be) measured quantitatively. This approach has worked well for concerned parties whose costs fall exclusively into these categories. However, for many other stakeholders, costs are not well expressed in conventional categories of risk assessment (e.g., environmental and noneconomic societal impacts). Consequently, methods of vulnerability assessment have sought to go beyond the limitations of conventional risk assessment (e.g., with community vulnerability maps). Much work remains to be done in the creation of integrated assessments of risk and vulnerability.

The following recommendations arise from this review of risk and vulnerability:

- Vulnerability studies conducted by federal, state, or local agencies should incorporate a broader set of potential losses and costs than is typical in traditional assessments. In addition to potential damage to the built environment, such a study should consider the characteristics of individuals and families at risk and environmental vulnerabilities of the community or region.

- Community vulnerability assessments should include evaluations of the circumstances and locations of concentrations of high-risk groups, such as the poor, elderly, handicapped, women living alone, female-headed households, families with low ratios of adults to dependents, ethnic minorities, renters, recent residents including immigrants, transients, tourists, and the homeless.

- Research is needed on the physical, emotional, and social effects of disasters on both men and women of varying age, ethnicity, and social class. Such research will explain the effects of social, economic, and political status on disaster response at the household, neighborhood, and community levels.

- Risk assessments of coastal hazards should delineate the uncertainty (e.g., confidence intervals) associated with the likelihood of disasters and the potential losses should a disaster occur.

- Existing research on business costs related to coastal hazards is quite limited, and that which is available focuses on businesses with fewer than 50 employees. Therefore, more studies should be undertaken focusing on the vulnerability and costs to large and small businesses of coastal hazards and the impacts of business interruption on the affected community.

- Communities should develop and maintain up-to-date databases of existing building stock, critical facilities such as hospitals and evacuation centers, public utilities, and public buildings. The recorded information should include location of these facilities, and property or replacement values. This information would be valuable as input to HAZUS and other GIS mapping tools. Community vulnerability maps should be developed that include the locations of high-risk households and congregate living facilities.

References

Abel, E., and M. Nelson, eds. 1990. *Circles of Care: Work and Identity in Women's Lives.* Albany: SUNY Press.

Anderson, M. B. 1995. Vulnerability to disaster and sustainable development: A general framework for assessing vulnerability. In M. Munasinghe and C. Clarke (eds.), *Disaster Prevention for Sustainable Development.* Washington, DC: IDNDR and the World Bank.

Baker, E. J. 1991. Hurricane evacuation behavior. *International Journal of Mass Emergencies and Disasters* 9(2):287–310.

Bates, F. L., C. Fogleman, V. Parenton, R. Pittman, and G. Tracy. 1963. *The Social and Psychological Consequences of a Natural Disaster: A Longitudinal Study of Hurricane Audrey.* Washington, DC: National Research Council.

Bates, F. L., and C. Pelanda. 1994. An ecological approach to disasters. In R. R. Dynes and K. J. Tierney (eds.), *Disasters, Collective Behavior, and Social Organization.* Newark: University of Delaware Press.

Bipartisan Task Force on Funding Disaster Relief. 1995. *Federal Disaster Assistance,* U.S. Senate, 104-4.

Blaikie, P., T. Cannon, I. Davis, and B. Wisner. 1994. *At Risk: Natural Hazards, People's Vulnerability, and Disasters.* London: Routledge.

Bolin, R. C., and P. Bolton. 1986. *Race, Religion, and Ethnicity in Disaster Recovery.* Boulder: University of Colorado.

Bolin, R. C., and L. Stanford. 1991. Shelter, housing and recovery: A comparison of U.S. disasters. *Disasters* 15(1):24–34.

Bureau of the Census. 1992. *Current Population Reports.* Washington, DC: U.S. Department of Commerce.

Bureau of the Census. 1996a. *Poverty in the United States: 1995.* Washington, DC: Department of Commerce.

Bureau of the Census. 1996b. *Population Projections of the United States by Age, Sex, Race, and Hispanic Origin.* Washington, DC: Department of Commerce.

Bureau of the Census. 1996c. *1990 Census of Population and Housing.* Summary Tape File 3A. Washington, DC: Department of Commerce.

Bureau of the Census. 1996d. *Households by Type, 1940 to Present.* (www.census.gov/population/socdemo/ hh-fam)

Cannon, T. 1994. Vulnerability analysis and the explanation of "natural" disasters.

In Varley, A. (ed.), *Disasters, Development and Environment.* New York: Wiley and Sons, pp. 13–30.

Cutter, S. L. 1998. Hazards of Place Assessment Project in Georgetown County, SC. Presentation to the Heinz Center Panel on Risk, Vulnerability, and the True Costs of Coastal Disasters, March 25, Charleston, SC.

Cutter, S. L., J. Tiefenbacher, and W. D. Solecki. 1992. En-gendered fears: Femininity and technological risk perception. *Industrial Crisis Quarterly* 6:5–22.

Dash, N., W. G. Peacock, and B. H. Morrow 1997. And the poor get poorer: A neglected Black community. In W. G. Peacock, B. H. Morrow, and H. Gladwin (eds.), *Hurricane Andrew: Ethnicity, Gender and the Sociology of Disasters.* London: Routledge, pp. 206–225.

Drabek, T. E. 1986. *Human Systems Responses to Disaster: An Inventory of Sociological Findings.* New York: Springer-Verlag.

Drabek, T. E. 1994. *Disaster Evacuation and the Tourist Industry.* Boulder: Institute of Behavioral Sciences, University of Colorado.

Drabek, T. E. 1995. Disaster responses within the tourist industry. *International Journal of Mass Emergencies and Disasters* 13(1):7–23.

Drabek, T. E., W. H. Key, P. E. Erickson, and J. L. Crowe. 1975. The impact of disaster on kin relationships. *Journal of Marriage and the Family* (August):481–494.

DuBay, D., A. Tweed, R. M. Schoch, and A. H. Lapinski, 1999. *Environmental Science.* New York: Scott Foresman Addison Wesley, p. 195.

Enarson, E., and B. H. Morrow. 1997. A gendered perspective: The voices of women. In W. G. Peacock, B. H. Morrow, and H. Gladwin (eds.), *Hurricane Andrew: Ethnicity, Gender, and the Sociology of Disasters.* London: Routledge, pp. 116–140.

Enarson, E., and B. H. Morrow (eds.). 1998. *The Gendered Terrain of Disaster: Through Women's Eyes.* Westport, CT: Praeger.

Faupel, C. E., S. P. Kelley, and T. Petee. 1992. The impact of disaster education on household preparedness for Hurricane Hugo. *International Journal of Mass Emergencies and Disasters* 10(1):5–24.

Finch, J., and D. Groves (eds.). 1983. *A Labour of Love: Women, Work, and Caring.* London: Routledge and Kegan Paul.

Flynn, J., P. Slovic, and C. Mertz. 1994. Gender, race, and perception of environmental health risks. *Risk Analysis* 14(6):1101–1108.

Fothergill, A. 1996. Gender, risk, and disaster. *International Journal of Mass Emergencies and Disasters* 14(1):33–55.

Geis, D. E. 1988. Flood plains, coastal area construction. In *Encyclopedia of Architecture: Design, Engineering, and Construction,* vol. 2. New York: John Wiley and Sons, pp. 460–474.

Geis, D. E. 1996. Helping local governments create sustainable and disaster resistant communities—the role of mitigation. In *Proceeding of the Second International Conference, Amsterdam, April 22, 23, 24, 1996: Local Authorities Confronting Disaster and Emergencies.* Amsterdam, the Netherlands: The International Union of Local Authorities, Section 10, pp. 11–16.

Geis, D. E. 1997. Disaster resistant communities: A community-based approach to hazard mitigation. *The CUSEC Journal, a publication of the Central United States Earthquake Consortium.* 4(1):1–2.

Girard, C., and W. G. Peacock. 1997. Ethnicity and segregation: Post-hurricane relocation. In W. G. Peacock, B. H. Morrow, and H. Gladwin (eds.), *Hurricane Andrew: Ethnicity, Gender, and the Sociology of Disasters.* London: Routledge, pp. 191–205.

Gladwin, H., and W. G. Peacock. 1997. Warning and evacuation: A night for hard houses. In W. G. Peacock, B. H. Morrow, and H. Gladwin (eds.) *Hurricane Andrew: Ethnicity, Gender, and the Sociology of Disasters* London: Routledge, pp. 52–74.

Hebert, P. J., J. D. Jarrell, and M. Mayfield, 1993. *The Deadliest, Costliest, and Most Intense United States Hurricanes of this Century (And Other Frequently Requested Hurricane Facts).* NOAA Technical Memorandum NWS NHC-31 (February). Coral Gables, FL: NHC.

Hoffman, S. M. 1993. Up from the embers: The aftermath of the Oakland Berkeley firestorm: A survivor anthropologist's perspective. Paper presented at the Society for Applied Anthropology annual meeting, San Antonio, TX.

Insurance Institute for Property Loss Reduction and Insurance Research Council. 1995. *Community Exposure and Community Protection: Hurricane Andrew's Legacy.* Wheaton, IL, and Boston: IIPLR and IRC.

Insurance Research Council. 1986. *Catastrophic Losses: How the Insurance System Would Handle Two $7 Billion Hurricanes.* Malvern, PA: Insurance Research Council.

Jarrell, J. D., P. J. Hebert, and M. Mayfield. 1992. *Hurricane Experience Levels of Coastal County Populations from Texas to Maine.* NOAA Technical Memorandum NWS NHC-46 (August). Coral Gables, FL: NHC.

Khondker, H. H. 1996. Women and floods in Bangladesh. *International Journal of Mass Emergencies and Disasters* 14(3):281–292.

Kunreuther, H. 1998. Program for Reducing Disaster Losses through Insurance. In H. Kunreuther and R. Roth Sr. (eds.), *Paying the Price: The Status and Role of Insurance against Natural Disasters in the United States.* Washington, DC: Joseph Henry Press.

Landsea, C. W., N. Nicholls, W. M. Gray, and L. A. Avila. 1996. Downward trends in the frequency of intense Atlantic hurricanes during the past five decades. *Geophysical Research Letters* 23:1697–1700.

Leatherman, S. P., R. Chalfont, E. C. Pendleton, T. L. McCandless, and S. Funderburk. 1995. *Vanishing Lands: Sea Level, Society, and the Chesapeake Bay.* Annapolis: University of Maryland. 47 pp.

Lecomte, E., and H. Gahagan. 1998. Hurricane protection in Florida. In H. Kunreuther and R. Roth Sr. (eds.), *Paying the Price: The Status and Role of Insurance against Natural Disasters in the United States.* Washington, DC: Joseph Henry Press.

Maskey, A. 1989. *Disaster Mitigation: A Community-Based Approach.* Development Guidelines, no. 3. Oxford: Oxfam.

Morrow, B. H. 1997. Stretching the bonds: The families of Andrew. In W. G. Peacock, B. H. Morrow, and H. Gladwin (eds.), *Hurricane Andrew: Ethnicity, Gender, and the Sociology of Disasters.* London: Routledge, 141–170.

Morrow, B. H. 1999. Identifying and mapping community vulnerability. *Disasters: The Journal of Disaster Studies, Policy and Management* 23(1):1–18.

Morrow, B. H., and Enarson, E. 1996. Hurricane Andrew through women's eyes: Issues and recommendations. *International Journal of Mass Emergencies and Disasters* 14(1):1–22.

Morrow, B. H., and W. G. Peacock. 1997. Disasters and social change: Hurricane Andrew and the reshaping of Miami? In W. G. Peacock, B. H. Morrow, and H. Gladwin (eds.), *Hurricane Andrew: Ethnicity, Gender, and the Sociology of Disasters.* London: Routledge, pp. 226–242.

Morrow, B. H., W. G. Peacock, and E. Enarson. 1994. *Assessing a Community Recovery Function for the ARC Disaster Response Plan.* Alexandria, VA: American Red Cross Hurricane Andrew Recovery Project.

National Research Council. 1994. *Science and Judgment in Risk Assessment.* Washington, DC: National Academy Press.

National Research Council. 1998. *Sustaining Marine Fisheries.* Washington, DC: National Academy Press.

Nature Conservancy, The. 1998. Information as a tool: Taking stock of our natural heritage [July 22]. (http://www.tnc.org)

Neal, D. M., and B. Phillips. 1990. Female-dominated local social movement organizations in disaster-threat situations. In G. West and R. L. Blumberg (eds.), *Women and Social Protest.* New York: Oxford University Press, pp. 243–255.

Nigg, J. M., and R. W. Perry. 1988. Influential first sources: Brief statements with long-term effects. *International Journal of Mass Emergencies and Disasters* 6(3):311–343.

Nigg, J. M., and K. Tierney. 1990. Explaining differential outcomes in the small business disaster loan application process. Preliminary Paper 156. Newark: Disaster Research Center, University of Delaware.

Oliver-Smith, A. ed. 1986. *Natural Disasters and Cultural Responses.* Studies in Third World Societies, no. 36. Williamsburg, VA: College of William and Mary.

Peacock, W. G., B. H. Morrow, and H. Gladwin. 1997. *Hurricane Andrew: Ethnicity, Gender, and the Sociology of Disasters* London: Routledge.

Peacock, W. G., and A. K. Ragsdale. 1997. Social systems, ecological networks and disasters: Toward a socio-political ecology of disasters. In W. G. Peacock, B. H. Morrow, and H. Gladwin (eds.), *Hurricane Andrew: Ethnicity, Gender and the Sociology of Disaster.* London: Routledge, pp. 36–51.

Phillips, B. D. 1991. *Post-Disaster Sheltering and Housing of Hispanics, the Elderly and the Homeless.* Final report to the National Science Foundation. Dallas: Southern Methodist University Press.

Phillips, B. D. 1993. Cultural diversity in disasters: Sheltering, housing, and long-term recovery. *International Journal of Mass Emergencies and Disasters* 11(1):99–110.

Phillips, B. D. 1996. Creating, sustaining, and losing place: Homelessness in the context of disaster. *Humanity and Society* 20(1):94–101.

Pielke, R. A. Jr., and C.W. Landsea. 1998. Normalized hurricane losses in the United States, 1925–1995. *Weather and Forecasting* 10:621–631.

Pielke, R. A. Jr., and R. A. Pielke Sr. 1997. Vulnerability to hurricanes along the U.S. Atlantic and Gulf coasts: Considerations of the use of long-term forecasts. In H. F. Diaz and R. S. Pulwarty (eds.), *Hurricanes: Climate and Socioeconomic Impacts.* New York: Springer, pp. 147–184.

Pielke, R. A. Jr., and R. A. Pielke Sr. 1997. *Hurricanes: Their Nature and Impacts on Society.* London: John Wiley and Sons.

Railton, P. 1990. Benefit–cost analysis as a source of information about welfare. In P. B. Hammond and E. Coppock (ed.), *Valuing Health Risks, Costs, and Benefits for Environmental Decision Making.* Washington, DC: National Academy Press, pp. 55–82.

Reskin, B., and I. Padavic. 1994. *Women and Men at Work.* Thousand Oaks, CA: Pine Forge Press.

Reuters News Service. 1996. Modern warnings system cut hurricane deaths in U.S. Reuters News Service, January 18.

Scott, J. M., F. Davis, R. Csuti, R. Noss, C., Butterfield, C., Groves, H., Anderson, S. Caicco, F. D'Erchi, T. C. Edwards, J., Ulliman, and R. G. Wright. 1993. *Gap Analysis: A Geographic Approach to Protection of Biodiversity.* Wildlife Monograph, no. 123. U.S. Department of Interior, 41 pp.

Sheets, R. 1995. Stormy weather. *Forum for Applied Research and Public Policy* 10:5–15.

Tierney, K. J. 1989. Improving theory and research in hazard mitigation: Political economy and organizational perspectives. *International Journal of Mass Emergencies and Disasters* 7(3):367–396.

Tierney, K., W. Petak, and H. Hahn. 1988. *Disabled Persons and Earthquake Hazards* Boulder: Institute of Behavioral Science, University of Colorado.

Tobin, G. A., and J. C. Ollenburger. 1992. *Natural Hazards and the Elderly.* Boulder: Natural Hazards Research and Applications Information Center, University of Colorado.

Varley, A. 1994. The exceptional and the everyday: Vulnerability analysis in the International Decade for Natural Disaster Reduction. In A. Varley (ed.), *Disasters, Development, and environment.* New York: Wiley and Sons, pp. 1–11.

Watts, M. 1983. On the poverty of theory: Natural hazards in context. In K. Hewitt (ed.), *Interpretations of Calamity from the Viewpoint of Human Ecology.* Boston: Allen and Unwin, pp. 231–262.

Williams, J. S., K. Dodd, and K. K. Grohn. 1991. *Coast in Crisis.* Circular 1075. Reston, VA: U.S. Geological Survey, 32 pp.

Chapter 5
Developing and Evaluating Mitigation Strategies

The previous two chapters provided a more complete picture of the costs and risks to communities facing coastal hazards than has been described in typical analyses. As indicated in chapter 3, the costs of coastal storms and hurricanes can be much greater than those traditionally measured and reported in the aftermath of disasters. Chapter 4 provided the scientific basis concerning risk assessments to complement this expanded treatment of costs. It revealed that coastal communities may be more vulnerable to serious losses from disasters than public- and private-sector agencies previously had suggested.

These findings highlight the importance of developing hazard mitigation strategies to reduce the vulnerability of coastal areas to future storms and hurricanes. Hazard mitigation is defined as "sustained action taken to reduce or eliminate the long-term risk to people and property from hazards and their effects" (FEMA, 1997). The Heinz panel is interested in developing a broad paradigm that enables communities to meet today's needs without jeopardizing capabilities to meet the needs of future generations. Building on the work of Mileti (1999) the panel defines the following five objectives of a sustainable hazard mitigation program:

1. *Maintain and, if possible, enhance environmental quality.* Environmental quality refers to the performance of the ecosystem of a specified area. The community must define more explicitly the desirable characteristics of an ecosystem in both the short and the long term.
2. *Maintain and, if possible, enhance quality of life.* A population's quality of life has many components, including its standard of living; health; safety; arts; education; and vulnerability to pollution, disease, disaster, and other

risks. Local communities need to define the quality of life they want for themselves and for future generations.

3. *Foster local resiliency to disasters.* Local resiliency to disasters means that a community is able to withstand an extreme natural event without suffering devastating losses, substantially diminished productivity, or long-term reductions in quality of life, and does not require a large amount of outside assistance.

4. *Identify intergenerational equity.* One needs to consider ways of preserving resources, reducing the consequences of future disasters, and preserving the natural systems to provide a satisfying quality of life for both this generation and future generations.

5. *Identify community concerns and issues.* By seeking wide participation in decision making by all of the interested parties, one can identify their possible concerns and issues while at the same time generating strategies for dealing with them.

This chapter examines strategies for addressing the above issues for communities threatened with coastal hazards. The first section suggests an expanded view of benefit–cost analysis for evaluating mitigation measures. The heart of the chapter outlines a set of strategies, including the creation of disaster resistant communities, that hold promise for reducing future losses. The concluding portion of the chapter raises some challenges for implementing mitigation measures and describes three complementary programs in the public and private sectors that hold considerable promise: the Federal Emergency Management Agency's Project Impact, Disaster Recovery Business Alliances, and the Institute for Business and Home Safety's Showcase Community Program.

Rethinking the Cost-Effectiveness of Mitigation Measures

Elements of Benefit–Cost Analysis

The importance of considering all the impacts of disasters is highlighted by the use of benefit-cost analysis as a technique for evaluating the relative merits of alternative mitigation strategies using a systematic process described in more detail in Boardman et al. (1996). The process begins with the identification of the different mitigation strategies being considered, including the status quo. Each alternative affects a number of individuals, groups, and organizations, all of whose benefits and costs need to be counted. Once these benefits and costs have been specified, the impacts are quantified and some value is attached to them for each of the affected individuals or groups. Some type of weighting procedure is required to aggregate these impacts to enable an approximation of how each alternative will affect society as a whole.

If the aggregate expected benefits of a mitigation measure exceed its expected costs, then it should be considered for adoption. However, limited resources and budget constraints, as well as political and social considerations, may preclude many of these cost-effective measures from being implemented. There are the obvious questions as to who pays for the mitigation measure and who benefits from it. The funders and beneficiaries may not be the same parties; hence, conflicts may arise concerning whether the measure is justifiable or implementable. This issue is not addressed in this report. Rather, the focus here is on why it is important to delineate the full range of costs of coastal hazards and all of the risks and vulnerabilities of the affected community when evaluating specific mitigation measures.

To highlight this point consider the following simple example: A coastal community is considering requiring that certain structures in the area undertake partial roof mitigation against future storms and hurricanes. Partial roof mitigation means improving the uplift resistance and strength of the roof without removing the roof covering. It includes bracing roof trusses and gable end walls, applying wood adhesive where the roof decking and roof supports meet, and installing hurricane straps or clips where the roof framing meets the top of the studs.

For what types of structures is this mitigation measure desirable? To answer this question one needs the following types of data:

- The chances of coastal storms of different magnitude. As reflected in scientists' best estimate of the probability distribution of coastal hurricanes and storms. It also may include the uncertainty surrounding these estimates.
- The best estimates and range of damage from storms or hurricanes of different intensities to structures with and without partial roof mitigation in place.
- The best estimates and range of indirect costs to the community of storms or hurricanes of different intensities with and without partial roof mitigation in place for structures.
- The best estimates and range of costs of partial roof mitigation to structures in the community.

Chapters 3 and 4 pointed out the challenges involved in providing these data to evaluate the cost effectiveness of specific mitigation measures. In the past, officials have tended to understate the benefits of mitigation by focusing almost entirely on the reduced costs of structural damage and ignoring the indirect costs. Some of these costs are associated with family and community disruption, which may be difficult to quantify in dollar terms but are still very real. When these additional costs are taken into account, different mitigation measures are likely to be seen as highly cost effective—measures that, when viewed solely on the basis of reduced structural damage, may be only marginally desirable or even undesirable. Furthermore, it is important to consider the time dimension on two levels when evaluating mitigation measures. Mitigation measures involve upfront expenditures but provide benefits over the entire life of a structure, which may be 30 to 50 years. Secondly, many of the indirect costs of disasters spill over long time periods, so one must consider more than the immediate losses from a disaster.

The results of a benefit–cost analysis will differ, depending on which stakeholder is being considered and which policy tools are in effect. For example, a municipality has little incentive to invest in mitigating impacts on its public buildings if officials know that, following a major disaster, the federal government will provide a grant to cover at least 75 percent of repair costs, the current disaster relief policy (U.S. Congress, 1995).[1] A homeowner may find that a mitigation measure is not cost effective because she has insurance to cover most of the losses and will not receive a large enough premium discount from the insurer to make the investment economically attractive.

An Illustrative Example

To illustrate these points, one can incorporate hypothetical data on risk and returns into an analysis of the cost effectiveness of partial roof mitigation. Suppose only one storm could affect the community, and that the probability of its occurrence is given by p. There is a wide range of estimates by the experts as to p ranging from $p_{min} = 1/200$ to $p_{max} = 1/20$. The storm would cause $50,000 of damage to a particular structure if that structure were not partially roof braced and $30,000 if it were mitigated. The house is expected to last for the next 25 years.

Let B equal the annual expected benefits of partial roof mitigation, in the form of reduced structural damage to the house. The value of B will range from $100 (i.e., 1/200 [$50,000–$30,000]) to $1,000 (i.e., 1/20 [$50,000–$30,000]) depending on what value of p one uses with respect to the storm. If one computes these expected benefits over a 25-year period and uses an annual discount rate of 5 percent to convert the annual reduction in damage into the present value, then the expected present value of benefits of investing in roof bracing over the lifetime of the house will range from

$1,400 to $14,000, depending on the value of B, which is determined by the estimate of p. [Note: the present value of the mitigation investment is determined by calculating $\sum_{1}^{25} B/(1 + .05)^t$.]

If the cost of partial roof mitigation to the structure were greater than $14,000, then a benefit–cost analysis would suggest the investment is not worthwhile, even if one used a value of $p = p_{max} = 1/20$. However, based on the material presented in chapter 3 on the true costs of disasters, the benefits of this or any other mitigation measure far exceed the reduction in damage to the structure itself. More specifically, consider the following indirect benefits of mitigation that need to be factored into the analysis:

- the savings in the costs of temporary housing from having the structure stand,
- the relief of family stress by enabling families to stay in their home because it was not severely damaged, and
- enabling businesses to continue to function over time because they were not substantially damaged.

There may be additional benefits to the entire community if all of its structures meet a particular mitigation standard, such as partial roof mitigation. Property values of all homes might be increased if potential buyers knew that they would be moving into a safer community. There would be less chance of community disruption from a disaster if damage to all homes and businesses in the area, not just those that voluntarily adopted the mitigation measure, were reduced.

There may be mitigation measures that go way beyond structurally improving a home or business that need to be considered to preserve both the built and the natural environments. With respect to the built environment, one needs to consider ways to reduce the disruption of infrastructure and lifelines, which can have huge effects on residents as well as businesses. A dysfunctional road can have major implications for the community: general loss of community productivity; disruption of access for businesses and citizens; disruption of residents' ability to get to work or to their daily activities; prevention of access by emergency vehicles (which could cause immense health and safety problems); and disruption of the basic supplies, such as food, needed by all communities on a daily basis. Losses in power and electricity pose major problems to the functioning of families and the operation of businesses (Chang et al., 1997).

There is also a need to consider the benefits from specific mitigation measures that will help preserve natural resources, coastal forests, wetlands, and endangered ecosystems. These environmental considerations cannot be quantified as easily as can dollar damage to structures, but they are critically important when developing long-range mitigation strategies.

Finally, if homeowners and businesses believe that they will receive substantial disaster assistance in the form of low-interest loans or grants from the federal government, then they will have less incentive to invest in mitigation measures. If their expectations of this relief turn out to be ill-founded, then they will learn too late that they should have invested in these measures. If they are correct, then citizens in other parts of the state or country are subsidizing their recovery process.

Alternative Mitigation Measures

In developing a strategy for reducing losses from coastal hazards, a community needs to look at a package of mitigation and preparedness measures that will involve a number of different interested parties, each of which has a stake in the outcome. This point was made many years ago by Gilbert White (1964), who pointed out the importance of combining different adjustments for dealing with the flood hazard. This approach remains valuable today for any hazard that a community faces. There need to be enough economic and social incentives in both the short and the long term to convince all of these different groups to buy into the programs and promote and implement these concepts.

The Role of the Built Environment in Developing Coastal Hazard Mitigation Strategies

Appropriate design and management of a region's built environment are at the heart of coastal hazard mitigation. By developing a mitigation package to make a community more disaster resistant (see box 5.1), officials can reduce the true costs of coastal hazards. The costs to be reduced include the direct costs to the built environment itself, as well as the indirect costs identified in chapter 3—social, business, and environmental—incurred as a result of the damaged, destroyed, or functionally ineffective built environment. The following sections describe mitigation measures, many of which have been implemented, for reducing losses from coastal hazards. This chapter reviews traditional approaches such as building codes, insurance, tax incentives, and land-use management measures, as well as innovative programs that can be undertaken to mitigate damage to natural resources from natural disasters.

Many of these measures have an impact on more than one of the four sectors that were introduced in chapter 3: the built environment, the business

Box 5.1. Creating Disaster Resistant Coastal Communities

A disaster resistant community (DRC) is a community built to reduce losses to humans, the environment, and property as well as the social and economic disruptions caused by natural disasters. It is the safest possible community that can be designed and built given the status quo and budget and resource constraints. The DRC concept reflects the integral relationship between how humans shape communities (the relationship to natural systems, development patterns, form, configuration, function, use, and capacity), and the capacity of those communities to resist the damage caused by an extreme natural hazard. This concept can be implemented through the planning and development processes in place in almost every community (Geis, 1994).

FIVE STEPS TO A DISASTER RESISTANT COMMUNITY
The following steps provide a framework for achieving a DRC. To be successful, the process must include a full range of local players—government officials, developers, the citizenry, financial and insurance institutions, and business leaders, as well as the support and involvement of the state and federal governments.

1. **Promote public awareness.** Educating the public—through mitigation communication materials, media activity, and other means—will ensure that planning efforts go beyond the local government to reach the entire community. When community members are involved in the vision-development and decision-making process, they will feel empowered to participate fully in civic affairs, and they will become additional resources to the local government in the process of planning DRCs.

2. **Maintain a comprehensive perspective.** Local governments must account for the entire community in the process of developing and implementing an effective mitigation strategy. It is extremely important for communities to look beyond individual buildings to consider the entire built environment—the block, neighborhood, and community; the streets, parks, and infrastructure that connects them; and other systems and components that unify and define this complex system.

3. **Integrate mitigation planning into the local decision-making process.** Local governments must ensure that at each step in the planning and decision-making process—from zoning and codes to capital budgeting, from transportation planning to facilities management, and from subdivisions to strategic plans—the values and priorities of the stakeholders are reinforced and implemented. These decision makers must be involved in the process, discuss the ramifications of their decisions in the short and long term, strive for consensus around actions, and ready the necessary planning tools to implement those actions.

4. **Conduct a community risk assessment.** Local governments must understand the community's vulnerabilities—cost implications, resources, and opportunities—with regard to coastal hazards. With a

(continues)

Box 5.1. Continued

well-documented risk assessment for the community in hand, local authorities can document lessons learned and translate those lessons into development and design guidelines, which can be integrated into the community's unique planning and decision-making process.

5. **Create and use a disaster resource network.** Local authorities must improve their access to state-of-the-art information in developing and implementing a mitigation strategy. This information includes local, national, and international resources: research, literature, specialists, local experts and teams of experts, case studies across the globe, and useful methodologies.

DESIGN/MITIGATION CONSIDERATIONS AND GUIDELINES
An effective mitigation strategy requires that more attention be given to the various systems and components of the community, where and how they are designed, how they serve and relate to each other, and how they fit into ecological and geological systems. Built-environment mitigation measures have two parts; (1) The goal oriented design considerations and guidelines associated with shaping growth and development and (2) the regulatory and administrative tools, such as building codes, zoning ordinances, and subdivision regulations, needed to implement these guidelines.

Goal oriented design considerations and guidelines should include the following:

- the relationship between the built and natural environments;
- designing and building to complement ecological systems and their workings;
- community–regional support systems for development;
- transportation and utility design, hierarchy and location;
- community development and growth patterns;
- design and patterns of open space;
- housing and neighborhood design;
- individual and group building design;
- emergency management function design; and
- community facility design, location, and capacity.

These principles also apply to retrofitting of existing development (see box 5.2).

community, the social environment, and natural resources and ecosystems. Each community faces its own set of hazards, has a unique past history, and features special sets of institutional arrangements, and, accordingly, needs to develop a mitigation strategy that suits its circumstances.

Box 5.2. Hazards Mitigation Meets Historic Preservation: The Community Sustainability Center in Charleston, South Carolina

While autumn evokes images of blazing foliage in much of the country, it is a harbinger of the hurricane season for coastal South Carolina. Hurricane Hugo, which struck the South Carolina coast in September 1989, left a legacy greater than the widespread destruction to people's homes, tree-lined neighborhoods, and beloved beaches. One of the lasting effects has been the community's increased awareness of the risks involved in living in a low-lying, hurricane-prone city by the sea.

This awareness is evidenced in an old house in the middle of historic downtown Charleston. The two-story house, built in about 1875, has become a living example of how simple retrofits to traditional frame buildings can reduce the threats of flood, wind, and earthquakes—natural hazards affecting the South Carolina coast. The house, now known as 113 Calhoun Street: A Center for Sustainable Living, showcases low-cost tools and techniques for natural hazards mitigation, sustainable building practices, and sustainable living.

"What is remarkable about the project is the emphasis on retrofit of historic buildings," comments Bob Bacon of the South Carolina Sea Grant Consortium Extension Program. Typically, historic preservation guidelines prohibit major renovations that might conflict with the integrity of the structure or the historic fabric of the community. In this case, Clemson University Extension Service, along with the city of Charleston, the South Carolina Sea Grant Consortium, the South Carolina Emergency Preparedness Division, and the Federal Emergency Management Agency (FEMA) worked together to develop a project that both met historic preservation provisions and reduced the risk to natural hazards.

Once completed, 113 Calhoun Street will serve as a resource center where architects, contractors, engineers, and the general public can learn about old and new mitigation technologies. For example, the floors and wall along the east side of the building will be exposed, allowing visitors to see how the chimney, foundation, and connections between the floors have been reinforced.

According to Bacon, solidly connecting the foundation, floors, roof, and chimney to one another is the key to the structural retrofit. "You can't lose the roof if it's attached to the walls, if they are, in turn, attached to the floors and the foundation," he explains. Making the individual parts into one continuous structure strengthens the entire building.

Elevating the house posed a particular challenge. According to National Flood Insurance Program regulations, houses undergoing major renovations in floodplains are required to be raised above the Base Flood Elevation, a measurement used by FEMA in its Flood Insurance Rate Maps. If the designers of 113 Calhoun Street had adhered to FEMA's guidelines, the historic value of the house would have been compromised. Using

(continues)

Box 5.2. Continued

FEMA's flood elevation cost–benefit analysis software, engineers at Clemson determined that by raising the house a mere 7 inches, they could reduce the risk of flooding by over 60 percent. Officials determined that there would be no significant loss of historic value, and the house was raised.

Other retrofits to the house include:

- The foundation, constructed out of unreinforced masonry, has been replaced with reinforced block bolted to the building frame.
- The original framing, which consists of mortise and tenon joinery, is reinforced with metal connectors and plywood shear walls.
- The existing plank roof is being replaced with plywood. For demonstration purposes, the plywood will be attached to roof rafters using a combination of methods, including nails, screws, and adhesives.
- Windows will feature a variety of glazing and window covering options, from traditional wooden shutters over impact-resistant glazing, to steel storm shutters, to plywood window coverings.
- Electrical outlets and other important fixtures on the first floor will be elevated to prevent potential flood damage.
- Interior fixtures and furnishings such as file cabinets and bookcases will be attached to walls as an earthquake safety measure.

For more information, contact the South Carolina Sea Grant Consortium at (843) 727-2078.

Building Codes

A building code is a standard that guides the design, construction, and maintenance of new structures in a community. Some states have model codes that are adopted at the local level, some at the state level. Other states let local governments design and implement their own standards. Building codes establish minimum acceptable standards necessary for preserving public health, safety, and welfare and for protecting property. In addition, building codes: (1) promote a level and predictable playing field for designers, suppliers, and builders; (2) promote a degree of comfort for buyers, who are entitled to rely upon minimum construction standards for the safety and soundness of a building; (3) allow economies of scale in the production of building materials and construction of buildings; and (4) contribute to the durability of buildings.

Good building codes have little value if they are not enforced. Independent studies of damage following Hurricane Andrew and the Northridge Earthquake revealed that lax code enforcement and poor construction contributed to the total damage. To make sure that building codes are enforced, it is necessary to thoroughly inspect a property for items that can contribute to structural performance prior to issuing a certificate of occupancy. Today, enforcement of building codes is limited in many communities because of a shortage of inspectors. Communities on the Atlantic coast, particularly in Florida, have become more mindful of the need for inspection, given that over 25 percent of the damage from Hurricane Andrew could have been prevented if the existing building codes had been adhered to by builders (Insurance Institute for Property Loss Reduction and Insurance Research Council, 1995). One way to encourage the adoption of cost-effective mitigation measures would be to incorporate them into building codes and provide some type of seal of approval to each structure that meets or exceeds these standards. By inspecting a building to see that it has incorporated critical elements and then giving it a seal of approval, the government provides accurate information to the property owner.

Building codes also help mitigate the intangible (social, emotional) losses that insurance does not cover, but which often make the claims adjusting process more difficult for insurers. According to the Insurance Institute for Property Loss Reduction (IIPLR), builders often oppose changes in building codes on grounds that the proposals: (1) do not produce benefits commensurate with the cost or (2) make buildings so expensive that potential buyers are forced out of the market. The incremental costs of many code improvements are nominal, and in the context of the final cost of the property to a buyer they are inconsequential. However, the benefits of such improvements may have far-reaching effects on life-safety and property-damage issues. For example, a requirement that roof coverings withstand commonly encountered winds and hail would not only protect the roofing material from damage, but would also keep wind and rain from entering and doing major damage to the interior. The same holds true for requirements that door and window openings be secure enough to prevent penetration by wind-borne objects. A survey by IIPLR revealed that 91 percent of homeowners in hurricane-prone coastal areas believe builders should be required to follow stricter building codes even though it might add as much as $5,000 to the cost of a $100,000 home (Insurance Institute for Property Loss Reduction, 1996).

A seal of approval may have the added benefit of increasing the property value of a home, because buyers can be expected to pay a premium for a safer structure. A July 1994 telephone survey of 1,241 residents in six hurricane-prone areas along the Atlantic and Gulf coasts provided data that lends support to the argument for this type of program. More than 90 percent of the respondents felt that local home builders should be required to follow building codes, and 85 percent considered it very important that local building departments conduct inspections of new residential construction (Insurance Institute for Property Loss Reduction, 1995).

It is much less costly to implement mitigation measures for planned structures than to retrofit existing ones. Hence there has been a reluctance by states or communities to require current property to meet specific standards that might be applied to new construction. There are exceptions to this general rule when communities feel that the benefits of preserving a particular structure is worth the expense. Box 5.2 illustrates why Charleston, South Carolina, retrofitted one of its homes in the historic part of the city.

The Role of Insurance

In theory, insurance rewards individuals after a disaster. If these individuals incur losses to their structures, then they receive claims payments for the insured portion of their damage. Insured individuals can expect to receive a reduced premium for adopting mitigation measures prior to a disaster because the potential losses to the insurer are reduced. Indeed, insurers have the option of refusing to provide coverage unless the prospective policyholder undertakes certain protective measures to lower the potential losses. This was common practice with respect to fire coverage in the nineteenth century. For example, one company, the Spinners Mutual, insured risks only where automatic sprinkler systems were installed. The Manufacturers Mutual in Providence, Rhode Island, developed specifications for fire hoses and advised mills to buy only from companies that met these standards (Bainbridge, 1952). Today, most insurers have been reluctant to deny coverage on these grounds.

There are a number of ways that insurance can encourage mitigation activities. The following are several examples that address the concerns for a more efficient allocation of resources while still addressing equity or distributional concerns. A more detailed discussion of how insurance can be coordinated with other policy tools for reducing losses from future natural disasters can be found in Kunreuther (1998).

Premium Reductions Linked with Long-Term Loans

Insurance premium reductions based on the owner's taking loss prevention measures can be an important first step in encouraging property owners to adopt these measures. There are also other ways to make this measure financially attractive to the property owner. If a homeowner is reluctant to incur the up-front cost of mitigation because of budget constraints, then the bank could provide the necessary funds for mitigation through a home improvement loan, with a payback period identical to the life of the mortgage.

Consider the following example, in which the cost of bracing the roof on a property in a hurricane-prone coastal area is $1,500. If meteorologists' best estimate of the annual probability of a hurricane is 1/100, and the reduction in loss from bracing the roof is $27,500, then the expected annual benefit is $275. A 20-year loan for $1,500 at an annual interest rate of 10 percent would result in payments of $145 per year. If the annual insurance premium reduction reflected the expected benefits of the mitigation measure (i.e., $275), then the insured homeowner would have lower *total* payments by investing in mitigation.

Subsidized Loans for Low-Income Families

Many poorly constructed homes are owned by low-income families that cannot afford the costs of either mitigation measures or reconstruction should their house incur damage from a natural disaster. Equity considerations argue for providing this group with low-interest loans and grants so that they can either adopt cost-effective mitigation measures or relocate to a safer area. Because low-income victims are likely to receive federal assistance to cover uninsured losses after a disaster, subsidizing these mitigation measures can also be justified on efficiency grounds.

Community-Based Insurance Incentives

One way to encourage communities to develop and enforce building codes and land-use management measures is to reduce insurance premiums for all policyholders in an area based on the stringency of its building code standards and land-use regulations. The more effective a community program is in reducing future disaster losses, the greater the insurance premium reduction.

Such a Community Rating System (CRS) was created by the Federal Insurance Administration in 1990 as a way to recognize and encourage community floodplain management activities that exceed the minimum National Flood Insurance Program (NFIP) standards (Pasterick, 1998). Inspired by the CRS, the Institute for Business and Home Safety (IBHS) helped create the Building Code Effectiveness Grading Schedule for use in adjusting private-sector insurance premiums. This rating system, administered by the Insurance Services Office, measures how well building codes are enforced in communities around the United States. Although it is not yet fully implemented, the program is intended to ensure that property located in communities with well-enforced codes will benefit through lower insurance premiums.

Liability System

The liability system has the potential to be a powerful tool for encouraging key interested parties to enforce relevant standards and regulations. In theory, insurers would not be liable for claims if they could show that the relevant building code was not enforced. Contractors who did not follow a building code could be responsible for paying for the damage to poorly designed homes battered by a hurricane. Banks that did not require homeowners in high-hazard areas to purchase flood insurance on federally insured mortgages could be forced to pay the claims that the property owner would have collected from a flood policy.

Regulatory Measures

In practice the liability system has not been used in this way. However, there are signs that this may be changing. A step toward making banks more responsible for enforcing insurance requirements was taken in the Flood Disaster Protection Act of 1990, which levies fines on any financial institution that lets a policy lapse. Florida anticipates developing a statewide building code whereby contractors not meeting the standards would be fined and lose their licenses.

The Role of Tax Incentives for Mitigation

One way for communities to encourage residents to pursue mitigation measures is to provide them with tax incentives. For example, if a homeowner reduces the chances of damage from a hurricane by installing a mitigation measure, then this taxpayer would get a rebate on state taxes to reflect the lower costs for disaster relief. Alternatively, property taxes could be reduced for the same reason. In practice, communities often create a monetary disincentive to invest in mitigation. A property owner who improves a home by making it safer is likely to have the property reassessed at a *higher* value and, hence, will have to pay higher taxes. California has recognized this problem, and in 1990 voters passed Proposition 127, which exempts seismic rehabilitation improvements to buildings from reassessments that would increase property taxes.

The city of Berkeley has taken an additional step to encourage home buyers to retrofit newly purchased homes by instituting a transfer tax rebate. The city has a 1.5 percent tax levied on property transfer transactions; up to one-third of this amount can be applied to seismic upgrades during the sale of property. Qualifying upgrades include foundation repairs or replacement, wall bracing in basements, shear wall installation, water heater anchoring, and securing of chimneys. Since 1993, these rebates have been applied to 6,300 houses, representing approximately $4.4 million in foregone revenues to the city (Earthquake Engineering Research Institute, 1998).

The principal reason for using tax rebates to encourage mitigation is the broader benefit associated with these measures. If a house is not damaged because it is elevated or protected in some way, then the general community gains much larger savings than just the reduced damage to the house. For example, residents who would have had to leave their unmitigated homes after a disaster, but who instead are able to remain in their protected homes, do not have to be fed or housed elsewhere. These added benefits cannot be captured through insurance premium reductions, which normally cover damage only to the property. Taxes are associated with broader units of analysis, such as the community, state, or even federal level. To the extent that the savings in disaster costs accrue to these units of government, tax rebates are most appropriate.

The Role of Land-Use Management

A study by Burby (1998) shows that communities can achieve large reductions in losses from natural disasters by adopting land-use plans while at the same time achieving environmental and other goals. As pointed out in chapter 1, the NFIP requires participating communities to regulate the location and design of future floodplain construction to reduce losses from floods. Based on a national sample of 10 cities in flood-prone areas that attempted to plan for and manage flooding hazards, the study revealed that floodplain development was reduced by over 75 percent of what would have occurred without the local planning programs. A benefit–cost analysis revealed $11 million in reduced property damages per year, with annual administrative and private costs totaling only $1.3 million.

Burby's study (1998) notes that there are serious barriers to adopting this approach on a broad scale. Few local governments are willing to adopt land-use measures to protect against natural hazards unless they receive strong mandates to do so from higher-level governments. Land-use approaches require the accurate identification of areas affected by hazards, but hazard zone mapping is too expensive for most municipalities. An additional barrier to the adoption of these measures is that hazards do not respect political boundaries.

Mitigating Health and Social Post-Disaster Impacts

A number of steps can be taken prior to a disaster to enable a community to respond to the health and social needs of disaster victims. A public announcement system can be prepared ahead of time to discourage the influx of unneeded people and supplies into an affected region. Aggressive outreach programs are needed to reach isolated populations as soon as possible. Shelters must be screened carefully to determine their capability to weather the storm. Plans for distributing food stamps need to include more effective ways for determining qualification.

Prior to a storm, educational campaigns that address health and safety issues likely to be encountered in the aftermath of a disaster should be implemented. The need for long-term mental health programs after a major storm should be anticipated by local, as well as federal, responding agencies. Employee assistance programs and organizational practices—including shorter work rotation periods, retreats, and counseling services—should be pre-planned to help responders deal with stress.

Mitigation Techniques to Protect Natural Resources

Damage to natural ecosystems and resources during and after a hurricane or major storm is inevitable. However, some damages, especially indirect environmental damage caused by poorly sited or constructed development and infrastructure, can be avoided. Communities, public agencies, and private parties can reduce the vulnerability of natural ecosystems and resources to coastal hazards by preventing the release of hazardous waste through proper handling, storage, and contingency planning. Sound planning and siting of development and infrastructure consistent with realistic coastal disaster scenarios is an important environmental protection tool. For example, preservation of undeveloped floodplains and wetlands allows these areas to serve as storm and erosion buffers and as temporary storage for floodwaters. Resilient buildings that meet strict building codes will result in less debris released into the environment and less damage to building contents (which would end up using valuable landfill capacity).

Protection of beaches, dunes, and native vegetation, and appropriate building construction setbacks that respect natural coastal processes, help minimize damage to critical habitats. These measures also lessen the need for expensive beach restoration projects that might degrade turtle nesting and shorebird habitat. These few examples point out that, while some damage to ecosystems and natural resources during coastal disasters cannot be avoided, there are strategies and tactics that can help minimize losses and take advantage of the inherent mitigation functions and value of nature's infrastructure. A list of mitigation strategies that communities may want to consider to protect natural resources from coastal disasters follows in box 5.3.

Box 5.3. Mitigation techniques to protect natural resources

BEACHES

1. Ordinances that restrict withdrawal of fill material after storms.
2. Prohibition of activities that would reduce or alter beach/barrier configuration and dune height (such as removal of vegetation or construction of groins and jetties that prevent sediment transport).
3. Enhancement of sediment sources and/or transport processes that naturally maintain coastal barriers and shorelines (such as use of dredged spoil from navigation channels and beach sand fencing).
4. Post-storm beach nourishment in areas that provide critical habitat for sea turtles and shorebird rookeries.
5. Sensitivity analysis of critical beach habitats to establish pre- and post-storm priorities for protection and restoration of habitats at greatest risk.
6. Restoration of vegetation on beaches and barriers after storms to prevent loss of sediment and to aid in dune/beach recovery.
7. Establishment of baseline understanding of ecological features and processes to ensure that mitigation measures are designed properly and to enable post-storm monitoring.

WETLANDS

1. Ordinances that protect coastal wetlands and buffer zones from development.
2. Sensitivity analysis of wetland vulnerability to storms to establish priorities for restoration after storms and to restrict activities that might degrade or destroy important wetlands.
3. Revegetation, sediment nourishment, exotic species control, and other activities to restore those wetlands that provide critical functions (e.g., storm buffer for coastal communities and endangered species habitat).
4. Development of plans for removal of structures and vessels that are stranded in wetlands after a storm so that wetland habitat is not destroyed.
5. Enhancement of sediment accretion processes that naturally restore coastal wetlands after a storm, such as redistribution of sediments that clog navigation channels.

FORESTS

1. Management of forest stand structure (spacing/stocking density particularly) to reduce damage due to windthrow; careful selection of silvicultural treatments such as thinning that might increase windthrow.

(continues)

Box 5.3. Continued

2. Management of species composition (e.g., culture and maintenance of species that are more tolerant of storms in areas populated with red-cockaded woodpecker such as longleaf pine rather than loblolly).
3. Use of prescribed burns to minimize fuel accumulation. This helps manage understory growth and enhances desirable herbaceous plants.
4. Development of plans and obtaining of regulatory approval prior to storms for salvage operations and prescribed burns to remove forest debris.
5. Use of artificial nesting cavities to compensate for cavities in trees lost during and after storms.

FISHERIES

Molluscan Shell Fisheries
1. Develop plans for closures of oyster and clam fisheries following storms (because of high fecal coliform levels) in collaboration with fishers so they can focus on families and know what to expect after a storm.
2. Encourage development of business plans to accommodate temporary closure of shellfisheries.
3. Develop plans for depositing shell/clutch material to renourish shell-fish beds following storms.

Shrimp Fisheries
1. Develop plans for the provision of ice and generator power for fish-houses, cold storage, and live-bait operations.
2. Retrofit/rebuild docks and other onshore facilities to reduce future losses and fisheries downtime related to storms.
3. Post-disaster debris clearance of fishing grounds and waterways to prevent damage to vessels, open commercial vessel traffic, and reduce damage to nets.
4. Establish gear compensation fund and loans for commercial fishers to repair vessels, gear, and onshore support facilities.

Finfish
1. Minimal impacts occur here compared to other fisheries. However, fish stocking has been used to mitigate losses in some cases.

RECREATIONAL FISHING
1. Develop provisions/strategies for replacing recreational piers that are important to the local economy.
2. Develop plans to construct or reconstruct piers, boat launches, and other recreational facilities that are more capable of withstanding storm surge and high winds.

WATER QUALITY
1. Take actions to minimize pollutant discharge during storms (e.g., sewage discharges that result in shellfish closures), retrofit facilities as prescribed by pre-storm assessment of potential releases.
2. In calculating allowable pollutant discharges from point and nonpoint sources, consider the cumulative loading of pollutants in estuarine/coastal sediments that may be released during storms.
3. Develop standards and emergency measures to prevent the release of toxic pollutants during storms.

Implementing Mitigation Measures

This section discusses the importance of developing a mitigation plan and understanding the decision processes of the different stakeholders to increase the chances that loss-reduction measures will be implemented. The chapter concludes with an illustrative example from the fictitious town of Waterville that suggests how key interested parties could work together in promoting mitigation measures.

Establish a Planning Process for Mitigation

Coastal communities differ greatly from one state or locality to another. Some are free-standing municipalities, some are outlying areas of larger mainland towns or cities, and some are unincorporated areas under county jurisdiction. Seldom do political units of any type coincide with coastal physical features such as barrier islands, coastal ecosystems, or coastal floodplains. The challenge is to achieve some degree of harmony among these different governmental authorities. Integrated planning also requires that higher levels of government, when necessary, preempt certain actions by lower levels that threaten to undermine coastal management objectives. Thus, when a local government or county approves (and encourages) the construction of high-rise condominiums on a disappearing coastal barrier like North Topsail Island, North Carolina, the state or federal government may need to override that action.

One important step that a community can take is to establish a hazard mitigation committee. The membership needs to include individuals representing key interested parties from the community as well as state and federal officials who have expertise in hazard mitigation and understand how their units of government can interface with the community. The committee will play a key role in developing and evaluating mitigation strategies in a way that increases the chances that they will be implemented. By ensuring that all relevant interests are represented in the planning process, the committee increases the likelihood that some consensus will be reached regarding how to proceed (Burby, 1998).

Understanding the Decision Processes of Key Stakeholders

Each of the interested parties deals differently with the hazards facing a given community. Before developing a mitigation strategy, it is important to understand the nature of each group's concerns and how each of these groups processes information. Considerable empirical evidence suggests that homeowners in hazard-prone areas believe that the disaster "will not happen to me" while they are living in their structure (Palm, 1995; Kunreuther, 1996). In addition, property owners are very reluctant to incur the upfront costs of investing in a mitigation measure because they either face budget constraints or they underestimate the benefits of the measure, the latter because of a high discount rate or the expectation that they will reside in a particular structure for only a short length of time (Kunreuther et al., 1998). These factors suggest that it will be extremely difficult to encourage homeowners to adopt mitigation measures voluntarily unless the strategies are relatively inexpensive and the individuals are particularly concerned with the threat of natural disasters. The July 1994 telephone survey discussed earlier in the "Building Codes" section of this chapter, revealed that 62 percent of respondents indicated that they had not installed hurricane shutters, used laminated glass in windows, installed roof bracing, or made sure that side walls were bolted to the foundation, either before or after Hurricane Andrew (Insurance Institute for Property Loss Reduction, 1995).

Other interested parties have little incentive to call attention to the potential natural hazard threat. Real estate agents are reluctant to point out the hazard to potential buyers unless they are forced to by law. Even then, many of them mention that the house is in a hazard-prone area only after the buyer has committed psychologically to purchasing the structure (Palm, 1981). Engineers and builders have limited economic incentives to design safer structures, because doing so normally means incurring costs that they feel will hurt them competitively (May and Stark, 1992). Local officials revealed that they tend to view natural hazards as a minor problem relative to other concerns such as crime, housing affordability, and education (Burby, 1998). One study indicated that, on average, local officials rank natural hazards thirteenth in importance among community problems, just behind pornographic literature (Rossi et al., 1982). Of course, after a disaster (when it is too late), the issue of recovery is at the top of a community's list of concerns.

On the other hand, insurers have every reason to want accurate information on the hazards facing a community to determine the appropriate rates to charge and how large a portfolio of risks they should assume without incurring an unacceptably high risk of insolvency. Banks and financial institutions should want to know the real risks they face when issuing a mortgage, although there is little empirical evidence suggesting that they actually take this factor into account in decision making.

A Mitigation Strategy for Waterville

Suppose the hypothetical town of Waterville would like to encourage its residents to adopt mitigation measures to reduce future damage from hurricanes and severe storms. Building codes could be well-enforced by the town. Banks and financial institutions in Waterville could require that structures be inspected and certified that they met the existing standards specified in the codes as a condition for obtaining a mortgage. This inspection, which is a form of buyer protection, is similar in concept to the termite and radon inspections normally required when property is financed. The success of such a program requires the support of the building industry, realtors, and a cadre of inspectors, who are well-qualified to provide accurate information on the condition of the structure. Property in Waterville will receive special reductions in insurance because the community will score high on the Building Code Effectiveness Grading System administered by the Insurance Services Office.

Insurers may want to limit coverage to only those structures that are given a seal of approval or a certificate of disaster resistance. If property owners in Waterville are willing to undertake additional cost-effective mitigation measures, then the local banks could provide long-term loans tied to the mortgage and insurers could reduce premiums. If the state insurance commissioners approve a set of rates based on risk, then the annual payments on the mitigation loan can be expected to be less than the savings in insurance premiums.

Illustrative Examples of Community Mitigation Programs

Several programs have been initiated in the past several years with the principal objective of making communities more resistant to natural disasters. These programs have recognized the importance of involving the key stakeholders concerned with disaster losses and implementing a set of economic incentives that make the mitigation measures appealing to these concerned parties. The programs are also based on a much broader set of costs and benefits than traditionally has been considered in evaluating mitigation measures. In this sense, they provide models for a future sustainable mitigation strategy that recognizes the true costs of disasters.

Project Impact

Project Impact was initiated by the Federal Emergency Management Agency (FEMA). This initiative challenges the country to undertake actions that protect families, businesses, and communities by reducing the effects of natural disasters. Project Impact has three primary tenets: mitigation is a local issue, private sector participation is essential to mitigation efforts, and mitigation is a long-term effort requiring a long-term commitment.

Project Impact seeks to achieve the goal of loss reduction through a community-based partnership consisting of key stakeholders from the private sector; nonprofit organizations; and local, state, and federal governments. The community must first examine its risk of natural disasters and identify its vulnerabilities to those risks. Next, it must identify and prioritize risk-reduction actions and mitigation activities. Finally, local leaders must build support for these actions and publicize their successes to ensure continued cooperation and support.

There are currently 118 Project Impact communities in different stages of development, and as of 1999, FEMA has appropriated $57 million for the initiative. Several pilot communities, including Deerfield Beach, Florida; Pascagoula, Mississippi; and Wilmington, North Carolina, are focusing on loss-reduction strategies to mitigate the effects of hurricanes. Each community has different resources, and, as a result, very different approaches.

For example, in Deerfield Beach, a strong group of business contingency planners has developed a strategy targeting public awareness and education. As part of a volunteer effort, they have installed hurricane shutters, donated by a local manufacturer, on homes in a low-income neighborhood. Pascagoula, a small shipbuilding community, has concentrated on developing a risk assessment capability while initiating collaborative prevention projects with local businesses. Wilmington has a partnership with the National Oceanic and Atmospheric Administration's Coastal Services Center to develop a comprehensive risk assessment tool. The community also recently adopted more comprehensive building codes aimed at reducing property losses.

The Showcase Community Program

The Institute for Business and Home Safety is an initiative of the insurance industry dedicated to reducing losses from natural disasters. Because much of the impetus for loss reduction must come from the local level, IBHS has established the Showcase Community Program to realize the goals of its strategic plan. The program has three main objectives:
• to help a community reduce its vulnerability to natural disasters,
• to generate a "me too" attitude among other communities by showcasing the successful efforts of communities that participate in this program, and
• to learn what works and what does not work to reduce the economic and emotional devastation of natural disasters.

To support the Showcase Community Program, IBHS developed statements of understanding with a number of groups, including the Central United States Earthquake Consortium (CUSEC), the American Red Cross (ARC), the Electric Power Research Institute (EPRI), the Disaster Recovery Business Alliance (DRBA[SM]), the American Society of Civil Engineers, and the American Society of Home Inspectors. These organizations provide professional expertise, additional personnel, and energy needed to sustain locally driven efforts. In addition, IBHS member companies are engaged in the Showcase Communities program by supporting retrofits of child daycare centers, sponsoring DRBA[SM] activities, and providing speakers at community events, as well as through other activities.

Evansville/Vanderburgh County, Indiana, and Deerfield Beach/Broward County, Florida, were the first two pilot Showcase Communities in 1997 and 1998, respectively. Rhode Island became the first Showcase State in the country in December 1998 with the governor's Executive Order listing the 14 initial areas around which the state will organize itself. Box 5.4 contains a brief description of mitigation initiatives undertaken as part of this pro-

---

Box 5.4. Showcase Communities

EVANSVILLE/VANDERBURGH COUNTY, INDIANA. The Evansville designation followed a meeting of public- and private-sector representatives in April 1997, organized by the CUSEC. The participants articulated the community's vision of a disaster resistant community by agreeing to use FEMA's HAZUS loss estimation model, incorporating local data sets that would enable a much more accurate hazard and risk assessment for the community. The community leaders agreed to take natural hazards into

(continues)

Box 5.4. Continued

account in the community's land-use decisions and to apply for participation in the NFIP's Community Rating System (CRS). As a CRS community, Evansville/Vanderburgh County policyholders will become eligible for flood insurance premium credits. Evansville/Vanderburgh County also adopted the 1997 version of the UBC building code.

An important leadership role has been played by the business community, which has founded a southwestern Indiana Disaster Recovery Business Alliance (DRBA^{SM}). Composed of major corporations, members are assessing their vulnerability to natural disasters and developing plans to enable regional economic recovery following a disaster. The DRBA^{SM} is working closely with the public sector. Collaborative efforts include the development of business information for use in the loss estimation models and the development of an emergency pass system that would allow businesses to enter damaged areas in a timely manner, in order to accelerate economic recovery.

DEERFIELD BEACH/BROWARD COUNTY. In Florida, the IBHS Showcase Community designation of Deerfield Beach/Broward County complements the work of FEMA's Project Impact program in Deerfield Beach and the Florida Department of Community Affairs (DCA) showcase community initiative. The DCA is promoting a number of initiatives that support the criteria for the IBHS Showcase Communities. One of these is the formulation of a county-wide mitigation strategy, called the Local Mitigation Strategy, with input from each community in the county. The strategy includes methodologies for evaluation of the actions taken.

Two statewide IBHS initiatives should have an impact on the Deerfield Beach/Broward County Showcase Community program. The DCA has contracted through IBHS to hire a coordinator for a statewide incentives committee, composed of multiple private sector entities that might be interested in offering financial incentives for structural mitigation to homes. The task of the committee is to develop a package of financial incentives for homes retrofitted for wind resistance through the DCA Residential Construction Mitigation Program (RCMP). Ultimately, the goal is that homeowners who incorporate the mitigation features of the RCMP on their own will receive these incentives.

In addition, IBHS and members of the Florida insurance industry have joined in an unprecedented partnership with the state of Florida, FEMA, and local not-for-profit organizations to conduct a statewide public awareness campaign. The Florida Alliance for Safe Homes, or FLASH, will provide Florida residents with the information and resources they need to help make their families, homes, and communities safer from hurricanes and other severe winds. FLASH will continue through November 30, 1999.

IBHS is also working with Broward County as it develops a county-wide Business Emergency Preparedness Network. The purpose of the network is to open up communication between businesses and the public sector around needs for disaster response and recovery. County officials are reaching out to chambers of commerce and local businesses. IBHS is sharing information on how Rhode Island's Disaster Recovery Business Alliance is working, in order to help the county with strategies for a successful network.

RHODE ISLAND SHOWCASE STATE. Recognizing that states play a key role in supporting communities as they move toward disaster resistance, IBHS has worked with the Rhode Island Emergency Management Agency (RIEMA), Rhode Island Sea Grant at the University of Rhode Island/Coastal Resources Center, and FEMA Region I to create a Showcase State, the first of its kind in the country. Modeled after the Showcase Community program, the 14 elements were adapted to outline state actions that could create the right atmosphere for local action. In December 1998, the governor of Rhode Island signed an executive order to make Rhode Island a Showcase State for disaster resistance.

The groundwork for the Showcase State was laid by the work of RIEMA and RI Sea Grant over the past few years. Together, they developed a methodology for communities to create mitigation strategies that could be integrated into their state-mandated local comprehensive plans. The Rhode Island Joint Reinsurance Association, also known as the RI FAIR Plan, contributed financing for a demonstration of wind and water retrofit measures at a state-owned home, demonstrating the insurance industry commitment to mitigation in RI. The next step was to garner the leadership of Narragansett Electric and AT&T Wireless Services to become charter members of the first statewide Disaster Recovery Business Alliance in the country. A Business Needs Assessment workshop set the agenda for the next year, which local chambers of commerce have begun to implement. This business leadership provided the catalyst for the governor and lieutenant governor to become advocates for the Showcase State, and ultimately to endorse and sign the executive order. At the executive order signing, the RI FAIR Plan announced a major contribution to provide support for the Business Alliance to become a self-sustaining organization. An action strategy for the 14 elements of the Showcase State will be developed by the public and private partnership at the beginning of 1999.

gram in Evansville/Vanderburgh County, Deerfield Beach/Broward County, and the state of Rhode Island.

Disaster Recovery Business Alliances (DRBA^{SM})

Public sector emergency authorities, utility service providers, emergency medical teams and other first responders have well-developed emergency response procedures, and they generally coordinate well with disaster relief organizations. However, the recovery of essential commerce and trade is traditionally left to chance, market forces, or ad hoc liaisons created in the chaotic aftermath of the event. Quick and coordinated recovery of basic commercial networks—utilities, food and water distribution, telecommunications, financial services, transportation and fuels, and broadcast media—is the key to timely recovery of other businesses, the viability of neighborhoods, and the continuity of government.

An increasing number of communities are examining the feasibility of establishing a DRBA^{SM}. The objective is to bring together the leadership and expertise of the business, emergency preparedness, and engineering and scientific communities to develop a public/private partnership. This approach reduces the vulnerability of businesses and the community's marketplace to flooding, tornadoes and severe weather, earthquakes, and other hazards. The purpose of such an alliance is to provide a forum within which local leaders and planning experts can identify and mitigate risks to essential channels of commerce serving the community and surrounding counties. In addition to this basic planning, the DRBA^{SM} may develop unique sharable expertise related to a particular natural, technological, or human-caused risk, such as recovery of industrial refrigeration following earthquakes, tornadoes, ice storms, or floods.

Before, during, and after emergencies, a DRBA^{SM} provides members with access to proven and emerging technologies in support of loss mitigation, disaster monitoring, geographic information applications, and sustainable energy and communications. It accelerates socioeconomic recovery through coordinated exchange of status and resource information between business members, public sector emergency authorities, and volunteer organizations active in disasters.

Conclusions and Recommendations

The previous findings and recommendations highlight the importance of developing hazard mitigation strategies to reduce the vulnerability of coastal areas to future storms and hurricanes. Hazard mitigation as defined by

FEMA is "sustained action to reduce or eliminate the long-term risk to people and property from hazards and their effects."

A community-based approach along with an improved understanding of natural systems and appropriate siting, design, and construction of the built environment are essential to advances in hurricane and weather-related hazard mitigation.

The domain of benefit–cost analysis must be expanded to include the evaluation of the relative effectiveness of different mitigation strategies. As the panel has recommended, the concept of costs must be broadened to incorporate many of the hidden costs and impacts of coastal disasters. A successful mitigation strategy requires that interested parties interact so that each feels net gains will be achieved if specific measures are implemented. The Project Impact program run by FEMA, the IBHS Showcase Community program, and the Disaster Recovery Business Alliance are new initiatives that bring key stakeholders together to develop strategies for reducing future losses from coastal hazards.

Based on its analysis of mitigation strategies, the panel makes the following recommendations:

- Communities can follow a number of general steps to help plan and create a disaster resistant community (DRC). To be successful, the plan must be developed and supported by a full range of local players—government officials, developers, the citizenry, financial and insurance institutions, business leaders, and state and federal governments. The five steps in such a process are:
  1. promote public awareness;
  2. maintain a comprehensive perspective;
  3. integrate mitigation planning into the local decision-making process;
  4. conduct a community risk analysis; and
  5. create and use a disaster resource network.
- Existing community-based hazard mitigation planning models should be expanded to include not only the risk to the built environment but also business, social, and natural resource or ecosystem risks and vulnerabilities.
- Communities should consider establishing a local hazard mitigation committee composed of individuals who represent key stakeholders from the community as well as state and federal officials who have expertise in hazard mitigation. Such a committee can play an important role in developing and evaluating mitigation strategies.
- Existing building codes must be enforced.
- Empirically based model programs for reducing the risk of coastal hazards

are needed. These programs should factor in the impacts and costs associated with the built environment, business, social concerns, and natural resources.

- All levels of government (federal, state, and local) should examine their current programs and policies to determine whether they are acting as disincentives to mitigation efforts.

- To reduce the indirect effects of a coastal hazard event, community disaster plans should provide for prompt response to the social needs of the affected community by placing a higher priority on the restoration of schools, recreational facilities, family counseling programs, daycare centers, and shelters for abused women and children in addition to hospitals. The plans also should promote neighborhood-level response networks and initiatives.

- To deal with the broader set of costs of coastal hazards, there is a need for a mitigation strategy that combines a number of policy tools, including building codes, land-use planning (e.g., zoning), incentives (e.g., subsidies, fines), taxation (e.g., property taxes), and insurance. Developing and implementing these policy tools will require an integrated effort by a number of the concerned parties, including contractors and developers, real estate agents, banks and financial institutions, insurers, and public-sector agencies.

- A partnership with the insurance industry should be developed and an analysis of the industry undertaken to determine how it can play a more creative role in encouraging mitigation through linkages with other policy tools as well as with other interested parties, such as financial institutions, developers, and the real estate community. Insurance rates should reflect the risk associated with the hazard so that appropriate premium reductions can be given to property owners who adopt loss-reduction measures. If rates are suppressed in high-hazard areas, as they appear to be in some states, then one cannot expect insurance to be used effectively as a policy tool for encouraging adoption of mitigation measures.

Note

1. For catastrophic events, such as Hurricane Andrew in 1992 and the Mississippi floods of 1993, the federal government covers the entire cost of public facility repairs.

References

Bainbridge, J. 1952. *Biography of an Idea: The Story of Mutual Fire and Casualty Insurance.* Garden City, NY: Doubleday.

Boardman, A. E., D. H. Greenberg, A. R. Vining, and D. L. Weimer. 1996. *Cost Benefit Analysis: Concepts and Practice*. Saddle River, NJ: Prentice-Hall Business.

Burby, R. 1998. *Cooperating with Nature: Confronting Natural Hazards with Land-Use Planning for Sustainable Communities*. Washington, DC: Joseph Henry Press.

Chang, S., A. Rose, and M. Shinozuka. 1997. *Infrastructure Life Cycle Cost Analysis: Direct and Indirect User Costs of Natural Hazards in Structural Engineering*. Structural Engineers World Conference Proceedings, July 19–23, 1998. Amsterdam: Elseviar.

Earthquake Engineering Research Institute. 1998. *Incentives and Impediments to Improving the Seismic Performance of Buildings*. Oakland, CA: Earthquake Engineering Research Institute.

Federal Emergency Management Agency (FEMA). 1997. *Report on Costs and Benefits of Natural Hazard Mitigation*. Washington, DC: FEMA (Mitigation Directorate).

Geis, D. E. 1994. Planning Disaster Resistant Communities: Lessons for Local Authorities. In *Proceedings: Local Authorities Confronting Disasters and Emergencies International Conference*. Tel Aviv, Israel: International Union of Local Authorities.

Insurance Institute for Property Loss Reduction. 1995. *Homes and Hurricanes: Public Opinion Concerning Various Issues Relating to Home Builders, Building Codes and Damage Mitigation*. Boston: IIPLR.

Insurance Institute for Property Loss Reduction. 1996. *Natural Hazard Mitigation Insights*. Boston: IIPLR.

Insurance Institute for Property Loss Reduction and Insurance Research Council. 1995. Coastal Exposure and Community Protection: Hurricane Andrew's Legacy. Wheaton, IL: IRC; and Boston: IIPLR.

Kunreuther, H. 1996. Mitigating disaster losses through insurance. *Journal of Risk and Uncertainty* 12:171–187.

Kunreuther, H. 1998. A program for reducing disaster losses through insurance. In H. Kunreuther and R. Roth Sr. (eds.), *Paying the Price: The Status and Role of Insurance against Natural Disasters in the United States*. Washington, DC: Joseph Henry Press.

Kunreuther, H., A. Onculer, and P. Slovic. 1998. Time insensitivity for protective measures. *Journal of Risk and Uncertainty* 16:279–299.

Louisiana Department of Natural Resources. 1998. T'was the night after Christmas. *Louisiana Coastlines*. Baton Rouge: Coastal Restoration Division, pp. 5–6.

May, P., and N. Stark. 1992. Design professions and earthquake policy. *Earthquake Spectra* 8:115–132.

Mileti, D. S. 1999. *Disasters by Design: A Reassessment of Natural Hazards in the United States*. Washington, DC: Joseph Henry Press.

Palm, R. 1981. *Real Estate Agents and Special Studies Zones Disclosure*. Boulder: Institute of Behavioral Science, University of Colorado.

Palm, R. 1995. *Earthquake Insurance: A Longitudinal Study of California Homeowners*. Boulder: Westview Press.

Pasterick, E. 1998. The National Flood Insurance Program. H. Kunreuther and R. Roth Sr. (eds.), *Paying the Price: The Status and Role of Insurance Against Natural Disasters in the United States*. Washington, DC: Joseph Henry Press.

Platt, R. 1982. The Jackson Flood of 1979: A public policy disaster. *Journal of the American Planning Association* 48:219–231.

Rossi, P., J. Wright, and E. Weber-Burdin. 1982. *Natural Hazards and Public Choice: The State and Local Politics of Hazard Mitigation.* New York: Academic Press.

U.S. Congress. 1995. *Federal Disaster Assistance.* Report of the Senate Task Force on Funding Disaster Relief. Washington, DC: USGPO.

White, G. 1964. *Choice of Adjustments to Floods.* Department of Geography Research Paper, no. 93. Chicago: University of Chicago Press.

Chapter 6

A Framework for Community Planning

The need for a fresh approach to the coastal hazards problem is urgent. Storms cause billions of dollars worth of damage along the nation's coast every year. At present, damage assessments are based on insured losses and federal reimbursements to local governments, a practice that overlooks many additional costs to the affected residents, businesses, and natural environment. Building on the first five chapters of the report, this chapter recommends a comprehensive framework that will enable communities vulnerable to natural disasters to incorporate risk assessment, vulnerability analysis, and a broad-based cost study in the development and implementation of mitigation strategies to reduce future losses. Although the Heinz panel focused on coastal hazards, the framework is designed to address a broader range of natural hazards and incorporate the concerns of the key interested parties. It is recommended for use by local planners and decision makers to help strengthen community mitigation programs.

Elements of the Framework

The framework builds on Pielke (1997) who proposed that risk and vulnerability result from a combination of natural and societal conditions. It is depicted in figure 6.1 and is organized around the following three principles.

- It is important to characterize potential losses from disasters of different magnitudes by linking risk assessment with the vulnerability of a region.
- An assessment needs to incorporate a very broad range of economic, business, social, and environmental costs (both immediate and those incurred

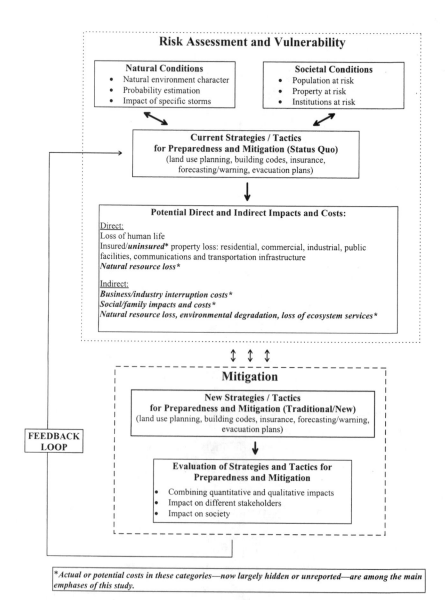

Risk Assessment and Vulnerability

Natural Conditions
- Natural environment character
- Probability estimation
- Impact of specific storms

Societal Conditions
- Population at risk
- Property at risk
- Institutions at risk

**Current Strategies / Tactics
for Preparedness and Mitigation (Status Quo)**
(land use planning, building codes, insurance,
forecasting/warning, evacuation plans)

Potential Direct and Indirect Impacts and Costs:

Direct:
Loss of human life
Insured/*uninsured** property loss: residential, commercial, industrial, public
facilities, communications and transportation infrastructure
*Natural resource loss**

Indirect:
*Business/industry interruption costs**
*Social/family impacts and costs**
*Natural resource loss, environmental degradation, loss of ecosystem services**

Mitigation

**New Strategies / Tactics
for Preparedness and Mitigation (Traditional/New)**
(land use planning, building codes, insurance, forecasting/warning,
evacuation plans)

**Evaluation of Strategies and Tactics for
Preparedness and Mitigation**
- Combining quantitative and qualitative impacts
- Impact on different stakeholders
- Impact on society

**FEEDBACK
LOOP**

*Actual or potential costs in these categories—now largely hidden or unreported—are among the main
emphases of this study.*

Figure 6.1. Risk and Cost Assessment Framework.

over time) associated with weather-related hazard events when evaluating alternative mitigation and preparedness strategies.

• It is important to develop a broad set of alternative mitigation and preparedness strategies, recognizing the relevance of the status quo but not being restricted by current policy.

Risk Assessment and Vulnerability

Risk and vulnerability to weather-related coastal hazards are defined as the potential for loss of life, property, business capacity, social and family stability, environmental quality, and political stability as a result of hurricanes and extratropical storms. More specifically, this module in the framework links the process of risk assessment with the vulnerability of both the natural and the societal conditions.

Risk Assessment

Two elements need to be considered in any risk assessment: the chances of the event occurring and the consequences of the event if it does occur. There is tremendous uncertainty associated with the risks of severe storms or hurricanes hitting a particular location over even a relatively long period of time such as 10, 20, or 50 years. Given the infrequency of these events, there are limited data on which to base an estimate of the probability of, and potential damage from these storms in the future. To the extent possible, one needs to quantify the uncertainty and ambiguity of these estimates by specifying confidence intervals or bounds to reflect differences among experts and lack of scientific information. The Corps of Engineers is currently doing this in the analysis process of their water resources projects. The Corps has manuals, guidelines, and procedures for applying statistical risk and uncertainty analysis for flood control, shore protection, navigation, and environmental restoration projects (U.S. Army Corps of Engineers, 1996).

If there are good causal models of the risk, then there is a possibility of providing estimates of the chances and consequences of future storms using a combination of scientific analysis with historical data. In the past few years, scientists and engineers have made considerable progress in estimating the risk of damage to different structures, but there is still considerable uncertainty regarding these figures. The consensus in the scientific community is that there has been a downward trend in the frequency of severe storms and hurricanes since 1991 (Pielke and Landsea, 1998) and that the increased losses in recent years are because of population growth in coastal areas (Karl et al., 1997). Even though there has been a downward trend in storm frequency and hurricanes, community leaders must be made aware of a 50-year planning horizon during which several severe storms could hit their community. The severity of coastal hazards in the last decade has to be viewed with this long-term perspective in mind, even though these recent events may be the most memorable and have a major impact on individuals' behavior.

Vulnerability Analysis: Natural Conditions

Major climatic events, such as severe storms, are part of the natural geological and ecological processes that constantly shape coastal lands and vegetation. The extent of the risk that coastal hazards pose to natural systems and the built environment is related directly to the degree that land uses alter and degrade the environment. To analyze this risk, it is necessary to assess the characteristics and resilience of the natural environment. More specifically, natural features such as soils, elevations above sea level, and vegetative cover need to be inventoried. The intensity of land use, and the extent that hydrology, water quality, and habitats are altered, must all be evaluated. Land uses that extensively modify natural systems make these systems much more vulnerable to coastal hazards than do those that preserve and perpetuate natural ecological processes. The natural environment may be affected adversely immediately after the disaster as well as over the long term. Some of the damage may be irreversible, whereas other adverse impacts may be only temporary.

Vulnerability Analysis: Societal Conditions

Hurricanes, storms, and other natural events become "hazards" when they affect human society in adverse ways. Communities are vulnerable to these hazards to the extent that they are subject to potential damage to, or disruption of, normal activities. Societal conditions reflect human settlement patterns, the built environment, and day-to-day activities. These conditions include the institutions established to deal with natural hazards during both preparations and response.

The vulnerability of a community includes the potential for direct damage to residential, commercial, and industrial property as well as schools, government, and critical facilities. It also includes the potential for disruption of communication and transportation following disasters. Any disruption of the infrastructure, such as a loss of electric power or break in gas lines, can interrupt business activity and cause stress to affected families, particularly if they are forced to evacuate their residences and are subject to shortages of basic supplies. If the destruction of the infrastructure causes additional damage (e.g., property destroyed by fires caused by breaks in the gas lines), then this vulnerability needs to be taken into account. One also has to consider the exposure of the population to each hazard type and the potential number of fatalities and injuries to different socioeconomic groups.

Potential Direct and Indirect Impacts and Costs

When a severe storm makes landfall, its impacts are a function of the vulnerability of coastal communities and the surrounding environment—the combination of natural and societal conditions that exist at the time. The same is true for less severe, but chronic, hazards.

Nature of Impacts

Disasters create both direct and indirect impacts. As pointed out in chapter 3, *direct impacts* are the damage and losses that can be directly attributed to the storm itself; examples include injuries and loss of life, damage to property and infrastructure, and losses of natural habitats or fish and wildlife populations. *Indirect or secondary impacts* are those that occur over time; examples of indirect impacts on people include family trauma and social disruption, business interruptions, and shortages of critical human services. With respect to indirect environmental effects, fish and wildlife populations may be slow to recover and the loss of an erosion-buffering beach or wetland may alter the future vulnerability of the community. It is important to recognize that there may also be some benefits to certain sectors arising from disaster. For example, for the first two years after Hurricane Hugo, which hit the Charleston, South Carolina, area in 1989, the construction industry boomed amid the enormous demand for repairs and reconstruction. Then there was a significant slowdown in activity.

Some direct impacts of hurricanes and similar natural disasters are easy to quantify because they can be expressed in monetary units—insured losses to homes, businesses, and industry; bridge and highway repairs; cost of new equipment or repairs; and, dollar value of crop loss. The costs of other direct impacts and many indirect impacts may have to be expressed in quality terms. For example, how does one quantify the stress on families due to loss of homes? or fear and anxiety about having another home destroyed in a future hurricane? or the loss of "community" associated with the wholesale destruction of neighborhoods?

Developing Strategies and Tactics for Preparedness and Mitigation

The framework depicted in figure 6.1 is a vehicle for analyzing the impact of different mitigation and preparedness strategies (including maintaining the status quo) on the community at risk. These strategies include public and private actions that decrease the potential for loss of life, property, business capacity, social stability and services, environmental quality, or political stability; and that hasten recovery should a disaster occur.

In developing alternative mitigation and preparedness strategies, one starts with the status quo to examine how well the current set of programs performs. One then varies some of the elements to see what difference this makes in the projected performance. There is a need to be concerned with effective planning for actual events (e.g., forecasting improvements, evacuation planning for hurricanes) as well as long-term planning to reduce future exposure or increase the community's resiliency over time (e.g., land-use planning and implementation, building code strengthening and enforcement).

Although there are some advantages to studying the impact of individual programs, such as insurance, one needs to recognize that policy instruments are interconnected and that they should be developed in tandem. Consider the relationship between building codes and insurance. By developing and enforcing stricter codes for all structures in hazard-prone areas, a community is likely to reduce future disaster losses significantly. This will have two desirable effects. First, it will reduce the magnitude of the losses from future disasters and enable insurers to provide additional coverage to property owners. This, in turn, will reduce the need for reinsurance and funds from other sources, such as the capital market and state pools. If insurance rates are based on risk, then insurers also will be able to offer property owners lower premiums for the same amount of coverage.

Evaluation of Strategies and Tactics for Preparedness and Mitigation

For any given set of preparedness and mitigation strategies, one can evaluate the direct and indirect impacts (both quantitatively and qualitatively), and the associated costs and benefits to different sectors of the community from economic, environmental (natural and built), and social perspectives for hurricanes of different magnitudes. By constructing a series of different scenarios to evaluate individual events (e.g., ministorms, catastrophic hurricanes) one can determine the expected losses from and impacts of the spectrum of events that can affect a given locality (i.e., the consequences of each storm multiplied by its probability). Sensitivity analyses need to be performed to deal with the uncertainty associated with the risk of coastal hazards.

Measuring social welfare solely on the basis of higher income seems to reflect a rather impoverished view of how humans derive meaning from their lives. It is important to ask whether the compensation and benefits actually do have a significant effect on the community's general position, participation, and influence in the larger society before accepting the premise that a higher income automatically means "better off." Elizabeth Anderson (1993), for example, points out that when it comes to issues associated with health, safety, and the environment, simply providing more money to individuals will not fully accommodate their concerns. People may have intrinsic attitudes toward their surrounding environment, perhaps awe and admiration of nature or beauty, which cannot be translated into monetary terms should the environment be despoiled. For many individuals poorly built facilities that pose health and safety risks raise significant moral concerns that simply cannot be counteracted with dollars.

Feedback Loop

There is a need for feedback from the evaluation of mitigation strategies to the design of alternative programs. After evaluating the current strategy, a community needs to consider a set of alternative programs that may reduce its risk and vulnerability. The choice of a particular strategy can be determined only by performing the types of analyses outlined earlier. As new information on the risk and vulnerability of a community becomes available through improved risk assessment techniques, geographical information systems, and modeling approaches, the proposed strategy is also likely to change.

Using the Framework

To illustrate how a community could use the framework to evaluate alternative strategies, the Heinz panel developed a scenario for the hypothetical city of Bristol Pier. The scenario is designed to enable the reader to appreciate the challenges and opportunities facing communities in developing a sustainable mitigation plan.

Nature of the Problem

A development company has made a proposal to the city of Bristol Pier to extend a sewer line to a low coastal area of older, low-density housing to support the construction of a planned housing development with lakefront amenities, including a restaurant and tennis and beach club on the coast and a marina on the bay side. To access this area, the sewer line must be extended across a bay and along a narrow isthmus between the coast and the bay.

The developer has prepared and presented a plan that shows significant economic benefits to the city. These benefits take the form of increased tourism, a larger property tax base, job creation, benefits to other property owners (e.g., access to the sewer line and increased property value), elimination of potential problems with on-site septic systems, and assurances that the installation of the sewer line under the road will allow the housing development to be landward of the erosion setback line. The developer assures the city that the housing will meet flood elevation standards and building codes.

The city of Bristol Pier is a coastal community where officials are aware of hazards such as erosion and severe storms, including hurricanes. Although a serious storm has not struck this area in 24 years, the community participates in the National Flood Insurance Program and the state has established an erosion setback line. There is only one narrow, unpaved road leading out to this coastal area. The city officials are aware that access to this area could be cut off by persistent erosion or a storm surge, which might lead to loss of lives.

The city conducts an internal review of the project including review by the police, fire, parks, planning, and building departments. It also requests input from the Water Authority, Drain Commission, Road Commission, Health Department, School District, and State Department of Environmental Protection. In weighing the project presented by the development company in conjunction with the master plan, zoning ordinance, and emergency preparedness plan, city officials find a number of benefits and costs that need to be considered. The city of Bristol Pier will hold a public hearing and then make a decision on how to proceed.

Risk Assessment and Vulnerability

To determine whether the proposed extension of the sewer line and new developments in the area are worth pursuing, the community must determine the likely risks to the area affected by the proposed developments. The following questions need to be addressed:

- What are the chances of hurricanes and storms affecting Bristol Pier, and what is the uncertainty surrounding these estimates?
- What are the characteristics of the population, property, and institutions at risk from these hurricanes and storms if the status quo is maintained or the proposed sewer line extension is approved?
- What are the potential damages from these storms to the natural environment and the facilities located in the area if the status quo is maintained or the new proposal for a sewer line extension is approved?

Potential Direct and Indirect Impacts and Costs

To determine whether the city of Bristol Pier should allow an extension of the sewer line, the community needs to determine the direct and indirect benefits and costs associated with this action relative to maintaining the status quo. By involving all of the interested parties listed earlier, the residents of Bristol Pier feel confident that all of the relevant impacts are on the table. The key benefits and costs that need to be considered are as follows:

Direct Benefits
- Tax revenues to Bristol Pier
- Employment opportunities
- Revenues to construction companies and real estate industry

Direct Costs
- Traffic congestion
- Sewage treatment plant enlargement and upgrade to accommodate new sewer line
- Widening of narrow road to facilitate evacuation
- Adverse impact on valuable wetlands from widening the road
- Loss of lives from a severe storm or hurricane
- Cost of shore protection
- Costs of emergency services and relief agencies

Indirect Costs
- Break in the sewer line and pollution of the bay
- Degradation of the wetlands or bay necessitating remediation
- Losses to businesses from storms (e.g., decreased revenues, uninsured inventory, closure for repair, interrupted cash flow for salaries, utilities, taxes)
- Bankruptcy of some businesses as a result of storms
- Loss of habitat due to debris and pollutants deposited into waters and wetlands
- Increased storm impacts such as overwash on habitat areas due to loss of buffering from developed coast
- Damage to fish and wildlife populations
- Loss of beach due to erosion
- Loss of tourism due to loss of recreational beach from hardened structures
- Loss of employee work time to address family and housing needs
- Displacement of neighbors resulting in loss of community solidarity

If the indirect costs from development in hazardous coastal areas were considered, along with the more obvious direct costs by the city, would the decision change? Although we cannot know in advance, of course, it seems clear that decisions can be based on firmer ground if the residents and city officials are aware of the true cost of coastal hazards. Although losses from coastal hazards occur yearly on a national scale and, therefore, are on the political agendas of agencies such as the Federal Emergency Management

Agency (FEMA), local governments experience disasters infrequently. Therefore, coastal hazards generally seem to be less pressing to local officials, especially when a severe storm has not affected the community recently. But the officials making land-use and infrastructure decisions need to be fully aware of the true range of costs if they are to balance short-term gains against unexpected short- and long-term losses.

Strategies/Tactics for Preparedness and Mitigation

Two proposals are being evaluated for the city of Bristol Pier:

1. Maintain the status quo by not extending the sewer line to a coastal area of older, low-density housing.
2. Extend the sewer line to the low coastal area and construct a planned housing development with lakefront amenities.

These proposals will be reviewed and compared by a number of interested parties. These include:

- Relevant municipality departments (e.g., police, fire, parks, planning and building, health, environmental protection)
- Relevant state, which would be involved with the building setbacks because of erosion concerns, the marina because it affects public trust waters and the sewer line
- Federal Insurance Administration, which administers the National Flood Insurance Program covering water damage from storms and hurricanes
- Insurance industry, which offers protection against wind damage from storms and hurricanes
- Contractors and developers, who will build the new structures if Proposal 2 is approved
- Real estate agents, who will sell the new structures if Proposal 2 is approved
- Banks and financial institutions, which will provide mortgages to the new owners if Proposal 2 is approved
- Current residents of Bristol Pier

Evaluation of Strategies and Tactics for Preparedness and Mitigation

Once the benefits and costs have been specified in relation to the two proposals, one needs to quantify the impacts and assign a dollar value to them for each of the affected individuals. Sometimes these values can be determined directly; an example is the cost associated with constructing a project. When it comes to other impacts, such as valuing a human life, a wide range of dollar figures (e.g., from \$100,000 to \$15 million) have been used by economists.[1]

Contingent valuation (CV) is the method now sanctioned by many federal agencies to evaluate qualitative effects such as environmental impact. Under this procedure, an individual is asked to specify the maximum he or she is willing to pay to achieve a desired impact (e.g., avoid environmental destruction following an earthquake). When these dollar figures are aggregated across all of the affected individuals the total gives some insight into how much certain improvements are worth. The CV method has been controversial in recent years, so there is no consensus regarding whether this approach should be widely applied.[2] The CV method has not been used to evaluate impacts such as family tensions and stress following a disaster. Rather than trying to quantify all of these impacts, the community may want to characterize them in qualitative terms.

Feedback Loop

As new information becomes available on the probabilities and consequences of severe storms and hurricanes, Bristol Pier may want to reevaluate its options with respect to developing the low coastal area if it initially decides to maintain the status quo. Should the city choose to extend the sewer line and construct a planned housing development, then it may want to consider a set of well-enforced building codes and mitigation measures if the costs of protective measures decline or there appears to be a greater chance of major damage to the area than was originally anticipated. If Bristol Pier would like to be a resilient community that is capable of dealing with disasters primarily with its own resources, then it will have to be vigilant and use new information as it becomes available to reevaluate its mitigation and preparedness strategies.

Thus, the Heinz panel framework can be used to analyze the impact of different mitigation and preparedness strategies on the community at risk. These strategies include public and private actions that will decrease the potential loss of life, property, business, social stability and services, environmental quality, and political stability, and that will hasten recovery should a disaster occur.

Notes

1. See Viscusi (1993) for a comprehensive review of this literature.
2. For a description and critique of the CV approach see Portney (1994) and Diamond and Hausman (1994).

References

Anderson, E. 1993. *Value and Ethics in Economics.* Cambridge: Harvard University Press.

Diamond, P., and J. Hausman. 1994. Contingent valuation: Is some number better than no number? *Journal of Economic Perspectives* (Fall):45–64.

Karl, T., N. Nicholls, and J. Gregory. 1997. The coming climate. *Scientific American* (May):79–83.

Pielke, R. A., Jr. 1997. Reframing the U.S. hurricane problem. *Society and Natural Resources* 10:485–499.

Pielke, R. A. Jr., and C. W. Landsea. 1998. Normalized hurricane losses in the United States, 1925–1995. *Weather and Forecasting* 10:621–631.

Portney, P. 1994. The contingent valuation debate: Why economists should care. *Journal of Economic Perspectives* (Fall):3–17.

U.S. Army Corps of Engineers. 1996. *Shoreline Protection and Beach Erosion Control Study.* Alexandria, VA: Institute for Water Resources.

Viscusi, K. 1993. The value of risks to life and health. *Journal of Economic Literature* 31:1912–1946.

Appendix A

Persons Interviewed at The Heinz Center Panel Meeting Workshop and Questions Distributed

March 25–27, 1998
Charleston, SC

Laurel Addy, SC Department of Social Services

Dana Beach, SC Coastal Conservation League

Frank Brigman III, Small Business Owner

John Brumgardt, The Charleston Museum

Don Cameron, Charleston Housing Authority

Paul Campbell Jr., Alumax Primary Aluminum Corporation

George Campsen Jr., Small Business Owner

Larry Cannon, SC Department of Social Services

Charles Chase, Charleston Historic Preservation Office

John Cook, Charleston Commissioners of Public Works

Wayne Fanning, Trident District Environmental Quality Control

Foster Folsom, SC Department of Natural Resources

Yvonne Fortenberry, Charleston Planning Office

Alice Faye Fosh, The Salvation Army

David Gerhardt, Westvaco

David Gordon, U.S. Fish and Wildlife Service

Lamar Goude, The Salvation Army

Debra Hernandez, SC Ocean and Coastal Resource Management

Lee Jedziniak, SC Insurance Commission

Timothy Kana, Baird and Associates

Gered Lennon, College of Charleston Department of Geology

Billy McCord, SC Department of Natural Resources

Mark Permar, Permar and Ravenel

Jim Sadler, Unisun Insurance

Douglas Smits, Charleston Inspector's Office

David Soutter, Wachovia Bank

Glen Stapleton, Francis Marion National Forest

Dawn Teator, American Red Cross

Deborah Waid, Crisis Ministries

Kaye Wallen, Charleston County Medical Society

David Whitaker, SC Department of Natural Resources

General Questions Asked of All Interviewees
- What were the impacts of the disaster on your sector and how could they have been mitigated?
- What surprises did you experience?
- What do you wish you had done differently prior to the event?
- What prevented you from taking these actions?
- Have you made these changes since Hugo?
- Should these changes be institutionalized, and if so, why?
- What information would you have liked to have had that you didn't?
- What, if anything, have you done post-Hugo to get this information?
- How can your experiences be applied to help other communities?

Questions Asked of the Built-Environment Group

For our purpose, the built environment includes all physical development in your community—buildings and infrastructure: roads, public transit, utilities and facilities, housing, businesses, health and safety facilities, public buildings. It is your community's "physical plant." Our focus is to identify vulnerable areas and subsequent costs to the built environment (damage and destruction) that would occur as a result of a natural disaster, particularly a hurricane. We are also interested in the indirect costs, such as social and economic disruption and natural-environmental damage, caused by the destruction and damage to the built environment.

1. Knowledge about vulnerability toward disasters
   - What systems or components of your community built environment are most vulnerable to natural hazards and disasters? (Transportation; utility and communication lines and support facilities; housing and residential areas; private business and commercial; health and safety facilities; government buildings; educational buildings, etc.)
   - What direct costs would you need to be prepared to deal with as a result of damage and destruction to your built environment (buildings and infrastructure) caused by a natural disaster?
   - What indirect costs would you need to be prepared to deal with as a result of damage and destruction to your built environment (buildings and infrastructure)? (Social, economic disruption and losses, natural environmental damage, loss of businesses, loss of tax base, function and operation, etc.)
   - What elements of your community built environment represent the largest financial investment to your community?
   - What elements of your community built environment are most important? (a) during and after an event; (b) to your community's economic viability; (c) to your citizen's health and safety; (d) to the effective functioning of your Emergency Management Plan.

2. Past experience with natural disasters
   - What impact and associated costs have past natural disasters had on your community's built environment?
     —Direct (buildings and infrastructure)
     —Indirect (social and economic disruption, loss of businesses, natural-environment damage, loss of tax base, etc.)
   - What lessons did your community learn as a result of these past experiences?

3. Actions taken to protect your community against future disasters
   - What steps has your community taken (or is in the process of taking) to minimize the direct and indirect vulnerabilities and costs from a potential natural disaster? (a) vulnerability and potential cost assessment; (b) use of mitigation techniques in your planning–development

process; (c) appropriate design and code regulations; utilization of disaster resistant community principles, etc.

4. Desirable features of disaster planning
   - Do you see a relationship between how your community is planned and built and its capacity to minimize the direct and indirect losses and costs caused by natural disasters?
   - Are you aware of the principles and techniques of creating disaster resistant communities?
   - Are you aware of the potential multi-benefits of implementing mitigation measures into your community's decision-making process? (For example: improved economic, environmental, and social viability; more effective use of built and natural resources, thus resulting in financial savings; capacity to recover more quickly should such an event occur; a safer and healthier community; a more sustainable and higher-quality-of-life community; improved business environment; expanded tax base; etc.)

5. Descriptive data
   - Past, present, or projected data: building stock and lifeline inventory; type/number of facilities; specific damage patterns from past and projected events (use of models); types of failure; involvement of business and community groups; availability and use of state-of-the-art material; results of risk/vulnerability assessment studies; business and social disruption estimates; specific mitigation steps being taken.

Questions Asked of the Business Impacts and Costs Group

- Did your business sustain uninsured losses? If so, how much?
- Did your revenue structure or cost structure change near-term or long-term after Hurricane Hugo?
- Did your productivity suffer as a result of Hurricane Hugo? And if so, how long did it take to correct and what were the costs?
- Does your business have a disaster plan? What hazards and issues does it address?
- In planning for possible natural disasters, do you consider damage to the natural resources and social and community disruption (e.g., clean water supply needs, employee/family disruption; transportation to your facility)?
- Are there internal or external constraints to hazard mitigation planning in your business (e.g., other higher priorities, lack of information or assistance)?

- What kinds of information, assistance, or other incentives would help you overcome these constraints?

Questions Asked of the Natural Environment Group

- In retrospect, did Hugo involve costs to natural resources or services that were (or still are) hidden and/or unreported? Examples?
- Who bore these costs?
- Were some natural resource damage costs reimbursed? By whom?
- Who should be tracking disaster impacts and costs to natural resources and how?
- How did Hugo's direct impacts and costs to natural resources compare to the indirect impacts and costs associated with cleanup, disposal, and recovery operations?
- What are the most serious lingering natural resource problems associated with the storm?
- How might information on the costs of disasters to natural resources and services be of use to communities, businesses, and others as they conduct disaster vulnerability analyses and develop mitigation strategies?
- Are there other important questions we are not asking to which you have answers or ideas?

Questions Asked of the Social Environment Group

1. Preparation/Evacuation
   - To what extent do you feel the households of Charleston were prepared for Hurricane Hugo? What about your own?
   - What can you share with us about the preparedness level of your organization or department at that time?
   - How would you describe the costs associated with ineffective preparedness and response at the household level? In your organization?
   - How would you describe the evacuation effort prior to Hugo?
   - Do you know the estimated dollar cost of evacuating the Charleston area at that time?
   - How effective was the sheltering associated with Hugo? How many people were sheltered? What organization(s) was (were) in charge? What were the costs, including expenses necessary to get the buildings back to their original uses?

2. Impact
- What were the death and injury statistics directly resulting from Hugo's impact? During the cleanup and recovery? Do you know of any medical cost figures attributed to Hugo?
- Do you have insights to share about the emotional and social cost on families? Do you know of any evidence of its impact on domestic violence? Child abuse? Male desertion? Divorce? Care of elderly parents? Foster parenting? Suicide? Relationships with kin? Neighbors?
- Did you perceive gender differences in the impact, and subsequent family responsibilities, within households? Were there differences in the relative demands put on women and men?
- Did you notice age differences in the effects of the storm and its aftermath? For example, how were small children, elementary age children, teenagers, middle age adults, and the elderly differentially impacted?
- Were there race/ethnicity differences in Hugo's impact? In your opinion what categories of families were most severely affected? Who tended to be the last to recover? How might they have been better helped?
- What was Hugo's impact on local hospitals? Nursing homes? Schools? Daycare centers? Public housing? Parks and recreational facilities? Zoos, museums, libraries, and other cultural facilities?
- What demands were put on local health and social service agencies as a result of Hugo? Do you have any cost figures?
- Do you have any information on the total costs associated with the response of local governments? The state of South Carolina? The federal response?
- What groups (including private and nongovernmental agencies) were instrumental in providing victim assistance? Do you have any estimates of the costs incurred in providing assistance to individuals and families?
- To what extent did these organizations and agencies attempt to coordinate their work to more effectively address the needs?
- Were some local health and social service agencies overwhelmed by the demands put upon them? To what extent were workers in these agencies overburdened and in need of personal assistance, such as counseling? Was there significant "burn out" among providers? What costs were associated with this?
- What were the short-term and long-term impacts of Hugo on local volunteerism? Charity fund-raising?

- What were the impacts on local schools? Teachers? Students?

3. Mitigation
   - Can you share with us some ways in which the hurricane readiness of health and social service providers in the Charleston area is different 10 years later?
   - How would you describe the current level of hurricane preparation of the health and social services agencies in the Charleston area? What about the households and families currently living in the area?
   - Did the Hugo experience result in significant long-range planning for future events?
   - Do you know of specific measures that have been taken to identify particularly vulnerable populations (such as the frail elderly, homeless, institutionalized, or public housing residents)? Any disaster preparation or mitigation initiatives targeting special populations? Do you have any estimates of costs associated with these measures?
   - Does the community have an active VOAD (Volunteer Organizations Active in Disasters) organization? Interfaith coalition?
   - Do you know of any specific expenditures (city, county, federal) incurred by the health and social services sectors related to hurricane mitigation and/or preparation?
   - Can you think of any other categories of "social costs" associated with disaster planning and response that we have not mentioned?

Appendix B

Private Models Used by the Insurance Industry and State Agencies

The descriptions below provide a sample of the types of models used by the insurance and reinsurance industries, as well as state agencies. Representatives of these companies participated in the panel's March 1998 workshop.

EQECAT's USWIND is a probabilistic model designed to estimate damage and insured losses caused by hurricanes along the U.S. Atlantic coastline. USWIND calculates "average annual damage and loss" estimates as well as annual probability exceedances using a database that is a combination of historical storms and more than 500,000 stochastic storm simulation results. Individual scenario and average annual damages and losses can be calculated for individual property sites or for entire portfolios of residential and commercial properties. The model uses scenario storms to estimate expected and probable maximum damage and loss due to a single event.

The storm database used by USWIND calculates wind speed probabilistic distribution using the important storm parameters. It utilizes an embedded commercial geographic information system (GIS) called Mapinfo to compute the latitude and longitude of each site analyzed. It provides the facility to define each of the property assets being analyzed in order to compute resulting damage. Damage can be calculated for structure, contents, time element (such as additional living expense or business interruption), and up to three additional user-defined coverage types. Insurance information in the form of insured values, limits, deductibles, and facultative and/or treaty reinsurance then are integrated with the probabilistic distribution of computed damage for each site to determine the probabilistic distribution of "insured loss" amount. Correlation is properly taken into account when aggregating individual site loss into an overall portfolio loss amount. For further information, call (415) 989-2000 or see www.eqecat.com.

Applied Insurance Research's (AIR) Catastrophe Modeling technology provides probabilistic risk information on event frequency and magnitude along with more traditional scenario-based information. The catastrophe loss estimation technology developed and continually updated by AIR is based on sophisticated simulation models of natural hazards, such as hurricanes, extratropical cyclones, tornadoes, hailstorms, earthquakes, and fire following earthquakes. These models encompass state-of-the-art knowledge in meteorology, seismology, and other physical sciences, and in wind and earthquake engineering. To estimate the complete probability distribution of losses for a peril in a given region, the model generates potential events in accordance with their relative probability of occurrence. The AIR catastrophe models generate thousands of hypothetical events and then estimate the property damages that would result from each of the simulated events.

The probabilistic loss analysis requires that a simulated catalog of potential events be generated. This catalog defines the frequency and intensity distributions of future events by geographical area. Then, the local intensity conditions caused by each simulated event are estimated for each geographical point of interest, usually either a geocoded latitude–longitude point or a zip code centroid. Once the local intensities are estimated, potential property damages can be calculated using vulnerability relationships developed by AIR. In the hurricane model, peak wind speeds and duration are estimated for each location, and damages are estimated for exposures falling into many distinct construction classifications. The damage functions incorporate the engineering relationships among wind speed, duration, and building damage. Finally, insured losses are calculated by taking into account deductibles and other policy conditions that affect the amount ultimately paid by a particular company or the industry as a whole. For further information, call (617) 267-6645 or see www.air-boston.com.

Risk Management Solutions' (RMS) Insurance and Investment Risk Assessment System (IRAS) is an expert system-driven analysis that utilizes RMS proprietary databases to model all aspects of financial risk associated with natural hazards. As with any complex physical model, uncertainty is involved in calculating the performance of a structure in a specific event. IRAS models this uncertainty in all of its calculations. IRAS can be divided into three primary subsystems—hazard, vulnerability, and financial—each of which uses specific inputs and knowledge bases to perform a part of the analysis.

The hazard model computes the impact of the peril on a given site or location. Using geocoded measurements, IRAS retrieves detailed information on local conditions from its proprietary databases. The hazard model then simulates specific events and, using the local condition data, determines the impact of the individual event at each site. The vulnerability model then uses specific structural information for the site—general construction class, occupancy type, number of stories, and age of construction, as well as detailed structural characteristics when available—and computes the resulting damage. Once the physical damage is determined for each site or location, the financial model determines insured losses to the relevant parties. IRAS calculates these losses based on the financial terms and conditions for each individual policy or account, including all coverage of site-specific limits and deductibles, and all per-risk reinsurance certificates. For further information, call (650) 617-6500 or see www.riskinc.com.

Watson Technical Consulting's The Arbiter of Storms (TAOS) is a meteorological hazard model intended to assist emergency managers, land-use planners, and meteorologists in assessing the risks associated with meteorological hazards. TAOS is designed using an object-oriented approach, which allows a user to select the methods most appropriate to the problem, or use multiple methods to create an ensemble approach. TAOS consists of numerous user-configurable modules such as wind, wave, tide, hydrology, rainfall, damage, statistical, and forecast. Each module contains flexible components, such as specific wind-field and wave models, that are chosen to best suit the user's goals. Typical applications include real-time tracking, track forecasting, and modeling of storm effects including probabilistic aspects for assessing real-time, seasonal, and overall historical risks. Fundamental to TAOS is its integration of GIS technology as the database-management system for the model.

TAOS can simulate tropical systems on a variety of scales, from a very small scale of 1 arc second (30.8 meters) per cell through a 5 arc minutes (9850 meters/cell) scale, which is large enough to include the entire Atlantic basin. Version TAOS/C models wind, wave, and rainfall; another variant, TAOS/R, is an ultra-high-resolution research version that also simulates non-tropical storm systems, rainfall runoff and riverine flooding, coastal erosion, and tsunamis. TAOS has been used to assess hazards for projects in the Bay of Bengal, Indian Ocean, Australia, Central America, the Caribbean, and the United States, most recently for the Florida High Resolution Tropical Cyclone Hazard Mapping Project. For further information, call (912) 826-4462 or see www.methaz.com.

Glossary

Atmospheric Pressure. The pressure exerted by the atmosphere at a given point. Its measurement can be expressed in several ways. One is in millibars. Another is in inches or millimeters of mercury (Hg). Also known as barometric pressure.

Beach. The zone of unconsolidated material that extends landward from the water line to the place where there is marked change in material or physiographic form, or to the line of permanent vegetation. The beach includes foreshore and backshore.

Beach Nourishment. The process of replenishing a beach. It may be brought about naturally by longshore transport or artificially by deposition of dredged materials.

Bluff. A high, steep bank or cliff.

Chronic Hazard. An enduring or recurring hazard, such as beach, dune, and bluff erosion; gradual weathering of sea cliffs; and flooding of low-lying lands during major storms.

Coast. A strip of land of indefinite width that extends from the shoreline inland to the first major change in terrain features.

Coastal County. A county is defined as coastal if (1) at least 15 percent of its total land area is located within the nation's coastal watershed or (2) a portion of its land accounts for at least 15 percent of a coastal cataloging unit. The United States has 673 coastal counties.

Coastal Zone. All U.S. waters subject to the tide, U.S. waters of the Great Lakes, specified ports and harbors on inland rivers, waters that are navigable by deep-draft vessels, including the contiguous zone and parts of the high seas, and the land surface or land substrata, ground waters, and ambient air proximal to those waters.

Coastline. (1) Technically, the line that forms the boundary between the coast and the shore. (2) Commonly, the line that forms the boundary between the land and the water.

Depression. In meteorology, it is another name for an area of low pressure, a low, or a trough. It also applies to a stage of tropical cyclone development and is known as a tropical depression to distinguish it from other synoptic features.

Dunes. Ridges or mounds of loose, wind-blown material, usually sand.

Ecosystem. A discrete environmental unit, consisting of living and nonliving parts that interact to form a stable system. The term can be applied at any scale, from a drop of pond water to the entire biosphere (i.e., the Earth can be viewed as a single ecosystem).

Ecosystem Services. Goods (such as food) and services (such as waste assimilation) that benefit human population either directly or indirectly. Ecosystem services are derived from ecosystem functions, which are the biological or system properties and processes of ecosystems.

Erosion. The loss of sediment from the beach, dunes, and bluffs.

Flooding. A general and temporary condition of partial or complete inundation of normally dry land areas from the overflow of inland or tidal water or rapid accumulation or runoff of surface waters from any source.

Geomorphology. That branch of both physiography and geology that deals with the form of the Earth, the general configuration of its surface, and the changes that take place in the evolution of landform.

Groin. A shore protection structure built (usually perpendicular to the shoreline) to trap littoral drift or retard erosion of the shore.

Harbor. Any protected water area affording a place of safety for vessels.

Hazard Mitigation. Actions taken to reduce or eliminate long-term risk to people and property from hazards and their effects.

Hazard Reduction. Strengthening structures and providing safeguards to reduce the amount of damage caused by natural hazards, including altering the coastal environment through erosion control devices, beach nourishment, flood control works, floodproofing, windproofing, or elevating.

Hurricane. A tropical cyclone in the Northern Hemisphere with sustained winds of at least 74 mph (64 knots) or greater in the North Atlantic Ocean, Caribbean Sea, or Gulf of Mexico. These winds blow in a large spiral around a relatively calm center of extremely low pressure known as the eye. Around the rim of the eye, winds may gust to more than 200 miles per hour. The entire storm, which can be up to 340 (550) in diameter, dominates the ocean surface and lower atmosphere over tens of thousands of square miles. Hurricanes draw their energy from the warm surface water of the tropics (usually above 27 Celsius) and latent heat of condensation, which explains why hurricanes dissipate rapidly once they move over cold water or large land masses.

Hurricane Straps. Clips at the intersection of the roof and the top of the wall used to keep the roof in place under high wind conditions.

Jetty. Massive, constructed rock structures built to stabilize and protect harbor entrances, usually built perpendicular to the shore to stabilize a river mouth.

Natural Hazards. Episodic and chronic destructive natural system events such as hurricanes, beach erosion, tsunamis, and severe storms.

Northeaster (nor'easter). A type of severe winter storm that affects the Mid-Atlantic and New England states of the United States.

Overwash. When a portion of the water that rushes up onto the beach following the breaking of a wave carries over the crest of a berm or of a structure.

Retrofit. Strengthening of structures to mitigate natural disaster risks.

Revetment. A sloping surface of stone, concrete, or other material used to protect embankment, natural coast, or shore structure against erosion by wave action or currents.

Scour. Removal of underwater material by waves and currents, especially at the base or toe of a shore structure.

Shore. The narrow strip of land in immediate contact with the sea, including the zone between high and low water lines. A shore of unconsolidated material is usually called a beach.

Shoreline. The intersection of a specified plane of water with the shore or beach. The line delineating the shoreline on National Ocean Service nautical charts and survey approximates the mean high-water line.

Storm (Hurricane) Shutters. Coverings for windows to protect them from flying debris during a storm event.

Storm Surge. The local change in the elevation of the ocean along a shore due to a storm. The storm surge is measured by subtracting the astronomic tidal elevation from the total elevation. It typically has a duration of a few hours. Since wind-generated waves ride on top of the storm surge (and are not included in the definition), the total instantaneous elevation may greatly exceed the predicted storm surge plus astronomic tide. It is potentially catastrophic, especially on low-lying coasts with gently sloping offshore topography.

Topography. The configuration of a surface, including its relief and the positions of its streams, roads, buildings, etc.

Tsunami. A series of waves generated by an impulsive disturbance in the ocean, usually an earthquake occurring near or under the sea.

Turbidity. Water that is thick or opaque with roiled sediment.

Watershed. The entire region that drains into a river, river system, or water body.

Wetland. An ecosystem that depends on constant or recurrent shallow inundation or saturation at or near the surface of the substrate.

Acronyms

DNR (Departments of Natural Resources)

EMTC (Environmental Management Technical Center, [USGS Biological Resources Division])

FEMA (Federal Emergency Management Agency)

GAP (Gap Analysis Program [USGS Biological Resources Division])

HUD (Housing and Urban Development)

NFIP (National Flood Insurance Program)

NMFS (National Marine Fishery Service)

NOAA (National Oceanic and Atmospheric Administration)

USACE (US Army Corps of Engineers)

USDA (US Department of Agriculture)

USEPA (US Environmental Protection Agency)

USFS (US Forest Service)

USFWS (US Fish and Wildlife Service)

USGS (US Geological Survey)

Note: Within federal agencies, field offices tend to have the most relevant information regarding regional studies.

About the Contributing Authors and Project Staff

Contributing Authors

Howard Kunreuther, Chair, is the Cecilia Yen Koo Professor of Decision Sciences and Public Policy and codirector of the Risk Management and Decision Processes Center at The Wharton School of the University of Pennsylvania. Dr. Kunreuther's research focuses on the effect of insurance regulatory and liability questions on risk-management decisions, particularly those concerning energy and environmental issues and industrial risk management policies. He brings to the panel special expertise in risk assessment, risk spreading techniques such as insurance, and strategies for managing risk through loss-reduction methods. Dr. Kunreuther has served on a number of national boards and committees advising industry and government, and is currently a member of the National Research Council's Board on Natural Disasters. Dr. Kunreuther received his A.B. from Bates College and holds a Ph.D. in economics from the Massachusetts Institute of Technology.

Rutherford Platt, Vice Chair, is professor of geography and planning law at the University of Massachusetts at Amherst. He specializes in the management of land and water resources and has focused much of his research on problems of floodplain, wetland, and coastal management. Before coming to the University of Massachusetts in 1972, Dr. Platt spent four years as staff attorney for the Open Lands Project, where he specialized in advocacy of open space preservation, farmland conservation, and highway and power plant siting. He has served on numerous National Research Council committees, including the Committee on Coastal Erosion Zone Management, the Committee on Flood Insurance Studies, and the Committee on Water

Resources Research Review. He holds a J.D. from the University of Chicago Law School and a Ph.D. in geography from the University of Chicago.

Stephen B. Baruch is president of his own consulting company in Los Altos, California. He specializes in helping businesses plan for, and recover from, natural and person-caused disasters, as well as mitigating the economic and community infrastructure impact from these disasters. Dr. Baruch is a founder of the first national business recovery program in the United States, the Disaster Recovery Business Alliance, which is a public/private partnership of the business community and local, state, and federal government agencies. Before forming is own company, Dr. Baruch worked at Electric Power Research Institute as team leader, Community Technology Solutions, where he directed programs in disaster planning and mitigation, economic development, and airport modernization. He was also the executive assistant to the senior vice president, Technical Operations. Dr. Baruch received his B.A. from Brooklyn College, M.P.A. in air pollution control administration from the University of Southern California, M.P.H. in environmental health from Yale University, and D.Env. degree in environmental science and engineering from the University of California–Los Angeles.

Richard Bernknopf is staff economist, Western Region Geologic Mapping Team, Geologic Division, U.S. Geological Survey. He is also co-director of the Center for Earth Science Information Research and a consulting professor at Stanford University. Dr. Bernknopf's recent research focuses on estimating the societal value of geologic map information, developing debris flow map units, formulating earthquake hazard mitigation plans, and assessing uncertainty in groundwater vulnerability. He has published a number of articles in refereed journals and has served as a guest lecturer at Carnegie Mellon University, George Mason University, the University of California at Riverside, and the University of Vermont. Dr. Bernknopf received his B.A. and Ph.D. degrees from the George Washington University.

Michael Buckley is division director, Hazard Identification and Risk Assessment Division, Mitigation Directorate, U.S. Federal Emergency Management Agency (FEMA). In this capacity, he is responsible for a broad range of activities and programs to identify and assess risk from all natural hazards, with an emphasis on floods and flood-related hazards, earthquakes, hurricanes, and wind. Major programs include the Hazard Mitigation Grant Program, National Flood Insurance Program, Hurricane Program, and Dam Safety Program. Prior to joining FEMA in 1980, Mr. Buckley worked with a public and private consulting engineering practice on a broad range of responsibilities involving water resources engineering and land development.

Virginia Burkett is chief of the Forest Ecology Branch at the National Wetlands Research Center of the U.S. Geological Survey, U.S. Department of the Interior, where she has worked since 1990. She supervises a team of forest scientists, ecologists, and computer modelers who conduct research related to the ecology, management, and restoration of forested wetlands. Her expertise includes wetland forest ecology and restoration, coastal wetland ecology, coastal management, and wildlife and fisheries management. Her current research involves bottomland generation in frequently flooded sites of the Mississippi River floodplain. Previously, Dr. Burkett served as the secretary/director of the Louisiana Department of Wildlife and Fisheries, the director of the Louisiana Coastal Zone Management Program, and assistant director of the Louisiana Geological Survey. She received an M.S. in botany from Northwestern University and a Ph.D. in forestry from Stephen F. Austin State University.

David Conrad is water resources specialist for the National Wildlife Federation (NWF), the nation's largest conservation education organization. His areas of activity in recent years include the water resource development programs of the U.S. Army Corps of Engineers and the Bureau of Reclamation and federal river protection and floodplain management programs. Most recently, he has been involved in legislation and a range of policy-related activities in response to the 1993 Upper Mississippi River basin floods, as well as recent floods in California and the Upper Midwest, particularly with a focus on helping communities seeking assistance to relocate high-risk residences and businesses out of flood-prone areas. Currently, Mr. Conrad is working on a study of the nation's repetitive flood-loss problems and the potential for greater use of nonstructural approaches to reducing flood risk. Prior to joining the NWF, he was legislative representative and water specialist for Friends of the Earth. Mr. Conrad received a B.A. in environmental sciences from the University of Virginia.

Todd Davison recently was appointed as the director of the Mitigation Division in Region IV, Federal Emergency Management Agency (FEMA). Previously, he served as chief of the Technical Assistance and Compliance Branch in the Mitigation Directorate of FEMA headquarters. Mr. Davison has been employed by FEMA for nine years, and has worked extensively on compliance and technical standards for the National Flood Insurance Program, Hazard Mitigation Grant Program, Hurricane Program, technical assistance contracting, and mitigation planning. He has served as deputy federal coordinating officer for mitigation in major disasters and, prior to his tenure with FEMA, worked for the Department of Natural Resources in Maryland and Louisiana in floodplain and coastal zone management. Mr. Davison received his B.S. and M.S. degrees in geography and coastal geology from Louisiana State University and is enrolled in a coastal hazards–related Ph.D. program at the University of Maryland.

Ken Deutsch is the manager of mitigation and community disaster preparedness in the Disaster Services Department, American Red Cross National Headquarters in Virginia. He is responsible for developing and sustaining Red Cross mitigation and community disaster preparedness policies and programs nationwide to help make people and communities safer from disasters. In this capacity, he works closely with officials from the Federal Emergency Management Agency (FEMA), other federal offices, state government offices, and the private sector. His primary responsibilities are to promote and encourage local, state, and national efforts that reduce the vulnerability of people and communities to natural hazards such as hurricanes, floods, and earthquakes. Formerly, he was a career military officer with extensive experience in infantry command positions as well as high-level planning and operations staff assignments. His last assignment was in the Office of the Secretary of Defense, where he oversaw major personnel policies associated with Operation Desert Shield. He retired from the U.S. Army in 1994 at the grade of Colonel. Mr. Deutsch is a graduate of Campbell University and earned his graduate degree in business management from Webster University. He is also a graduate of the Army Command and General Staff College, Army War College, and the Harvard University Senior Executive Fellows Program.

Donald E. Geis is an independent consultant in Potomac, Maryland, specializing in sustainable and quality-of-life community development, and disaster resistant community planning—hurricanes, flooding, and earthquakes. His professional and academic experience include four years as director of community planning programs for the International City/County Management Association; eight years as the principal of his own consulting firm, Geis Design-Research Associates; eight years as program director for community and environmental design research at the American Institute of Architects Foundation; and eight years on the faculty of the Urban and Environmental Planning Department, School of Architecture, at the University of Virginia. He has written and lectured extensively both in the United States and internationally and has received numerous honors and awards for his work. He received his B.S. in architecture from the University of Cincinnati, and a Master of Architecture in urban design from Carnegie Mellon University.

James Good is coastal resources specialist, Extension Sea Grant Program, and coordinator, Marine Resource Management Program, Oregon State University. In this capacity, his responsibilities include education and applied research in ocean and coastal resources management as well as overall program direction for the Marine Resource Management program. Current research activities include: shore protection policy and practices in Oregon, coastal natural hazards management in Oregon, and long-term erosion impacts of El Niño on the Oregon coast. Formerly, he was an associate professor with Oregon State University, and, prior to that, executive director for the Columbia River Estuary Study Task Force. He received his B.A. in chemistry from Susquehanna University, M.S. in marine resource management from Oregon State University, and Ph.D. in geography from Oregon State University.

Martin Jannereth is chief of the Great Lakes Shorelands Section for the Michigan Department of Environmental Quality. His responsibilities include the administration of programs addressing Great Lakes hazards, including areas subject to erosion and flooding; programs affecting important habitats along the Great Lakes, including wetlands and sand dunes; and programs affecting the bottomland resources of the Great Lakes. Mr. Jannereth has experience managing and implementing programs involving shore protection, coastal processes and geomorphology, wetlands, and environmental planning and analysis. He also has experience managing large-scale projects involving photogrammetric data and analysis. Recently, statewide responsibilities for wetland protection and aquatic nuisance treatment regulations have been added to this position. Mr. Jannereth is also head of the division-wide computer advisory committee. He holds a B.S. in forestry and an M.S. in forest ecology from Michigan State University.

Anthony Knap is senior research scientist and director, Bermuda Biological Station for Research (BBSR), Inc. His research interests include organic geochemistry, long-range transport processes and deposition of chemicals to and in the ocean, effects of chemicals on the marine environment, global climate change, and business–science interactions. Dr. Knap has been with BBSR since 1977, serving as its director since 1986 and as director of the Atlantic Global Change Institute since it was started in 1990. Recently, he and a colleague founded the Risk Prediction Initiative, a collaborative effort of the reinsurance industry and scientists to provide new information on climate-related events. Dr. Knap is the author of more than 80 peer-reviewed scientific publications in the areas of marine pollution, atmospheric pollution, and global change. He is chairman of the Intergovernmental Oceanographic Commission of United Nations Educational, Scientific and Cultural Organization/United Nations Environment Programme's Group of Experts for Methods, Standards and Intercalibration (GEMSI), a member of the steering committee of the U.S. Joint Global Ocean Flux Study, and a member of the health of the ocean panel for the Global Ocean Observing System. He received his B.S. from Wisconsin State University, M.S. in oceanography from the University of Southhampton, U.K., and Ph.D. in chemical oceanography from the University of Southampton, U.K.

Hugh Lane Jr. is president of the Bank of South Carolina, a position he has held since 1986. Formerly, he was executive vice president of the Citizens & Southern National Bank. In addition to his responsibilities as bank president, Mr. Lane serves as a member of the Advisory Committee for the Ashepoo-Coosaw-Edisto Basin National Estuarine Research Reserve, Trustee for the Belle W. Baruch Foundation, co-chairman of the Community Relations Committee, and advisory committee member of the Storm Eye Institute of the Medical University of South Carolina. He is also a former member of the South Carolina Coastal Council, an appointment he held for seven years. Mr. Lane received an honorary doctorate from Charleston Southern University and an honorary doctorate from The Citadel. He also received the 1997 Distinguished Citizen Award from the Wofford College Alumni Council. He received his B.A. in economics from the University of Pennsylvania.

Greta Ljung is senior research statistician at Applied Insurance Research (AIR), Inc., in Boston. While serving on the Heinz Center Panel, she was vice president of statistical services at the Institute for Business and Home Safety (IBHS), where she was responsible for developing and maintaining a national database of paid insured losses from natural catastrophes. Other projects included a flood insurance survey of Grand Forks, North Dakota, homeowners following the April 1997 flooding of Red River North. Prior to joining IBHS in 1996, Dr. Ljung taught statistics for ten years at Massachusetts Institute of Technology. She has also been a faculty member at Boston University and the University of Denver. Her work has been published in *Biometrika, Journal of Royal Statistical Society,* and other leading statistical journals. Dr. Ljung is an active member of the American Statistical Association and has served on the editorial board of several statistics journals. She received her undergraduate degree in psychology from Abo Academy in Finland and her M.S. and Ph.D. degrees in statistics from the University of Wisconsin–Madison.

Molly Macauley is senior fellow with Resources for the Future in Washington, D.C. Her research interests include energy economics, regulation of toxic substances, environmental economics, advanced materials economics, and urban economics. She also conducts research on the design of incentive arrangements to improve space resource use, valuation of nonpriced space resources, and public/private space commercial enterprise. Dr. Macauley has served on numerous national advisory committees and boards and received a top 25 "rising star" award from the National Space Society in 1994. She has also been elected to Corresponding Membership for the International Academy of Astronautics. Dr. Macauley received a B.A. in economics from the College of William and Mary and M.A. and Ph.D. degrees in economics from Johns Hopkins University.

Dennis Mileti is professor of sociology, director of the Natural Hazards Research Applications and Information Center, and chair of the Department of Sociology at the University of Colorado at Boulder. He has a range of practical experiences related to natural hazards mitigation and preparedness and is currently coordinating a national effort to assess natural hazards knowledge and research needs. Dr. Mileti is chair of the Board of Advisors to the Federal Emergency Management Agency's Emergency Management Institute and is the former chair of the National Research Council's Committee on Natural Disasters. Dr. Mileti is the author of more than 100 publications, most of which focus on the societal aspects of emergency preparedness and natural and technological hazards mitigation. He received a B.A. in sociology from the University of California–Los Angeles, M.A. in sociology from California State University at Los Angeles, and Ph.D. in sociology from the University of Colorado.

Todd Miller is the executive director of the North Carolina Coastal Federation, a nonprofit environmental group that advocates sustainable resource management along the North Carolina coast. In this capacity since 1982, he is responsible for financial planning and staffing, organizational and program development, formulation and advocacy of policy positions, and partnerships with related coastal organizations. Recently, he has been highly active in a number of pressing issues, including hog farm regulations, land-use planning, fisheries habitat, and estuary protection. He received his B.A. in environmental studies and M.A. in city and regional planning from the University of North Carolina at Chapel Hill.

Betty Hearn Morrow is research associate at the International Hurricane Center and associate professor of sociology at Florida International University. With a research interest in family sociology, she focuses on the social creation of disaster vulnerability, particularly at the household level, including the effects of gender on disaster response and impact. She is a coauthor of *Hurricane Andrew: Ethnicity, Gender and the Sociology of Disaster* (Routledge, 1997) and coeditor of *The Gendered Terrain of Disaster: Through Women's Eyes* (Praeger, 1998). Of particular reference to The Heinz Center project is her article "Identifying and Mapping Community Vulnerability," appearing in *Disasters: The Journal of Disaster Studies, Policy and Management* in 1999. Dr. Morrow received her B.A. from Ohio State University, M.Ed. from the University of Miami, M.A. from Florida State University, and Ph.D. from the University of Miami.

Joseph Myers is division director of the Florida Division of Emergency Management. In this capacity, he has focused on enhancing state and local preparedness and response for catastrophic disasters by strengthening the State Emergency Response Team, developing rapid response teams, and implementing the rapid impact assessment teams following major emergencies. During emergencies he serves as the Florida governor's authorized representative and state coordinating officer. His 21 years of experience in emergency management includes service as a state director in North Carolina. Mr. Myers is a member of the National Hurricane Conference Executive Committee, a member of the Florida Commission on Hurricane Loss Projection Methodology, president of the National Emergency Management Association (NEMA), and chairman of NEMA's National Mitigation Committee. He also serves on the advisory panel for the National Academy of Public Administration's exploratory study for the role of the National Guard in emergency response. He received his B.S. in education from Western Carolina University.

Roger A. Pielke Jr. is a scientist at the Environmental and Societal Impacts Group at the National Center for Atmospheric Research in Boulder, Colorado. He also holds an affiliate professorship in the Department of Political Science at the University of Colorado. His research focuses on the relationship between scientific information and public- and private-sector decision making. His current areas of research are societal responses to extreme weather events, domestic and international policy responses to climate change, and U.S. science policy. He currently serves on the American Meteorological Society's Committee on Societal Impacts, the American Society of Civil Engineers Task Committee on Mitigating Hydrological Disasters, and the U.S. Weather Research Program's Science Steering Committee. He is coauthor of *Hurricanes: Their Nature and Impact on Society* (Wiley & Sons, 1997). He received a B.A. in mathematics and Ph.D. in political science from the University of Colorado.

Anthony Pratt is the program manager of the Shoreline Management Branch of the Delaware Department of Natural Resources and Environment Control. In this capacity, he oversees programs related to beach construction regulation, technical engineering services, dune building and maintenance, and coastal hazards mitigation. Formerly, Mr. Pratt was the first full-time administrator of Delaware's Coastal Management Program and served as chairman of the Ad Hoc Committee on Beach Management/Sea Level Rise for Delaware's Environmental Legacy. He was a member of the National Governor's Association Committee on Global Change, the National Research Council's (NRC) Committee on Beach Nourishment and Protection, and the Delaware Beach Replenishment Project. He now serves on an NRC committee focusing on coastal engineering practices. Mr. Pratt received his B.A. in natural science from Hampshire College.

James T. B. Tripp has been a staff attorney at the Environmental Defense Fund (EDF) since 1973 and has served as its general counsel since 1985. His current interests include ecosystem restoration, wetland protection, land-use management, and transportation. Prior to joining the EDF, he was assistant U.S. attorney for southern New York state for five years. Mr. Tripp has served on a number of National Research Council boards and committees, including the Committee on Restoration of Aquatic Ecosystems and the Committee on Ground Water Quality Protection. Mr. Tripp obtained his LL.B. from Yale Law School and an M.S. in philosophy from Yale.

Project Staff

Sheila D. David is a fellow and project manager at The H. John Heinz III Center, where she is currently managing studies for the Center's Sustainable Coasts Program. Prior to joining The Heinz Center in 1997, she was a senior program officer for 21 years at the National Research Council's Water Science and Technology Board, where she was the study director for approximately 30 committees that produced reports on topics such as managing coastal erosion, restoration of aquatic ecosystems, protection of groundwater, water quality and water reuse, natural resource protection in the Grand Canyon, wetlands, characteristics and boundaries, valuing groundwater, and sustainable water supplies for the Middle East. Ms. David has served as an adviser and board member of the Association for Women in Science (AWIS) and as editor of AWIS magazine. She is also a founder of the National Academy of Science's annual program honoring women in science and engineering.

Allison Sondak, now attending law school at Tulane University, was a research assistant for The H. John Heinz III Center's Sustainable Coasts Program. Prior to working at The Heinz Center, she was a project assistant for the National Research Council's Board on Biology. She worked previously on fisheries and environmental policy for the U.S. Senate and on park management at the National Park Service. Her interests include coastal zone policy and natural resource management. She received a B.A. in environmental policy from Duke University and studied marine science and policy at the University of Copenhagen, Denmark.

The Board of Trustees
of
The H. John Heinz III Center for Science, Economics and the Environment

John Sawhill, Chair, President and CEO, The Nature Conservancy
Jared Cohon, President, Carnegie Mellon University
John Flicker, President, National Audubon Society
Teresa Heinz, Chair, Heinz Family Philanthropies
Samuel C. Johnson, Chair, S.C. Johnson & Son, Inc.
Fred Krupp, Executive Director, Environmental Defense Fund
Kenneth L. Lay, Chair and CEO, Enron Corporation
Simon A. Levin, Director, Princeton Environmental Institute, Princeton University
William Merrell, President, The Heinz Center
Paul O'Neill, Chairman and CEO, Aluminum Company of America
Phyllis Wyeth, Washington, D.C.

Secretary to the Board
Mary Hope Katsouros, Vice President for Programs, The Heinz Center

Heinz Center Staff
William Merrell, President
Mary Hope Katsouros, Vice President for Programs
Robert Friedman, Vice President for Research
Mary C. Eng, Treasurer
Sarah Baish, Research Assistant
Heather Blough, Assistant Project Manager
Glenn Boledovich, Fellow
Sheila D. David, Fellow and Project Manager
Stephen Dunn, Deputy Project Manager
Susan Hanna, Fellow and Project Manager
Daman Irby, Staff Assistant
Suzanne Jacobson, Fellow
Robert Kates, Senior Fellow
Mercedes Ilagan, Executive Assistant
Robin O'Malley, Fellow and Project Manager
William Seitz, Senior Fellow
Allison Sondak, Research Assistant
Robert White, Senior Fellow
Kate Wing, Research Assistant

Index

Building Code Effectiveness Grading
  Schedule, 151
Built environment
  in cost assessment, 51, 52, 58–68, 70
  costs of Hurricane Hugo, 64–65
  costs of preparedness, 74, 75
  delayed damage assessment, 34–35
  effects of earthquakes, 69
  effects of Hurricane Hugo, 32–35,
    64–65
  eight categories of the, 58–59
  Heinz panel workshop questions,
    182–184
  linkages to other costs, 65–68,
    113–114
  role in mitigation strategy development,
    144–148
  vulnerability of the, 111–114
Business Emergency Preparedness Network,
  163
Business environment, 68–73, 132
  in cost assessment, 3, 51, 52
  customer access, 69, 72
  direct costs, 49, 70
  effects of Hurricane Hugo, 35–36,
    71–73
  employee impacts, 29, 67, 69, 70, 72,
    73, 76, 78
  financial aid, 71
  Heinz panel workshop questions,
    184–195
  indirect costs, xxxi, xxxiii, 29, 49,
    69–73
  influx of construction workers and
    contractors, 37–38, 81
  interruption costs, xxiv, 4, 36, 49, 62,
    72
  loss of complementary business, 70,
    72
  offices and facilities. *See* Built
    environment
  public–private collaboration, xxix, 1
  supplies, 69

California
  earthquake damage, 69, 124
  jurisdiction of coastal region, 6
  tax incentives for mitigation, 152–153
  types of coasts, 4
Cars and trucks, 59, 64

Case studies
  mitigation framework for a hypothetical
    city, 175–179
  mitigation strategies, 157–164
  risk assessment by insurers, 123–127
Catastrophe Paid Loss Database, xxvi, 54,
  55–56
Charleston Chamber of Commerce, 71
Chemical pollution. *See* Hazardous
  materials; Pollution
Child abuse, 76, 79, 109
Cleanup. *See* Recovery
Coastal Barrier Resources Act of 1982, 14,
  19
Coastal Barrier Resource System, 14
Coastal development. *See also* Population
    density issues
  of barrier islands, 14, 19
  effects of. *See* Fisheries, degradation of;
    Pollution; Recreational areas; Traffic
    congestion; Visual blight; Wetlands,
    degradation of
  federal incentives for, 19
  interactions with the environment,
    122–123
  trends in, 112–113
  types of, 4–8
Coastal Engineering Research Center, 12
Coastal States Organization, 11
Coastal Zone Management Act of 1972, 16,
  18
Coastal Zone Management Program
    (CZMP), 10, 16, 18–19, 130
Coastal Zone Reauthorization Act of 1990,
  18
Coasts, 193. *See also* Shoreline protection
  natural influences on, 120
  percent of total national insurance
    coverage, 16
  types of, 4–5, 11
Communication
  disruption of, 67
  telephone service, 34, 65, 67
  in vulnerability assessment, 111
Communities
  coastal, 5–6, 14, 15
  fast-growing, 117
  insurance incentives for, 151–152
  loss of functioning services, 66, 76,
    77–78

Island Press Board of Directors

SUSAN E. SECHLER, *Chair*
Vice President, Aspen Institute

HENRY REATH, *Vice-Chair*
President, Collector's Reprints, Inc.

DRUMMOND PIKE, *Secretary*
President, The Tides Foundation

ROBERT E. BAENSCH, *Treasurer*
Professor of Publishing, New York University

CATHERINE M. CONOVER

GENE E. LIKENS
Director, The Institute of Ecosystem Studies

DANE NICHOLS
Chairman, The Natural Step, U.S.

CHARLES C. SAVITT
President, Center for Resource Economics/Island Press

VICTOR M. SHER
Environmental Lawyer

PETER R. STEIN
Managing Partner, Lyme Timber Company

RICHARD TRUDELL
Executive Director, American Indian Resources Institute

WREN WIRTH
President, The Winslow Foundation